GW00468221

THE MIXED ECONOMY

It is well known that all Western economies are now mixed economies. What is less well known is why they have opted for a system of mixed ownership, partly State, partly private. This book seeks to provide theoretical justification for that system and to illustrate it with examples drawn from a wide range of areas of economic life and policy. Thus Aubrey Silberston discusses the role of the British Steel Corporation in a mixed economy, Robert Millward seeks to compare the performance of public and private enterprise, and Charles Rowley looks at industrial policy in the mixed economy.

Anthony Culyer considers health services and George Psacharopoulos examines education; David Howell looks at energy and Andrew Bain at finance; Roy Hattersley seeks to situate the mixed economy in its political context, Brian Hindley and Derek Ezra to situate it in its world context, and Maurice Peston to construct a theoretical case for an inescapable condition. In his introduction and in his own contribution Lord Roll of Ipsden ties the threads, analytical and descriptive, together, and indicates important guidelines for future thinking and research.

Recent Section F publications include the following

M. Gaskin (*editor*) THE POLITICAL ECONOMY OF TOLERABLE SURVIVAL
W. Beckerman (*editor*) SLOW GROWTH IN BRITAIN
E. Nevin (*editor*) THE ECONOMICS OF DEVOLUTION
W. Leontief (*editor*) STRUCTURE, SYSTEM AND ECONOMIC POLICY

THE MIXED ECONOMY

Proceedings of Section F (Economics) of the British Association for the Advancement of Science, Salford 1980

Edited by
Lord Roll of Ipsden

First published 1982 by
THE MACMILLAN PRESS LTD
London and Basingstoke
Companies and representatives throughout the world

ISBN 0 333 31540 5

Printed in Hong Kong

Contents

Notes on the Contributors vi

Introduction ix

1 The Mixed Economy *Lord Roll of Ipsden* 1

2 The Nature and Significance of the Mixed Economy *Maurice Peston* 18

3 Industrial Policy in the Mixed Economy *Charles Rowley* 35

4 The Comparative Performance of Public and Private Ownership *Robert Millward* 58

5 Steel in a Mixed Economy *Aubrey Silberston* 94

6 Politics and the Mixed Economy *Roy Hattersley* 113

7 Health Services in the Mixed Economy *A. J. Culyer* 128

8 Education and Society: Old Myths versus New Facts *George Psacharopoulos* 145

9 Energy Policy and the Mixed Economy *David Howell* 162

10 Finance in the Mixed Economy *Andrew Bain* 175

11 The Mixed Economy in an International Context *Brian Hindley* 187

12 The Mixed Economy and British Trade *Sir Derek Ezra* 206

Index 224

Notes on the Contributors

Lord Roll of Ipsden is a merchant banker and Chairman of S.G. Warburg and Co. Ltd and its holding company, Mercury Securities Ltd, a director of Times Newspapers Ltd and of other companies. He has been a Civil Servant, retiring in 1966 from the post of Permanent Under-Secretary, Department of Economic Affairs, as well as having been an academic – he was a Professor in Economics at Hull University. Among his books are *A History of Economic Thought* and *Uses and Abuses of Economics.*

Maurice Peston is Professor of Economics at Queen Mary College, University of London. He is the author of *Theory of Macroeconomic Policy* (1974) and *Whatever happened to Macroeconomics* (1980). He has been a special adviser to the Secretaries of State for Education and Science and Prices and Consumer Protection.

Charles Rowley, B.A., Ph.D., graduated from the University of Nottingham with first class honours in 1960 and a Ph.D. in 1964. He has been a lecturer at Nottingham and Kent and a senior lecturer at Kent. He has also been a reader at the University of York. Since 1972 he has been David Dale Professor of Economics at the University of Newcastle upon Tyne. He has published in the fields of welfare economics, public economics and industrial economics.

Robert Millward is Professor of Economics and Chairman of the Department of Economics at the University of Salford, Lancashire. He is the author of *Public Expenditure Economics* (1970) and of several articles in the field of public finance. His recent interests have extended to problems of economic organisation, including the economics of long-run institutional change in European economic history. He also recently served as a member of the Severn Barrage Committee of the Department of Energy.

Aubrey Silberston is Professor of Economics at Imperial College, London. He is co-author of books on the motor industry, the patent system and the steel industry, and has published a number of articles on the economics of industry. He was a member of the Monopolies Commission 1965-8, of the Royal Commission on the Press 1974-7, and a part-time board member of the British Steel Corporation 1967-76.

Roy Hattersley is the Labour Member of Parliament for the Sparkbrook division of Birmingham. He has been Labour Party spokesman on Defence and on Education and Science and was Secretary of State for Prices and Consumer Protection from 1976-1979. He was a Visiting Fellow at the Institute of Politics at Harvard University in 1971 to 72.

Anthony Culyer is Professor of Economics and Deputy Director of the Institute of Social and Economic Research at the University of York. He has contributed many articles to economics and other journals and his recent books include *Need and the National Health Service* (1976), *Measuring Health: Lessons for Ontario* (1978) and *The Political Economy of Social Policy* (1980). He is co-editor of the new *Journal of Health Economics,* and is an economic adviser to several government and international agencies.

George Psacharopoulos is a lecturer in economics at the London School of Economics and Political Science. He is the author of *Returns to Education* (1973), *Earnings and Education in OECD Countries* (1975) and several journal articles on the economics of education and manpower planning.

David Howell, Conservative Member of Parliament for Guildford, is Secretary of State for Energy and a member of the Cabinet. He served formerly as Minister of State in Northern Ireland and as Parliamentary Secretary to the Civil Service Department. He is the author of many articles and pamphlets, was formerly on the editorial staff of the *Daily Telegraph* and before that in the economic section of the Treasury.

Andrew Bain is Walton Professor of Monetary and Financial Economics at the University of Strathclyde. He was a member of the Committee to Review the Functioning of Financial Institutions, and is the author of *The Control of the Money Supply* (3rd edn, 1980) and *The Growth of Television Ownership in the United Kingdom* (1964), and joint author of *Company Financing in the United Kingdom* (1976).

Brian Hindley is a Senior Lecturer in Economics at the London School of Economics and Counsellor for Studies of the Trade Policy Research Centre. He has published widely in the areas of trade policy and industrial policy and, most recently, 'Voluntary Export Restraints and Article XIX of the General Agreement on Tariffs and Trade', which appears in *Current Issues in Commercial Policy and Diplomacy* (Macmillan, 1980), edited by John Black and Brian Hindley.

Sir Derek Ezra is Chairman of the National Coal Board, of the Nationalised Industries Chairmen's Group and of the Nationalised Industries Overseas Group. In May 1978 he published a book entitled *Coal and Energy*. He has also written numerous articles and broadcasts on subjects associated with energy, economic and industrial affairs, overseas trade and the problems of management.

Introduction

All Western industrial nations have had mixed economies for many years. What is new is an acute debate concerning that mix and the breakdown of consensus with respect to the precise balance between the public and private sectors – in the limit between the command state and the night watchman state. When Section F of the British Association met in Salford in September 1980 to discuss the size, performance, composition and future of the mixed economy, it was doing so at a time of an apparent polarisation of attitudes as between left-wing collectivists and right-wing free marketeers. In that sense Section F was discussing not only the mixed economy but the compromise on which British economic policy had been based throughout the post-war period.

In the circumstances, it would be surprising if all the contributors to the discussions were in agreement on all the issues. Nor were they expected to be, for the purpose of an academic gathering such as the annual meeting of Section F is rather to air ideas than to arrive at decisive solutions. Nonetheless, the papers brought together in this volume do draw our attention to certain key topics in which the interest of all the contributors is engaged. Chief among these are the following:

Firstly, efficiency. Professor Millward makes clear how difficult it is to compare the performance of enterprises publicly-owned with that of enterprises in the public sector. In his paper, eschewing comparisons based on profitability (since governments have used public enterprises as instruments for the attainment of other policy objectives than profit maximisation alone, notably price stability), he opts instead for comparisons based on the relative cost-efficiency of public and private firms which supply the same product. Cases in point are not often found in the UK and the bulk of the evidence which he cites is drawn from the USA, Canada, Australia and Switzerland. His conclusion is that management in private enterprise would appear to be *less* cost-efficient than it is in the public sector (the exception seems to be refuse collection). A comparison based on relative profitability might, of course, yield different results, although the studies on the US electric power industry to which Professor Millward refers illustrate a case where the average rate of return in the state sector does not in practice differ widely from that in private enterprises. Professor Culyer, looking at the health services, returns a verdict similar in its positive attitude towards social provision: he argues that a national health service – contrary to much traditional economic analysis – is actually a more rational mode of organising health care services than would be a private system.

It would be wrong to discuss managerial efficiency in the mixed economy without considering that of politicians and bureaucrats as well. This topic is taken up by Professor Rowley. He draws attention to recent developments in political economy which call into question the omniscience and neutrality of governments and reminds the reader that government failure (a phenomenon less frequently discussed in the literature than is market failure) might result from the distortion of information flows on the part of self-seeking pressure groups and growth-conscious bureaucracies. He shows how state regulation (in the form of, say, tariffs or employment protection laws) may have the effect of ensuring rents to producers at the cost of consumers compelled as a result of the measures to pay supercompetitive prices; and he describes how vote-seeking politicians may have a perhaps unwelcome bias towards deficit finance and excessive expansion of the money supply. He also argues (in contrast to behavioural theorists who deny that market forces adequately discipline organisation men) that, in the perspective of agency theory, the market value of the manager himself is derivative from the performance of the firm he manages.

Professor Silberston, in his paper on the British Steel Corporation (of which he himself was a part-time board member from 1967 to 1976) takes up the theme of performance and politics. He acknowledges that the BSC has in the past failed on occasion to satisfy an unexpectedly high level of demand for steel and that it did not in its early years lay sufficient stress upon initiative and productivity. He blames politicans in part for these shortcomings – for intervening in investment and pricing policies, for example; for retarding closures which were in actual fact inevitable (notably those of works which were suboptimal in scale and employed obsolete technology); for placing excessive demands upon the valuable time of top management. He points out in addition that the very fact that the BSC was nationalised enabled trade unions to impose overmanning and high pay on the organisation in the knowledge that it – unlike its competitors in the private sector – was unlikely to be allowed to go bankrupt. At the same time, he also emphasises BSC's successes in the R and D field and its demonstrated ability to exploit economies of large scale.

The BSC faces competition from abroad: even if there were not significant private sector production, it is no more a natural monopoly than the National Coal Board, British Airways, British Shipbuilders, or British Leyland. The deleterious effects of privately-owned natural monopolies have often supplied an easy explanation of *why* industries are nationalised; and its unavailability in the case of industries producing internationally traded goods raises the issue of what policy goals, and what interests, nationalisation of such industries is intended to serve. Dr Hindley notes that nationalisation and nationalised industries have been used as means of protecting domestic industries against foreign competition; but he also argues that policy produces rough counterparts of these protective practices when privately-owned industries are pressed by imports. He therefore views these policies of nationalised industries as part of a wider problem, which is the unwillingness of many industrialised countries to adjust to changes in comparative costs. He suggests that protective policies in either the public or private sectors are designed to maintain or increase real wage rates in industries subject to international competition, and he concludes that the very extent of these policies (which some advocate should be further extended) makes it most unlikely that that aim can be achieved.

No one, as it happens, would say that public enterprise is unaware of the international dimension; and in his paper the Chairman of the National Coal Board, Sir Derek Ezra, draws attention to a little-noted contribution made by the nationalised industries – one independent of export performance and import substitution – to the balance of payments. This contribution is the sale of British technical expertise through consultancy and project-management schemes abroad; through the training of overseas personnel in the use of British equipment; and through the pooling and sharing of information with other nationalised industries at home.

Secondly, equity. A democratic society does not wish merely to attain its chosen economic objectives with no more than the minimal expenditure of scarce resources, it wishes also to do so in a manner fully consistent with generally accepted notions of fairness and social justice.

Justice is the theme of Dr Psacharopoulos' paper on education. He notes the high private rate of return to investment in human capital in all countries and, rejecting the market segmentation hypothesis, presents statistical evidence in support of the thesis that the provision of education to an otherwise poorer man will enable him in practice to receive greater lifetime earnings, even if he is in the short run subject to some graduate unemployment while waiting for a job. He notes that differentials for skill appear to be constant over long periods, suggesting that demand rises at the same time and rate as the supply of educated manpower. Every additional year of schooling brings with it incremental earnings; and, while the benefit is particularly great for the child schooled in the private sector of education, in all cases the provision of education contributes more to life chances than does family background.

Fairness extends beyond the scarce resource of money to spend on goods and refers as well to the whole institutional environment within which that money is earned. This is the essence of Roy Hattersley's contribution. Mr Hattersley calls for an increase in the number of autonomous, socially-owned companies, giving workers via collective ownership a vested interest in the economic success of their organisation; and argues that employee involvement, not state direction, is the way to harness enthusiasm and *morale* and thus to improve the performance of British industry. Mr Hattersley's paper – which seeks to show that self-interest and democratic socialism are not incompatible – was written at the very time that workers at Gdansk and Stettin were demonstrating their conviction that central ownership and bureaucratic control are not always and everywhere perceived to guarantee personal liberty and social equality.

Mr Hattersley is evidently convinced that competition is an important part of the just economy, and he joins his voice to several others in this volume in advocating effective restrictive practices legislation aimed at preventing undesirable concentration of economic power. He in addition proposes interventionist measures of a positive nature – measures such as regional policy or the provision of funds for industry. Clearly, he would be in agreement with Professor Peston's point that private economic transactions have public consequences; that property is to some extent held in trust; and that responsibility to the community cannot be neglected in any discussion of economic arrangements and regulations.

Thirdly, flexibility. An economic process is a dynamic, not a static thing. It is in good measure to be judged by how well it adjusts to unforeseen shocks. One of the most challenging tests in recent years has been the situation in the energy field since 1973, and the paper by the Secretary of State for Energy, Mr David Howell, is particularly illuminating in its attempt to present a Conservative case for rationing via the price mechanism. The market, he argues, encourages energy conservation, say, via home insulation, or via the substitution of the fuel-efficient vehicle for the huge 'gas guzzler', and the search for new sources of power. He adds, however, that a policy of market-determined energy prices must be accompanied by a degree of compassion towards those individuals and groups poorly placed to adapt quickly, together with government support to research and development schemes in areas as yet too risky to make them commercially viable. Mr Howell does not say that market signals are perfect guidelines along the road to change, but he is convinced that central planning would lead to worse errors.

Another illustration of flexibility is macroeconomic flexibility, the theme of Professor Bain's paper. He points out that, while publicly-owned financial intermediaries are in the UK the exception rather than the rule, they are nonetheless key participants in the mixed economy by virtue of their role in the process of credit creation. Although there is some uncertainty as to the sensivity of private-sector investment to small changes in rates of interest, there can be no doubt that the public sector is significantly less sensitive than is the private to the cost factor in the short run. Professor Bain's general opposition to narrowly-defined monetary targets on the grounds that they impede capital market flexibility is likely to prove particularly controversial.

Policies to foster macroeconomic flexibility have in recent decades become an important part of social regulation; and it is interesting that several papers in this volume favour incomes policy as opposed to the invisible hand when dealing with cost inflation and highly imperfect labour markets.

The mixed economy was not built to the specification of an architect; and its justification must be sought not in any fundamentalist doctrine, but in its responsiveness to the highly complex variety of objectives of man in society. This book does not seek to advocate any particular pattern of a mixed economy, but simply to say what it is and does and what it might in the future become.

London, December 1980 ERIC ROLL

1 The Mixed Economy

LORD ROLL OF IPSDEN

For its annual meeting in 1980, Section F of the British Association chose 'The Mixed Economy' as its theme, and during the course of the session a number of specific topics relating to the mixed economy were treated not only by academic economists, but also by business men and politicians.

In this introductory paper I want to touch upon a few general problems relating to the mixed economy. The first of these that deserves attention is the question why the mixed economy should currently be a matter of interest, indeed, debate, in our country as if it were something new. In fact, we have for about two hundred years had nothing but a mixed economy. That it has not and is not viewed with favour by what I might call the Left in politics and the social sciences, that is to say, by the advocates of the collective management of all our economic affairs, is nothing new. What is particularly striking today is that the mixed economy is under vigorous attack by what I might broadly call the Right of the politico/economic spectrum. The attack is inspired by a revival of extreme individualism in political philosophy with its concomitants of minimal government and a reliance on the 'invisible hand', working through free markets, to achieve an economically most efficient result.

Examples are numerous. In a recent booklet by one of the most consistent advocates of a completely free economy, is the statement that

> the mixed economy would be the desired objective if it combined state economy in public goods that yield collective benefits (defence, law and order, local roads, public health, some scientific research, etc.) with market economy in the mass of economic activity that yields personal benefits . . . But in practice the mixed economy has been used to enable the State to regulate, control, direct and run industry in ways that have distorted private initiative and prevented its prodigious productivity.

Here is another, more moderate, statement by the political commentator of a leading daily newspaper. 'The mixed capitalist economy brought so much prosperity to the nation in the 'fifties that socialism was a non-starter.' He goes on to say 'We are now in a very different scene. The mixed economy, as at present composed and arranged, has passed through a period of substantial failure.' To show that even on the political Right other views may be held, here is another example, coming from a practising politician. In a recent lecture, the Lord Privy Seal said:

> The extent to which help [that is to say help of a social character] is provided by way of subsidy, by insurance, or by voluntary bodies, or by self-help as a result of lower taxation and a more successful economy, and the extent to which social services are financed by taxation or charges, do not seem to me to be matters of fundamental principle.

And a little further on he speaks of a 'mixed or free economy as a necessary condition of freedom'.

There is much in these quotations that would deserve detailed analysis. For example, the parenthesis in my first quotation speaks of *local* roads, *some* scientific research, and ends with undefined etcetera. The second quotation makes the rather extraordinary statement that the mixed economy brought a great deal of prosperity in the 'fifties but for some reason has now passed through a period of substantial failure because it is 'as at present composed and arranged'. In Sir Ian Gilmour's quotation there is the equation or at least jointure of a 'mixed' with a 'free' economy. I do not propose to deal with these quotations any further. They are not only very puzzling in themselves, but show clearly the difficulties of the subject and the hazards to which one exposes oneself once one leaves the secure shelter of doctrinaire belief, be it in the 'night-watchman' state or in the 'command' economy.

Fortunately, or unfortunately, most of us, economists and businessmen and, as a rule, politicians, cannot take refuge in this shelter. We have to venture out. For my part, I do not propose to spend much time in debating the more doctrinaire attitudes; though in rejecting them, I do not propose to advocate any specific pattern for the mixed economy. My purpose is twofold: first to defend the principle and concept of the mixed economy as such; and second, to point out some of the problems for economics and for the relation between economics and politics which the maintenance of a mixed economy raises.

I suppose that I should have begun with a definition. But debates about definition are always dreary and rarely fruitful. A rough and ready distinction between two types must suffice. One relates to ownership and to the management of the economic activity of a society; the other is concerned with the instruments of economic policy, that is the means used by the State to influence a generally privately owned and managed economy. The limits of the first of these are set on one side by collective ownership of what are traditionally called the means of production, distribution and exchange, and the management of their use by central government or its agents; on the other side, by the institution of private property in the means of production, distribution and exchange, by the exclusive reliance on individual interest and private enterprise as the motive force in putting these to use. In most Western economies, and certainly in our own country, when we speak of a mixed economy, we mean that the structure of the economic activities of our society lies well within these two limits. It is unlikely that anyone today would wish to question Adam Smith's acceptance that defence (which, you will recall, came before opulence) was a proper field of state activity. (And when the replacement of Polaris by Trident is to cost £5000 million, one can hardly call it a non-economic activity.) But, defence apart, it is only extreme dogmatists who would wish to 'roll back' the frontiers of state activity until they are virtually coterminous with total inactivity.

We know that the decision where the frontiers of a mixed economy, within the broader limits I have indicated, are to lie raises not only philosophical problems and beliefs which divide people politically; it also raises practical problems which have troubled economists for a long time. The issue was succinctly put by Burke, when he spoke of it as 'one of the finest problems in legislation, namely to determine what the State ought to take upon itself to direct by the public wisdom and what it ought to leave with as little interference as possible to individual exertion'. I cannot dwell on the purely philosophic aspects of this issue, except to say that even among the most libertarian of modern social philosophers very important differences can be discerned. As Professor Partha Dasgupta has shown in a remarkable inaugural lecture, the ideas of, for example, John Rawls in his *Theory of Justice* are very different from those of Nozick or from those of Hayek. I believe that for my present purposes, and perhaps to a large extent for the theme that runs through many of the contributions to this session, the practical problem of the drawing of specific frontiers at a particular time and in specific circumstances is the decisive one.

I shall revert to this shortly. But at this point I should like to say that the second range of definitions, those which relate to instruments of economic policy, is at least as relevant as the first. I have spoken of instruments of economic policy and this implies a distinction between instruments and objectives. In practice this distinction is not easy to draw. Moreover, once objectives are included, it is difficult to distinguish between matters directly undertaken by the State and ends that are to be achieved by policy instruments in the narrower sense. As far as instruments are concerned, it would, I think, be unrealistic in the extreme to exempt the State from active concern with the creation of money. I know that in his more fanciful moments Hayek has evolved proposals for freeing even the creation of legal tender from the 'shackles' of the authorities. But I do not believe that for any practical purpose one can argue that a modern society can do without the regulation of money, or the levying of taxes. Nor can it do without a whole host of legislation and regulation built up over two hundred years, relating, for example, to safety, such as factory legislation, to a certain minimum of welfare, to the employment of children, and even in some cases to minimum wages. Nor can one ignore legislation on such basic elements of the commercial and industrial processes of society as the definition and punishment of fraud, or the laws relating to contract. All these are, potentially at least, instruments of economic policy; and to regard them merely as a 'framework' within which free private enterprise and free markets may flourish (the implication being that they are neutral), can be deceptive. What must be clear is that once taxation and the regulation of money are part of the inevitable appurtenances of government, the choice of how to balance the use to which these are to be put (to say nothing of some of the other more specific instruments of policy to which I have referred), becomes a major practical issue.

I have said that for my purpose the differences in definition of the mixed economy that relate to the use of instruments of economic policy is at least as relevant as that of the structure of ownership and management. The latter is, however, very actively debated at this moment in our country, when the government is committed to a policy, and has already started to a substantial degree to execute a policy, of getting government or government agencies out of both ownership and management of certain important segments of the economy. It seems to me that other countries are not nearly as much concerned at the present time with frontiers between government and private enterprise as such. I am speaking, of course, primarily of the highly developed industrialised countries of the West. It is not quite clear why the subject should be particularly worthy of debate as an issue of principle at the present time, since even in the United Kingdom the broad pattern of government enterprise, government ownership and goverment management has not changed very much in the last twenty years or so. But, I suppose that it is always worth looking at the frontiers of government enterprise. I happen to believe, and this will become clearer in other parts of what I have to say, that while these matters are proper, and at times very important, subjects for discussion, it is essential that this discussion should be of a practical character. They are not, in my view, as helpfully tackled if they are made part of some fundamentalist dogma. There are certain enterprises which have traditionally been acceptable to a majority of opinion, even a majority of orthodox economic opinion, as proper fields for government enterprise. The degree to which one may argue for expansion or contraction of these areas is bound to fluctuate with the economic fortunes of any particular country and with the political reflection of those fortunes and, therefore, to some extent with what political parties consider to be vote-catching or vote-repelling aspects of policy. We can all agree, for example, that the ownership of hotels by British Rail is an historical accident and that there is no compelling reason why these hotels should in fact be owned and run by a nationally-owned corporation; and the decision to part with the ownership of the British Transport Hotels can be accepted as a perfectly sensible one. There may be other enterprises ancillary to the main purpose of certain state-run corporations, such as in communications and even in the field of certain types of energy production, which would be hived off without any disadvantage to the main purpose of the enterprise, and, indeed, with some gain in efficiency and innovation.

Much more important, and much more difficult, is the question of how to treat the major enterprises themselves which happen to be in state ownership and, even if only indirectly, under state management. What happens in other countries is not particularly enlightening. In France and in Italy, for example, the vast majority of the large commercial banks are state-owned and, although they are not directly managed by the State, are, theoretically at least, in a much more direct line of control than they are here or in Germany or the United States. But this in itself is not decisive. It would be very difficult to detect any economically really significant sense in which state ownership of the French banks has made a difference to the way in which they are run. I have heard it said, no doubt semi-jocularly, that the private banks in France are much more likely to be obedient to the guidelines of the Banque de France and of the Ministry of Finance than are the nationalised banks. I have also heard it argued that the degree of control which the ownership of the French banks confers upon the authorities is virtually limited to the appointment of the chairman and to perhaps one or two other senior officials of the banks in question. But here again the practice of different countries differs, and there are many enterprises in which the hand of the State, although not directly present in management, has some influence on the choice of the chief executives.

It would seem to follow from this example that at least one important question which has to be decided in regard to the large state enterprises is whether a practically useful distinction can be drawn between management and ownership. In the light of the experience of this and of other countries, as well as on more theoretical grounds, I am not certain that clear rules can be laid down which could be applied in all cases at all times. There are enterprises in which the State has had a very considerable stake, indeed, at times a majority holding, such as British Petroleum. But it seems to me that from an industrial, commercial and financial point of view the management of that great and successful enterprise has been virtually indistinguishable from that of a company with private shareholders. Obviously, a company of the size and importance of British Petroleum, one involved in an area in which over the period in which it has been in existence not only major economic but also highly important political events have taken place, will get involved in matters of public policy and will have to take into account considerations which a different enterprise could ignore. But this is very different from believing that British Petroleum has in any direct sense been run by the British Government.

Again, the question whether the Bank of England is very significantly more under government control since its nationalization in 1946, compared with the inter-war period, is not easy to decide. Admittedly, under the Act of 1946, the Bank is subject to direction by the Chancellor of the Exchequer. But, already fifty-four years ago, when he wrote his celebrated essay *The End of Laissez-Faire,* Keynes was able to say

> The extreme instance perhaps of this tendency [the tendency of large enterprises to avoid criticism from the public rather than to serve its shareholders] is the case of an institution theoretically the

unrestricted property of private persons, i.e. the Bank of England. It is almost true to say that there is no class of person of whom the Governor of the Bank of England thinks less when he decides on his policy than of his shareholders. Their rights, in excess of their conventional dividend, have already sunk to the neighbourhood of zero.

I have for a long time believed, as did the late Sir Ronald Edwardes when he was chairman of the Electricity Council, and I have so argued in public, that the nationalised industries should be given much greater flexibility in their financing needs, and should be able to have access to financial markets rather than to be wholly dependent on the National Loan Funds. I believe this not out of any particular ideological conviction but simply because the decision of how much of the financing of any large industry, either already nationalised or considered suitable to have some degree of public ownership, should be sought in the market, is a wholly practical question. The answer to it must depend very largely on the past, present and prospective profitability of that enterprise and therefore its ability to attract private capital. I am, therefore, glad that this question is now being considered in a much more realistic and flexible way than it was under previous administrations, when it tended to be the victim of political dogmatism or bureaucratic convenience. However, even now it is bedevilled by the fact that to the extent to which for one reason or another funds have to be provided from public sources, the precise accounting methods by which this is done and the effect which this financing has on the budgetary situation and, therefore, on the fiscal policy of the government, is by no means clearly thought out. It does seem rather odd that a decision by government to provide several millions for a painting that is to be 'bought for the Nation' should have much the same accounting and therefore budgetary effect, with all its consequences for political controversy and debate, as does the question whether the National Coal Board should have flexibility in raising finance from private markets either in this country or internationally.

A further point which has complicated the question of the treatment of the great public utilities which have generally been regarded as potential candidates for nationalization is the relationship between the prices of their services and their financial management. Certainly, since the war, these matters have often become almost inextricably mixed up, whether under Labour or under Conservative administrations. Policies related to the fight against inflation, or to the creation of a state of affairs in which wage claims might be moderated if the cost of certain essential public services could be kept down, has become very much bound up with whether the relevant nationalised industries should have as their target the achievement of a specified profitability within any particular period of time.

Another question which deserves attention in any discussion of instruments of economic policy, is the question of the regulation, control, or suppression of monopoly. I mention it here since it affects to some degree the régime for nationalised industries. Many of the nationalised industries are what used to be called natural monopolies, that is to say, they are industries in which either a monopoly can be expected to develop or, because they involve the granting of certain rights, such as roads, gaslines, etc., which cannot be easily dispersed over a number of people, have been identified as monopolies from the start, therefore justifying either very detailed regulation or, in the limit, state ownership and management. However, in the course of their evolution some of these enterprises have tended to attach to themselves ancillary industries, sometimes closely related, sometimes only very distantly, if at all, related to their main purpose. The hiving off of these, in order to make them more accessible to competition, has been discussed from time to time in previous administrations, but has become a marked objective of policy under the present government. In so far as these secondary or ancillary industries are not readily brought within the ambit of natural monopolies, it is a perfectly reasonable objective of policy to say that they should not be sheltered from competition by being incorporated within the purview of an industry which is state owned and state managed or is an otherwise regulated monopoly. *Per se*, there is no reason why government policy should not be directed to getting rid of these industries to private enterprise.

The argument is, however, not always quite as simple as this. There are large private corporations which are subject only to a fairly limited degree of competition and which may be said, for a variety of reasons and not necessarily because of any special privilege granted by the authorities, to enjoy a degree of monopoly. These enterprises, which are not totally dissimilar from nationalised ones, have often incorporated within their group a fair diversity of other firms, diversity both in the sense of not having a direct affinity with the main industry, but also diverse in the sense that they may have different patterns of profitability. Thus, some paradoxes may appear when a nationalised industry is being enjoined to behave commercially, that is, to conduct itself as if it were a large-scale privately owned enterprise, while at the same time being prevented from doing certain things which a similar industry, if it were privately owned, might well do because it considered it to be commercially desirable.

I want to revert now to the question of instruments of policy, and here I would like to divide my remarks into two parts. First, I would like to say a few words on the present state of the debate, bearing mainly on the broader aspects of economic policy, and, second, on the implications of that debate for the existing state and future programme of economics. A systematic division of instruments of economic policy is not easy and can give rise to as many difficulties and paradoxes as it is designed to remove. Broadly speaking, one can distinguish between macro-economic policies and micro-economic policies. In my view, with a few exceptions, the macro-economic policies tend also to be those policies which have traditionally been associated with organised government, while micro-economic policies are of more modern origin and more subject to debate. Here it is further possible to distinguish between those which were largely the product of nineteenth-century industrialisation and those more recent ones which more extended and complex government intervention has put on the statute book or has added to regulatory practice.

The most important traditional macro-economic policies are those associated with spending and taxing by the State, and those associated with the regulation of money and credit, i.e. fiscal policy and monetary policy. There is very little argument among a broad range of economists and politicians that any modern policy designed to achieve certain economic objectives, such as growth, stability, avoidance of inflation and as far as possible the maintenance of a high level of economic activity and employment, must embrace both fiscal and monetary policy. The argument is about the precise mix and the application in regard to dosage and timing of this or that fiscal or monetary measure. Generally, it may be said that while monetary policy is exclusively aimed at the objectives that I have just described, fiscal policy is used for other purposes also, for example, to affect income and wealth through redistributive income and inheritance taxation, through the taxation of capital gains and transfers, as well as through the use of the public funds of the State to make certain social payments to improve the lot of this or that group of citizens. Indeed, traditionally, fiscal policy is used only for these other purposes, and it is part of the 'Keynesian revolution' (paradoxically originated by a monetary economist) that fiscal policy is now also addressed to the balance of the whole economy.

Whatever the argument may be about the precise mix and application in time of monetary and fiscal instruments, we can all agree that between them they are designed to correct the effect which certain changes, endogenous or exogenous, might have on the balance of production, the prospective level of economic activity and growth, international competitiveness, the balance of payments, and so on. In one way or another, by affecting demand, by altering profitability and thereby affecting, or supposedly affecting, the direction of investment and production, by altering income distribution and thereby affecting, or supposedly affecting, incentives, monetary and fiscal policies are designed either to restore a lost situation of balance or to produce a different balance which is considered to be economically, politically and perhaps socially more desirable. A great deal has been written on the different effects of fiscal and monetary policies and this is not the place for me to attempt to add anything new to this subject. There is, however, one point which I believe is worth stressing. History has shown that the crucial difference between the two policies tends to be the degree to which they bear directly upon those aspects of the economy that are to be influenced and the extent to which they only do so indirectly. Another distinction, sometimes equivalent to the first, is whether their results appear quickly or slowly. The matter is further complicated by the fact that direct and/or quick results or indirect and/or slow results do not follow a predetermined pattern in all circumstances.

Examples taken from our own recent experience are to the point. A reduction in the top rate of personal income tax was long overdue; and a modest shift in the burden of taxation from direct to indirect was also tolerable, and may indeed be desirable at a certain level of national income. But the expected direct effects on incentives and productivity are not yet visible. On the other hand, the effects of a strict monetary policy, especially one that relies so heavily on interest rates, have been, as could have been expected, very swift indeed. Yet, at the same time, they are indirect, for they bear on the profitability and liquidity of the corporate sector in the first place; and only through the transmission belt of corporate stringency affecting stocks, production and investment plans will they influence what they are intended to influence, namely, prices, wage settlements and the rate of inflation.

Another, perhaps more far-reaching, example is what happened in the industrialised countries of the West as a result of the oil price revolution. Everywhere, the objective of policy has been to absorb the effects of the oil price change as quickly as possible and without any lasting effect on the level of economic activity. This has meant trying to change the balance of incentives, rewards and punishments in the economic process in such a way that the income effects of the oil price change would be achieved as quickly as possible. In its simplest terms, to absorb the quintupling of the oil price in the first instance and the increases that have occurred since 1973/4 yet maintain, or quickly regain, the previous level of economic activity and the prospect of economic growth, together with the requisite competitiveness in international trade and payments, has required a decline in the real income of the mass of the population. I leave aside the question how that decline in real income is to be shared between income earners at different levels. This is by no means an unimportant question in social and political terms, but I address myself rather to the question as to how, igoring inter-class and inter-personal differences, a total decline in real income can be brought about which would be commensurate with the increase in the price of oil and last for a sufficient period of time to achieve the necessary changes in the patterns of production and distribution. Whereas in some countries this desired objective has been achieved by acting quickly and fairly directly upon the distribution of income, in other countries this has not been the case. The choice of economic policy instruments has thus determined the way in which the pattern of income distribution, and therefore the pattern of bearing the consequences of the oil price increase, are distributed throughout the population.

Generalising from the example of the oil price increase, one could argue, without exaggeration, that in a free and open economy adaptability of incomes is one of the most important problems of economic policy. For many years there has been much discussion whether what has become known as incomes policy should be added to fiscal and monetary measures as a major instrument of macro-economic policy. It is fair to say that no government in the Western industrialised countries of the world has in the last two or three decades been able to avoid getting involved in the problem of the adaptability of incomes to important changes in the general economic environment, whether the action of governments in response to this problem is called incomes policy or not. Since in our own country this particular phrase is at present highly unpopular, and government is consistently refusing to acknowledge that it has any intention of indulging in anything like an incomes policy, it may be worthwhile to say a few more words about an issue which I believe will continue to be with us and to be crucial to the health of a mixed economy.

I am well aware of the difficulties which our own and other governments have run into in the past in trying to influence the course of wage and salary settlements by one kind of incomes policy or another. The efficacy of what in America used to be called 'jaw-boning', or of 'guiding lights', 'norms', 'threshold agreement', 'statutory freezes' and 'social compacts' can justifiably be called in question, at least in terms of whether their effects are lasting or not. And there is certainly plenty of evidence of the difficulties caused by the erosion of traditional or acceptable income differentials, and the resulting 're-entry' problem when constraints on wage bargaining have, in the end, to be abandoned.

However, there is also evidence of the, at least temporary, effectiveness of certain forms of restraint. In this country the social compact produced an unprecedented fall of 8 per cent in real earnings in two years and made a major contribution to the reduction of inflation. Intercountry comparisons also support the case for some direct action on the incomes front. In Germany and Austria, while admittedly the deep-seated fear of inflation is a powerful cultural restraining factor, the structure of trade unions and the pattern of wage-bargaining have certainly produced a much better adaptability to change (such as the oil price increase) and greater freedom from inflationary pressures. And I would maintain that the institutional structures of Japan which have produced a much greater flexibility of real incomes have had a great deal to do with that country's industrial success, despite its exposed position in regard to energy and raw material supplies. Indeed, in our own country, despite the continued opposition to the principle of an incomes policy under the slogan of the sanctity of free markets (and despite also some considerable confusion in government statements about what is supposed to be the effect on inflation of monetary movements on the one hand and wages on the other), hardly a day passes that we are not told by government what is the desirable course of incomes. Moreover, government as an employer (or where it is for other reasons in a position to exert a direct influence) is, in fact, operating an incomes policy. It would be a gain in intellectual hygiene at least if this fact were more frankly acknowledged; as Arthur Burns, an unqualified supporter of the market economy both as an academic and as chairman of the Federal Reserve Board did when he said eight years ago that 'the hard fact is that market forces can no longer be counted on to check the upward course of wages and prices even when the aggregate demand for goods and services declines in the course of a business recession'. In theory, we have all learned in our first-year economics course, there is a price at which markets clear; in practice it may not always be so. It is rarely, if ever, the case as far as labour markets are concerned. It should, however, be said at once that in a country like ours or in the United States, any kind of policy that has as its object a restraint on the broad range of incomes will only be successful even in the short run if it is executed against a general pattern of policies that is adjudged to be broadly fair.

The last point which I have just made provides me with a useful bridge towards another topic I wish to raise, namely the relation of economics to the problems of policy in a mixed economy. Some twelve years ago when I spoke about the *Uses and Abuses of Economics*, I pointed to the discussions on wages in the 1930s, preceding and following the publication of the General Theory, on this very question. I then suggested that any economist who, building upon the somewhat fragmentary elements in Keynes and his contemporaries, was able to develop a new theory, would gain a very important place in the history of economic doctrine, and would, at the same time, be making a major contribution to the solution of some of our most perplexing policy problems. As yet there is no clear sign of a real breakthrough in this regard. Indeed, Peter Wiles, in a highly interesting article, *Ideology, Methodology and Neoclassical Economics*, has described as the greatest fault of neoclassical economics 'its total unwillingness to theorize about, or even to discuss, the complex of incomes policy and cost inflation'. It may well be that the problem is not capable of an analytical solution (at least in purely economic terms), but only of case by case empirical progress. But, at least, economists ought to be able to make some contribution to dissolving the veil of dogmatism that seems nowadays to surround this, as so many other problems, of the practical application of economics.

This is an area in which institutional, political, as well as strictly economic arguments coalesce. It would, therefore, be useful if more attention was given to it not only by theoretical economists but by those who have the ability to influence public opinion, and particularly the opinion of politicians. As I have already indicated, some inter-country comparisons may be useful. It may be found that the ability of countries to weather major fluctuations in the world economic scene is not so much a reflection – as some extreme economic free marketeers would claim – of their relative freedom from government intervention but is rather due to their ability, for institutional, social and, indeed, cultural reasons, to adapt incomes fairly quickly.

In another area much work is already being done, namely, on the question of the relationship between monetary and fiscal policy. I do not propose to go into this in any detail except to say that despite much effort and often rather acute controversy between protagonists of different views, no clear consensus has yet emerged. Perhaps one particular field in which the special skills of analytical economists might be more applied, is in the careful examination of certain aspects of the credit structure in this and other countries, of the way in which intermediation actually takes place, of the means by which the budget deficit, or what is nowadays called the public sector borrowing requirement, is in practice financed, and of the bearing of all these processes on the relatively simple – perhaps excessively simple – categories by which budgetary policy and and monetary policy are usually connected in theoretical discussions.

Another problem which it might be worth looking at afresh from the point of view of the current attack upon the mixed economy, particularly by those who believe in freedom of choice and freedom of markets, would be the area of monopoly and its control and the conditions under which competition may be sustained or re-established. Monopoly and competition are, of course, well-tilled fields of economic analysis; and in the light of modern theory of imperfect and monopolistic competition, one can no longer rely on the simple view that in the absence of state support monopolistic situations cannot be maintained. But there is much confusion about the practical application of economic analysis to certain policy objectives and about the objectives themselves; and these have not been dispelled by recent green papers and ministerial pronouncements. I am sure that further careful study could usefully be devoted to the effects of monopolies and restrictive practices legislation, to the practical operations of the Office of Fair Trading, and the ministerial decisions based on them, and also to the self-regulatory activities of the Take-Over Panel (and now of the Council for the Securities Industry) in the field of mergers. A great deal of case law, or at least case experience, has been built up; and I think it would be useful to re-examine that in the light of the categories of the economic theory of monopoly and competition, so as to throw more light on the basic purposes which all this intervention is designed to serve.

I spoke a few moments ago of inter-country comparisons, with special reference to the adaptability of incomes to major economic fluctuations. This whole area could well be further extended and explored. Far too often quite unsupported statements are made which would benefit from more careful analysis. For example, in a recent booklet which extols the virtues of the free market, the following statement appears: 'Even in the community of Western countries where private initiative, independent of the State, is more or less common, productivity and living standards broadly vary with the extent of the independence. Relative productivity in the four largest economies is broadly...', and there follows a table, which gives the United States as 5, Germany as 4, France as 3 and Britain as 2. Leaving aside the unexplained basis for this measurement, it may well be asked on what grounds such a close correlation is said to exist between these so-called measures of productivity (which, be it noted, are also equated with living standards) with what is described as 'independence' from state interference. I certainly know of no clear manner in which state interference can be measured as between the four countries mentioned. Furthermore, if productivity is to be used as the major yardstick (and I do not say that it should not), one may ask why Japan does not appear in this table. Is it perhaps because it could hardly be argued that the Japanese economy was in any significant sense free from a high degree of state intervention? Nor can one ignore the historical evolution of productivity. Leaving living standards out of account, which are, in any event, very difficult to define and to measure, the course of productivity in recent years in Japan, France, the United States, Germany and Britain shows no very clear trend that could be correlated with any one factor, certainly not with one so vague and so difficult to define as state interference.

More generally, I think the correlation of the 'performance' of an economy, however defined and measured, with either the structural or the policy mix of a mixed economy is a highly hazardous matter. It is certainly not one into which any responsible economic analyst would venture light-heartedly. However, it is precisely here where the publicists and politicians have a field-day. Facile comparisons are only too often invoked not only in regard to such specific objectives of economic policy as the fight against inflation, but even on more general matters such as securing growth with stability, or even the more difficult and fundamental matter as the balance between equality and efficiency, as the late Arthur Okun called it. In all these matters I see unfortunately a great gap between the patient work done by economists and its translation into the small change of political controversy between Right and Left. I fear that in this country the gap is greater today than it has been at any time in the last hundred years. I said in this country, because I do not believe the debates on the Continent, particularly in Germany and France, are as acute as they are here. Even in the United States there is less tendency to adopt extreme quasi-philosophical positions when discussing solutions to practical problems. In his important Godkin Lectures, *The Public Use of Private Interest*, in which Charles Schultze, the present chairman of the American Council of Economic Advisers, very effectively argues for the greater employment of private incentives and market mechanisms for the achievement of certain public goals, he expresses the belief that 'the American people can deal intelligently with issues when they are painted in hues more subtle than black and white'. To hear some politicans and publicists, that belief would be less justified here. As for the gap between economics and public policy one has only to think of the work done by Dennison in regard to growth, particularly in his latest study *Accounting for Slower Economic Growth*, to see how great the gulf is between what responsible economic analysts are prepared to say on the subject and what fills the columns of the daily press and of Hansard.

I say all this, although I am conscious of the fact that social scientists, including economists, are not among the most hesitant of scientists. Indeed, I am somctimes tempted to compare them, rather to their disadvantage, with modern biologists whom I see more tentatively discussing the findings of their discipline. But, economists are shrinking violets compared with politicians when it comes to the assurance with which propositions that are very hard to prove are pronounced as axioms. This contrast may well be unavoidable, for the audiences to which they address themselves are different. There is certainly a gulf between the broad thrust of the arguments in the economic sphere, the most important ones nowadays, of political parties, and what the general body of voters can comprehend and can decide that they want at any particular time. I very much doubt whether the voter, who undoubtedly wants to see inflation subdued or taxation reduced, or who may feel that the time has come for an improvement in social security benefits or in the range of activities of state-owned industries, is, or can be, fully aware of all the intricacies of policy which his very simple preferences may lead government to pursue.

Perhaps one has to accept that the rhetoric of the hustings must always be in absolutes; and perhaps only in this way can the precise mixture of a mixed economy be continually adjusted and corrected to correspond more closely not only to the changing desires of the electorate, but also to what is ultimately conducive to a prosperous and stable society. But it is a well-known phenomenon of our political system that the slogans of the electoral campaign tend to carry on into government for one or two years before the inevitable greyness of the economic landscape is borne in upon Ministers. This being so, there is some danger in adapting the mixture of a mixed economy by means of rather violent thrusts in one direction or its opposite. For the oscillations may becomes ever wider and with them the institution of policies which it would become difficult to reverse; thus leading to a polarisation of attitudes to the detriment of the minimum of consensus required for a stable society.

On the whole, therefore, I would hope that a greater infusion of the more refined economic analysis of some of the issues to which I have referred, into the daily political controversies could produce a better prospect for acceptance, survival, and development of the mixed economy. I say, I hope that it could, although I must confess that I cannot be entirely confident that this will happen.

2 The Nature And Significance Of The Mixed Economy

MAURICE PESTON
University of London

I am concerned in this essay with a decentralised economy containing a large number of economic units able to hire factors of production and produce and sell output. This happens via markets and a so-called price mechanism. Nonetheless, some of the producing units are extremely large so that resources are allocated inside them by direct control or planning methods. In addition, although the price mechanism is decentralised, it contains within it operating units, whether they be firms or trades unions, of considerable size and able to exert market power. The mixed economy is not the perfectly competitive system of elementary microeconomics.

In the case of the UK we are discussing an economy in which the 100 largest enterprises produce 40 per cent of total manufacturing output. In only five of the seventeen sectors in which industry may be classified do the top 100 firms produce less than 30 per cent of total output.[1]

Of the total labour force 53 per cent are members of trades unions, comprising 62 per cent of male employees and 38 per cent of female.[2] Currently, the Transport and General Workers Union has over two million members, and the Amalgamated Union of Engineering Workers nearly a million and a half. Altogether 26 trades unions have a membership of 100,000 or more.[3]

The mixed economy comprises a public sector and a private sector. The former may be thought of as comprising two parts; an enterprise section made up chiefly of the nationalised industries, and a political or governmental section. One, but not the only, way of assessing the relative significance of the public and private sectors is to note that, of the total employed labour force, 30 per cent is employed in the former and 70 per cent in the latter. Of the 30 per cent in the public sector, 8 per cent are in the public corporations and 22 per cent in what might be called government proper. A similar picture emerges if the income or value added generated by each sector is examined. In other words, the public-private split is approximately in the ratio of 1 to 2.[4]

Of course, as is well known, to confine the discussion to these measurements may present a misleading picture of the government. Thus, the government's role in controlling the economy will not be measured accurately by the number of civil servants or their incomes. A government may regulate and control the private sector extremely tightly using administrative and legal institutions, but not employing many people or spending much money. Equally, to the extent that the government raises taxes for distributive purposes (i.e. in order to make transfer payments), this may need to be measured directly. Thus, total government expenditure (including public corporations) is equal to about 45 per cent of total national expenditure when debt interest is ignored, and about 50 per cent when it is included.[5]

The mixed economy is a monetary economy in that most transactions involve an exchange of goods and services for money, or of paper assets of various kinds for money. It is useful, therefore, to distinguish a monetary (or financial) sector from a real (or producing and distributing) one. (It should be unnecessary to add that the fact that the mixed economy is based on the use of money does not lead to the conclusion that all its problems are monetary ones). Rather like the public sector, to measure the relative importance of the financial sector by its value added is to underestimate its significance. But for what it is worth it may be noted that insurance, banking, finance, and business services contribute about 7 per cent gross domestic product at factor cost.

Presumably, the economies are called mixed because both their private and public sectors are quite large. In none of them, however, does the public sector employ a majority of the work force or generate as much as 50 per cent of national income or value added. While public policy and the political process is important, the mixed economies are not pure socialist economies. Although private enterprise is subject to law, the legal restraints on what it can do are moderate, and do not prevent new firms entering most sectors of the economy. There is virtually no direct control of labour or on the movement of capital. Moreover, capital itself remains for the most part in private hands.

The mixed economy is a kind of hybrid of pure socialism and pure capitalism. To put it this way, however, is rather misleading. Firstly, as we have remarked in the previous paragraph, in all cases the private enterprise sector comprises significantly more than half of total economic activity. Secondly, as a matter of history all the mixed economies so far in the advanced industrial world have emerged as modified capitalism. No allegedly socialist state has so far allowed itself to be modified to such an extend that it would be correct to define it as a mixed economy.[6]

It is useful to remind ourselves at this point that, no matter what its ideological foundation, the mixed economy must in some sense or other solve what might be called the conventional set of economic problems. The production and distribution of goods and services (especially intertemporal and spatial resource allocation) and the division of income in all its forms are not avoided by the substitution of one institutional framework for another. All economic systems have these problems although they differ in how they attempt to solve them (and, indeed, in how they define solutions to them).[7] In the most abstract terms it may be possible to specify the economic problem set as quite independent of institutional structure; and theoretical analysis at this level can provide useful economic insights. Nonetheless, it is necessary to go beyond that and consider how problems are actually solved by individual people via institutions in society. Of particular importance in this regard for the UK are the issues centred around (a) inequality and incentives, (b) the fixing of wages and the role of collective bargaining, and (c) the need to generate a surplus to finance investment.

We have called the mixed economy a hybrid of socialism and capitalism. Each of these pure systems can be specified in ideological terms or as a rational account of how it proceeds as a problem solving mechanism. To put the matter at its simplest one may think of a centrally planned system optimising an objective function, or a decentralised system based on individual maximisation and exchange through competitive markets. Income distribution in the one case may be determined centrally and imposed, and in the other emerges from the past (via inheritance) together with the market mechanism. The ownership and accumulation of wealth is a matter for the state under socialism and the private individual under capitalism.

It would also be recognised that economists have shown at the theoretical level how forms of market mechanism socialism and planned capitalism could exist. In principle decision making in a socialist system could be decentralised with individuals following particular rules imposed from above. Equally, capitalism could be centrally planned via a vast data processing and computing system. The direct practical relevance of the theorems that have been proved in this area are of negligible significance to a world of uncertainty, and to a one in which conflicts of interest and the need for incentives arise. But it is worth remarking that within the individual enterprises of even the most extreme capitalist systems central planning and direct control occurs. Furthermore, all socialist systems, despite their central plans, have had to face the difficulties of coordinating the activities of individual planners and producers.

I have emphasised the theoretical and ideological purity that is claimed for socialism and capitalism in order to contrast it with the mixed economy which is by its very nature impure. The mixed economy is subject to attack on all sides because it supposedly lacks a logical foundation and a consistent justification. Its interventionary controls, and attempts to influence the distribution are anathema to the apologists for *laissez-faire*. Its acceptance of free enterprise, of profits, and considerable inequality of income and wealth offend the protagonists of pure socialism. The former attack it because the modifications of the free market have gone too far or even started at all; the latter attack it because the modifications have been insufficient and have not gone the whole hog.

Let us examine an example, namely the distribution of income. Public policy has endeavoured to influence this in a variety of ways: (a) by inheritance taxes, (b) by the progressive income tax, (c) by transfer payments, (d) by public expenditure (e.g. on education and training) affecting employability and productivity, (e) by institutional constraints such as minimum wage legislation and wages councils. Now, an important question is how effective these have been. Certainly, the data provided by the Royal Commission on the Distribution of Income and Wealth can be read either way, i.e. as showing a remarkable move towards greater equality or only the least that could be expected in the circumstances. There is also no agreement on what have been the causes of the changes that have actually occurred. But my main point is a different one. If the question is asked, Why have any of these policy measures been taken as far as they have, but no further?, it is difficult to find a satisfactory answer above the level of the trivial. Compared with such principles as 'all private wealth is inalienable so must not be touched by the state' or 'all wealth belongs to the community and must not be allowed to influence the economic and political power of individuals of the next generation', what is to be made of the moderate taxation of inheritance, the attempt to limit but not to abolish the intergenerational transmission of wealth within the family? To argue that what happens in practice arises from an attempt to balance the need for incentives, the preservation of freedom, and the diminution of inequality appears *ad hoc* and almost self-contradictory. Moreoever, the offence, if such it is, is compounded by the use of several policy measures. Investment is subsidised but inherited wealth is taxed. Higher education is subsidised but income is taxed progressively. Transfer payments are made, but particular items of expenditure by various people in need are also subsidised.

Of course, many policies in this area have emerged to meet particular circumstances (not excluding political ones) and it is not difficult to show that they cannot always be put together in a consistent pattern. Rational analysis and empirical studies may show after the event, so to speak, how some policy responses have ceased to be necessary given the existence or possible generalisation and extension of others. Points may be scored by asking, Why transfer purchasing power in general, but also subsidise particular goods and services?, since the former implies that the recipients are good judges of their needs, and the latter that they may not be.

While nothing to be said in this lecture should be regarded as antagonistic to such policy analysis, there are two further observations to be made. One is that it is a useful characteristic of the mixed economy that public policy tries to cope with problems as they arise and, perhaps, even when they are imperfectly understood. In the short term it may be easier to meet a fraction of the fuel bills of those on supplementary benefit than adjust the whole system of relevant transfer payments. The second is that the imperfections and uncertainty of impact of individual policy instruments suggests the need to try more than one even with respect to a single objective. Again, just in case fuel price rises are not correctly weighted in the appropriate cost of living index, supplementary benefits may be raised in line with that index, but the cost of fuel reduced somewhat as well for some groups in special need.

Having noted the rather messy nature of the mixed economy, it is important not to forget why it arises. The economic objections to free market uncontrolled capitalism can be listed briefly as follows:[8]

1 It fluctuates typically at a level of operation below full employment. There is also grave doubt about whether it has any significant tendency to move towards full employment even in the long run,

2 Income is distributed excessively unequally within it, and early inequalities are subsequently compounded by intergenerational transmission of wealth,
3 Competition is not easily sustainable in all sectors of the economy. In some it may be technically impossible (the so called case of natural monopoly), and in others is the result of cartels and restraints of trade (the case Adam Smith emphasised).
4 It fails to provide public goods and services (or more generally those involving external economies) either at all or on a sufficient scale. At the same time it does not limit sufficiently the production and consumption of goods involving significant external diseconomies.
5 While it may endeavour to meet consumer demand the validity of its efforts in this direction may be regarded as limited because of the use of some forms of advertising and marketing methods.

There is also an additional quasi-political observation that must be made. If free-market capitalism left to itself leads to increasingly large concentrations of economic power, the democratic political process may be imperilled.

Now the pure socialist regards these faults either as necessarily fatal (i.e. the Marxist position of the inevitability of the destruction of capitalism), or at least as making the system an entirely suitable target for attack and abolition. How then does the case for reform and transition to the mixed economy arise?

Historically, the answer is exceedingly simple. The mixed economy emerged as a reaction to circumstances, and often as a desire to preserve the *status quo*. It was only much after the event that an attempt was made to examine the changes for consistency, and to suggest that a new kind of system may have emerged.

The criticisms of capitalism are the case for not going back. What are the limits to going forward? The answer to this question lies in the following brief list of the defects of pure socialism, *soi disant*:

1. The central direction of economic activity is allocatively inefficient, almost certainly to a greater degree even than monopoly capitalism,
2. The virtual abolition of private enterprise implies in particular the abolition of the private process of innovation. A monopoly state process is a poor replacement.
3. State control of wealth and enterprise limit political freedom as much as if not more than private monopoly control does.[9] The

> other bulwark of political freedom, free trades unions operating within decentralised labour markets, is also undermined if not abolished altogether.

A final comment again concerns the distribution of income. Although it is not clear that it must be so, income (correctly defined as spending power) is not at all equally distributed in the socialist countries that exist. Indeed, income distribution in them may be more unequal than in some of the mixed economies.

The rationale for the mixed economy depends on both these sets of criticisms of its pure components. The attack on the mixed economy for its impurity can thus be seen to be ill-founded. It is precisely because of its refusal to go to either of the two extremes that it has any justification at all.

This does not mean that the mixed economy cannot be subject to criticism at all. Far from it. Since it sets itself precise and explicitly stated objectives, its performance may be assessed and its policy instruments continually examined for their effectiveness. In addition, the mixture itself must be investigated from time to time to see whether it needs changing drastically in one direction or another.

Before considering one or two examples of that kind, I must also mention that the mixed economy does have certain significant ideological aspects which cannot be ignored. The most important of them is the legitimacy of public intervention into private economic activity. It is here that the most clear-cut distinction between the advocacy of free enterprise capitalism and the mixed economy occurs. The essential point is that the private ownership of capital, while recognised as legitimate, does not imply total freedom to dispose of that capital in any way that the owner desires. To put the point differently, private economic transactions freely agreed to may nonetheless have public consequences which the government is entitled to examine, and, if necessary, modify. Yet another way of putting this is that, while capital is privately owned, it is also in trust, so that society and its representatives may enquire how it is being used, and change its use. If the question is asked, Why are public regulatory bodies allowed to exist?, the answer in the broadest possible terms lies in the socially responsible use of capital. If the alternative question is asked, Why is it not necessary to nationalise in a formal sense the means of production and distribution?, the answer is exactly the same. Indeed, nothing brings out more clearly the threatening nature of the mixed economy to the extremists of the right or left. Each regards the ownership of capital as sacrosanct, the difference being between the protection of private or public ownership. While recognising that ownership is important, the theorist of the mixed economy also stresses control, responsibility, and government intervention.[10]

This comment on the ideology of intervention extends much beyond the ownership of capital as such. It underlies the case for intervention in the process of price setting and income determination. While such intervention needs to be justified in particular cases for its effectiveness or efficiency, it also has a general justification in terms of the public interest. In terms of current debate, a price commission, an incomes commission, a supplementary benefits commission are all normal or natural components of the mixed economy as are the progressive income tax, wealth and inheritance taxes, and national insurance.

The second and seemingly contradictory ideological aspect of the mixed economy is its dominant concern with freedom. Corresponding to a principle of legitimacy of government intervention is a principle of legitimacy of private economic activity whether it be by firms, or trades unions. It is here that the protagonist of the mixed economy offends the pure socialist. While the community has a right to interest itself in any aspect of economic life, there is no *prima facie* reason why (with certain obvious exceptions) any single activity should be in the public sector. Private economic transactions may be interfered with, but equally they may not. In other words, while there is a general case allowing regulation and intervention, without additional evidence it does not necessitate it in all cases.

This leads me to a formal observation of a general nature which concerns the principle of consent for both private enterprise and public intervention that underlies the mixed economy. Put positively, this means that in broad terms what happens in the mixed economy requires the consent of the community at large. Put negatively, it means that the operation of the mixed economy or any of its component parts is limited by the need not to give extreme offence to the bulk of the community. This is not to say that individual people or institutions are not or may not be made to do things against their wishes. No community can avoid compulsion (of a legal kind, of course). It is to recognise that compulsion even by the state requires the consent of the community, and cannot be wholly offensive even to a small minority.

As an example, consider the attempt by the Labour Government as part of the social contract of 1974–9 to increase old-age pensions in real terms and relative to incomes in general. They certainly succeeded in this, and more generally transfer payments rose relative to national income and total public expenditure. During the first part of this period 1973–5 what is now called national disposable income fell, and even by 1977 was below its 1973 level. More significantly, the disposable income of workers did not return to its 1973–4 level until 1978. Thus, although it appeared that workers consented to what was essentially a transfer from themselves to the older dependent population (they themselves inevitably becoming members of that population in due course), when they came to count the cost, it seems probable that they thought the transfer had gone too far. Certainly, their attitude to wages and taxes by the end of the period made it clear that they did not favour taking the transfer any further. An attempt on the part of the government to raise pensions further could only exacerbate a cost-push inflationary process that was already in the process of building up. The government can lead; it can persuade, but ultimately it is constrained by the economic response of affected parties, on the one hand, and by the political process, on the other.

This example leads on more generally to the determination of incomes in various kinds of economies. Presumably, in pure socialism incomes are centrally determined. Experience in Eastern Europe does not suggest that they are set by free collective bargaining in various labour markets.[11] Pure capitalism is more difficult to assess. If the system is one corresponding to pure competition, there would be no monopoly on either side of the labour market. This does not mean either that full employment would always exist or that the resulting distribution of earned incomes (let alone unearned) would be satisfactory. But it is extremely unlikely that inflationary pressures will be of the cost-push type. Any realistic capitalist system, however, would be one in which monopoly elements were strong on both sides of the labour market. To avoid cost-push pressures it would have to follow the case of pure socialism and either make trades unions illegal or nugatory in the determination of incomes.[12]

One of the strongest forces moving a system away from capitalism towards the mixed economy is the determination of incomes and the desire to preserve the role of free trades unions and collective bargaining. If full employment is to be maintained, cost-push inflationary pressures reduced, and some degree of fairness of relative incomes established, there must be governmental involvement in the setting of incomes. This is so even if the power of trades unions were reduced drastically since the abolition of cost-push inflation leaves the questions of relative incomes and absolute poverty unsolved. But, despite current propaganda, it is doubtful whether, even temporarily, at least in the UK, the trades union movement could be made so weak that cost-push inflation would cease to exist.

The alternative is a mixed economy in which gross incomes are set by market forces, collective bargaining, and an incomes policy institution. The last of these would involve itself in setting norms, examining relativities, and arbitrating disputes. The macro-economic context would be set by government monetary and fiscal policy, and, of course, the latter would also be the basis for translating gross incomes into net ones.

It is easy to show that a macro-policy stance is directly related to a norm for average incomes and prices if full employment is to be maintained.[13] In the past the compatibility of the two have not been made sufficiently clear. The result has sometimes been expansionary (and then explosively inflationary) when too easy a macro-policy has gone hand in hand with too restrictive an incomes policy. At the present time the reverse is true – macro-policy is too restrictive and incomes policy has been too easy. (The government has started to recognise this in recent months and rather belatedly is working hard to establish income restraint especially in the public sector.)

Perhaps nothing shows more clearly the power of the forces that impel the government to become involved in the business of setting incomes than the experience of the present government. Having set their heart against it, they have drastically changed direction, although so far in an *ad hoc* and not thought out way, and without an appropriate institutional machinery.

Nonetheless, it must be said in their favour that, although it has been obvious for thirty-five years (since Beveridge's *Full Employment in a Free Society* and the acceptance of the full employment White Paper), an incomes policy is central to the working of a mixed economy, no one has yet succeeded in solving all of the problems associated with it. [14] One reason is that the trades union movement has not appreciated that free collective bargaining is only a viable approach to income setting if it is coupled with voluntary restraint. A government commitment to the maintenance of full employment at a particular level and rate of growth of nominal incomes has been interpreted too often as a signal for a free for all in the setting of nominal incomes and prices. But a second reason is that, if there is to be a voluntary and cooperative approach to the setting of incomes and prices in general, macro-economic policy cannot be the sole preserve of the government itself. Even at the height of trades union and employer cooperation with the Labour Government, there was little or no acceptance by the

Treasury that outsiders of any kind have a legitimate role in helping to determine the overall macro-economic position. The success of the social contract was remarkable, but it was doomed to failure since in the end the government was not willing to recognise the logic of its position that arms-length policy making could no longer succeed.

Incomes policy collapsed because the trades unions felt unable to accept the responsibilities involved, and the government would not develope a new style of cooperative policy making. More generally, of course, the painful business of explicitly discussing relativities both between various levels of earned income, and between earned income and profits was simply avoided. (In this connection the Royal Commission on the Distribution of Income and Wealth, whatever its academic merit in establishing the facts, was a disaster. Its role should and easily could have been one of policy analysis, and the clarification of the issues involved in setting relativities.)

The need for a policy on incomes is one of the justifications of a mixed economy. In the UK it defines a set of problems which have not so far been solved. An example concerns the behaviour of profits. If these are regarded as a residual (and, perhaps, on that account as a return to risky enterprise), they will fall in the down-swing of the trade cycle and rise in the up-swing. If, however, wage behaviour is such that a rise in profits at any time becomes a trigger for higher wage demands, the up-swing will be imperilled. Either there will be a real wage constraint on expansion causing so-called classical unemployment, or inflation will be exacerbated chronically. In addition, a shift away from profits will lower the share of private saving in national income. The result is either that average investment will be less at full employment (imperilling future output) or public savings (i.e. taxation) must be higher. All this is another way of making the elementary point that increased private consumption at full employment must be at the expense of investment or government expenditure on goods and services. Now, the division of full employment output, especially between public and private expenditure, and the division of full employment saving (again between public and private sectors) are subjects worthy of continual debate. They are central to the problem of the precise nature of the 'mixture' already mentioned. What is lacking is a recognition of their binding character and the need to develop machinery for discussing them and influencing policy with respect to them.

Of course, at less than full employment public and private expenditure can be increased simultaneously, and even at full capacity working the complementarity between the two forms of expenditure must be recognised as well as their competitiveness.[15] Nonetheless, on average, given the growth of productive capacity and the desire to maintain investment, an increase in public sector employment, unless these workers were to reduce their demands for private consumption expenditure (a most unlikely possibility), must cause a decline in private sector output. The excess demand for output can be met from overseas, but not permanently. In other words, the mixture undoubtedly involves consideration of what form the average person's welfare is to take. To ask for more public sector employment at full employment, but with no increase in overall productivity and no reduction in workers' living standards compared with what would otherwise be the case, is possible to a limited extent and for a short while as the living standards of 'non-workers' are reduced. Beyond that the effect would be to lower real national output, which, if the original demands were persisted in, would lead to an implosive contraction of the economy.

I have concentrated on real income as actually and conventionally measured. It is reasonable to argue that this is not the only measure of welfare. There are human costs to high productivity that a modern society may wish to avoid. It may also be the case that the incentives necessary for high productivity imply too high a degree of inequality of income and wealth. Our society may choose a relative lower level and rate of growth of real output and private consumption for the sake of other social and quasi-economic ends. What it cannot do is choose to be less productive, but make income demands contingent on its being more productive. That too has been part of the British dilemma of the past decade and a half and remains unsolved in our mixed economy.

I have referred to incomes policy as one area in which the mixed economy especially in its UK guise has posed for itself a series of problems which it has so far proved unwilling to come to grips with. I have also indicated the closeness of the relationship between incomes policy, the size of public expenditure, and the role of the public sector.

Let me now mention briefly one or two examples of problems of micro-economics which emphasise the strength and weakness of the mixed economy. The first concerns that favourite of the radical right – rent control. In conditions of sudden, unexpected shortage of accommodation either nationally or locally, while the response of a free market system would be a rise in rents and the obtaining of excess profits by landlords, the mixed economy might introduce a degree of rent control. Essentially, this transfers some of the surplus profits to tenants (although they may not always be able to realise them on the market). In itself, however, it does nothing to reduce the shortage itself. If this is the result of a reduction in supply, the problem can ultimately be solved only by an extension of supply. Moreover, given the cost of production of accommodation (including normal profit), either rents must cover this or there must be a transfer of funds from the general taxpayer to the tenant.

Looked at in this way, rent control has two functions. One is the temporary one of mitigating a market adjustment process. A second could be longer term if it is believed that landlords possess monopoly power relative to tenants. In the end, however, if people are to be properly accommodated, there must be no disincentive to private renting or sufficient public rentable housing has to be built. Either way the system as a whole is obliged to meet total costs. The weakness of the mixed economy is that it has not been able to approach this complex of issues systematically. The incentive to the private landlord has been seriously damaged, while public housing has been produced on too small a scale. Moreover, the latter, while rejecting ability and willingness to pay as its dominant principle of resource allocation, has gone to the other extreme and adopted what is overwhelmingly a queueing procedure. The contention being made is partly that the mixture may be wrong, but, more significantly, that the consequences of the mixture for housing policy are not allowed to go through.

A second example concerns the National Health Service. This has never been universal, and the private sector has continued to exist since 1948, albeit as an irrelevance to most people. What is puzzling about it is the lack of uniformity of provision within the service, differences appearing to be quite arbitrary. Experts within the service claim to be able to distinguish serious illness from 'cosmetic' or less serious medical problems. It is then said that the potential patient always gets the best available treatment for the former, but has to wait, often for quite long periods of time, for the latter. Those who are not willing to wait have the option of using the private sector.

The difficulty with this view is twofold. It is not the case that resources to be used for the treatment of serious illness are distributed equally across the country. Unless, therefore, it is argued that resources are irrelevant to medical practice, it cannot be the case that access to basic health is equally available to all. Furthermore, no one doubts that waiting lists for other treatments (e.g. tonsils, or varicose veins) vary widely between different regions. This can hardly be due entirely or even mainly to differences in the incidence of these conditions or to the preferences of patients. Why then three decades after the foundation of the NHS is so little done to change things? To put the point positively we have here another clear-cut case of the mixed economy not wishing to provide the aggregate of resources or to allocate them in ways corresponding to its own stated objectives.

It is easy to cite numerous examples of the imperfections of the mixed economy. It is nearly as easy to explain why they exist, or, more to the point, why they persist. The central reason is the political element which is so characteristic of decision making. This is not to justify what otherwise seems to be an irrational state of affairs, but is merely to indicate how self-interest comes to limit the efficient solution of problems. There is also the need to remember that the nonsense which is observed in a particular set of circumstances is almost certainly the undesirable by-product of what was otherwise a sensible policy initiative. This is shown by the examples that we have given. Thus, it is quite erroneous to start an attempt at improvement by expressing a desire to reinstate the *status quo*.

My final remarks are to do with future developments. No one doubts that the mixed economies of the advanced industrial world have been in difficulties for the past decade, and some would not hesitate to use the word 'crisis' in describing their recent history and present position. What is being debated is whether the solution to their difficulties lies in a move towards the more capitalist or more socialist end of the policy spectrum. Although I have definite views on that question, my purpose here is not so much to express them, but to state briefly what the argument is about.

The key developments that must be borne in mind are:

1. The dominant emphasis on real income and its distribution. In particular, the ability of inflation to solve the distributional struggle over shares in the available national cake has diminished. To put the proposition technically, money illusion is less important than it was. Price expectations rapidly adjust to the realities of actual inflation, causing demands for money wages also to react much more quickly. The ease with which distributional conflict was coped with in the 1950s and 1960s will not be re-established in the 1980s and 1990s.
2. The power of interest groups to protect their positions and to prevent change which they regard as adverse has grown strongly, notably in the public sector, and will not disappear even in the

light of large scale, chronic unemployment. The power to resist disadvantageous change (not exactly unknown to the professions) has spread to many more groups of organised workers.

3. The acceleration of technical advance of a labour saving kind will continue. The question of the ends of economic policy are far from settled, and the employment effects of technical change will make it more urgent to take a view on them. Should the normal working week and working lifetime be shortened? What is the role of permanent education and training? Will workers continue to express their demands mainly in terms of command over goods and services, as ordinarily defined, and is there a role for government in initiating a debate on the broad aims of economic activity, especially an improvement in the quality of working life?
4. For demographic reasons and also because of the adjustment problems of the economy to both short- and long-term changes, the relative size of the dependent population will be high for the next decade or so. The share of transfer payments in national income must rise (quite separate from their use to promote more equality). Can the social security system cope on this scale, and will there not be serious social consequences of these economic difficulties?

Related to all of this is the problem of energy and the future of the OPEC cartel. My own judgement is that in the longer term we shall return to an era of relative energy abundance. Matters will not be as easy as in the 1960s, and it is hard to believe that the monopoly power of OPEC will disappear altogether. But appropriate adjustments will occur. We have also remarked on the pace of technological change which is potentially exceptionally high. It might be inferred, therefore, that the potential long-term rate of growth of the real output of the mixed economies is high. To be set against this are the short-term problems of oil cost-push, attempts at anti-inflationary reductions in effective demand and the world recession, the possible rise of protectionism, the power of individual groups to resist change, the adverse effects on skill and attitudes to work of sustained periods of unemployment, and in some countries the diminution of industrial training and retraining. All of these factors reduce growth potential in the short and medium terms.

Thus, on the question of economic expansion there are two sorts of contradictions. The one is the technical one concerning what is the possible rate of economic expansion. There are grounds for predicting it to be historically high or low. (My own view for the 1980s would be 'low'.) The second is the normative one, concerning whether this is the time to shift economic policy from a dominant emphasis on the qualitative dimensions of economic welfare to the quantitative ones. Again there is room for argument as to whether in a time of adversity, qualitative aspects of life should be raised in esteem or lowered. (My own view is very much towards the qualitative and especially if it is coupled with further redistributive measures.)

Depending on what objectives are sought, the mixture of the mixed economy will move one way or other. My own assessment is that, although in the very short term change in the UK has been towards less government intervention and more capitalism, that is a transitory effect on a long-term trend the other way.

NOTES

1. S.J. Prais, *The Evolution of Giant Firms in Britain* (1976).
2. *Annual Abstract of Statistics* (1979) table 6.28.
3. *Ibid.*
4. *National Income and Expenditure 1979*, table 1.11.
5. *Ibid*, table 9.4.
6. Recent events in Poland suggest a glimmering of a counter-example.
7. M.H. Peston, 'When is a Problem of Economic Policy Solvable?', *Thames Papers in Political Economy* (Autumn 1979).
8. I hasten to add that I recognise there are many more objections to *laissez-faire* capitalism than the narrowly economic ones.
9. On the role of the mixed economy and the preservation and enhancement of liberty see M.H. Peston, 'Liberty and the Left', R. Leonard and D. Lipsey (eds), *The Socialist Agenda* (1980).
10. A. Crosland, *The Future of Socialism* (1956). My own views on this question are in the spirit of this seminal contribution. For the most part the so-called Clause IV of the Labour Party constitution, taken literally, is incompatible with a free democracy, and is irrelevant to existing problems. Happily there is no need to take it literally especially when it is placed in the context of social control of the use of capital. This is not to say that there is no case for the extension of public ownership especially in a non-monolithic form. But it is also not to give unequivocal support for the public ownership that exists.
11. Once again reference must be made to the Polish experience. It is noteworthy that just as in the past in the UK and other countries the trades unions are in the forefront of the struggle for freedom. In addition, it should not be forgotten that this struggle is being expressed in economic terms in the determination of wages in a labour market. It will be interesting to see, if the trades unions succeed in Poland, what form of an incomes policy will then emerge!
12. It is impossible to resist pointing out here as elsewhere how the radical right and the communist left seem to come to the same policy conclusion,

even if their methods of weakening the trades union movement are not the same.

13. M.H. Peston, 'Monetary Policy and Incomes Policy; Complements or Substitutes?', *Applied Economics* (1980).
14. Incomes policies in the UK are typically introduced in times of crisis and are weakened or abandoned when matters improve. It is obviously fallacious to infer from this that the policies are the cause of the crisis or that their removal is what leads to better economic performance.
15. A more critical view of this matter is taken by R. Bacon and W. Eltis, *Britain's Economic Problem: Too Few Producers* (1978).

3 Industrial Policy In The Mixed Economy

CHARLES ROWLEY
University of Newcastle upon Tyne

The mixed economy, for purposes of this paper, is taken to encompass, in varying form and degree, the economies of all non-communist societies. For purposes of comparison and contrast attention is here centred for the most part upon the mixed economies of the United Kingdom and the United States of America. In certain respects, this paper departs sharply from approaches which still dominate UK writings in the field of industrial economics, arguably with significant policy implications. Specifically, in *Section A* account is taken of recent developments in public choice analysis in analysing the actual policy interventions of governments and their bureaucracies, of recent developments in the economics of rent-seeking in analysing the actual responses of firms to regulatory initiatives, and of recent developments in the theory of property rights in analysing the predictable economic performance of corporate enterprise. In *Section B*, the paper explores the implications for industrial policy in its various aspects which are influenced by these perspectives and which render the development of an acceptable industrial policy ever more complex in the mixed economies. Some relevant proposals for long-term industrial policy are then outlined.

SOME RECENT RELEVANT PERSPECTIVES

THE PUBLIC CHOICE PERSPECTIVE

Welfare economics, in its conventional form, may be labelled most appropriately as a 'theory of market failure'. For analytical developments took the form, first, of rigorous statements of the necessary and sufficient conditions required for efficiency in the allocation of resources within an economy, given some distribution of income, and, secondly, of articulations of relationships among economic variables that failed to satisfy such conditions. In articulating such relationships, welfare economists have tended to avoid detailed institutional content. Nevertheless, by common acknowledgement, observed relationships in the capitalist sector of the mixed economy were deemed to indicate a marked degree of failure to achieve resource efficiency. In articulating such outcomes very considerable emphasis was placed upon the notion of self-seeking behaviour within the capitalist sector, with self-seeking not for the most part analysed broadly as utility maximising but much more narrowly as wealth (or expected wealth) maximising behaviour.

For the most part, demonstrations via welfare economics of the presence of market failure, rigorously defined, were held to justify the introduction via government of corrective measures. An idealised notion of a fully informed, welfare maximising government literally saturated the welfare economics literature throughout the first twenty years of the post-Second World War period. From Paul Samuelson through Kenneth Arrow, from Abba Lerner through Oscar Lange, economists lost their way in reckless pursuit of the joint logic of set theory and of the differential calculus, be it within the context of the mixed or of the communist society. It was only in the mid-1960s that the more realistic contributions by economists like Harold Demsetz [8, 18] began to impinge on the consensus, by raising questions concerning the omniscience and neutrality of government and insisting on comparative institutions analysis as a basis for determining the appropriate balance of the mixed economy. In such exercises the nature of government and its bureaucracy were subjected to a rigorous scrutiny and the so-called public choice school established a viable counterpart to the welfare economics tradition.

Indeed, public choice as developed during the 1906s and 1970s [3, 5, 16] has been designated by some proponents of that approach as a theory of 'government failure' that offsets the theory of 'market failure' that emerged from theoretical welfare economics. By replacing the concept of welfare maximising government with the (admittedly crude) notion of vote or plurality maximising political parties, public choice succeeded in puncturing the image of perfect government. By replacing the notion of omniscience with the notion that information flows are typically distorted by the self-seeking activities of pressure groups and growth conscious bureaucracies they further dented the notion that public intervention was the automatic panacea for so-called market failure. By employing relatively crude maximising assumptions for individual behaviour within the public sector as an analogue for the assumed wealth seeking behaviour of the private sector, public choice highlighted the essential fragility of theoretical welfare economics and established a powerful case for the comparative institutions approach. Although some of the generality of the policy implications of the former approach has been lost and has been replaced by a more circumspect case-by-case approach, nevertheless the debate has been conducted for the most part at a level of abstraction which has disturbed a number of economists.

In particular, Buchanan [6], who at one time was a firm proponent both of the theoretical welfare economics and of the public choice approach recently has castigated both schools for their use of the *homo economicus* construction in the highly restrictive forms which either require only economic arguments to appear in the individual preference function, or centre attention exclusively on such arguments whilst paying lip-service to the possible existence of other unspecified arguments. Of course the restrictive form offers greater generality in predicting the behaviour of economic man in response to specified environmental conditions. But is this generality purchased, asks Buchanan, at an excessive price in potential error, with dangerous implications for policy formulation? For, if altruistic motives chance to dominate the individual utility functions there may be no market failure or there may be no government failure even when the more restrictive approach indicates such existence.

The potential validity of Buchanan's criticism both of welfare economics and of public choice cannot be denied. Indeed, if counter-arguments really do outweigh the economic arguments in individual preference functions then even the marginal predictions of individual responses to small shifts in environmental parameters may be falsified and economists will have to go back to the drawing board to re-develop positive economics and positive public choice *ab initio*. However, the probability that this will prove the case must be extremely low. A wealth of evidence supporting the predictions of existing positive economic theory based on narrowly-defined *homo economicus* already exists. Less extensive (and as yet less convincing) evidence supporting the public choice predictions of spatial politics already is scattered through the literature. This paper therefore proceeds on the supposition that existing public choice theory must be paid close attention, if not blind obeisance, in the evaluation of industrial policy in a mixed economy. For sensual, self-seeking economic man is here to stay, at least where the market-place is concerned.

RENT SEEKING IN THE MIXED ECONOMY

It is argued in this paper that many of the regulatory interventions characteristic of the mixed economy in fact act as deterrents to competition by creating entry barriers and offer the prospect of monopoly profit (rents) to those who successfully negotiate their way through the regulatory constraints. Most clearly is this the case with public enterprise where potential entry is banned by statute and where capital market sanctions do not exist. But it is also the case with private enterprise where tariff and quota restrictions, planning restrictions, health and safety restrictions, fair trading restrictions, minimum wage restrictions, employment protection laws, environmental restrictions, etc. all combine to remove exisiting companies from and to deter new entry into the industrial sector.

It might be thought that such monopoly rents, arising as a consequence of government interventions, create little damage within the industrial sector, with the dead-weight losses due to higher prices accounting perhaps for only one per cent of gross domestic product. Unfortunately, the social cost significantly exceeds the dead-weight loss conventionally associated with monopoly. For the existence of an opportunity to obtain rents will attract resources into efforts to obtain monopolies. Obtaining a monopoly often is a competitive activity with the cost, at the margin, exactly equal to the expected profit of being such a monopolist. Where such rent seeking expenditures have no socially valuable by-products monopoly rents, instead of representing for the most part simply a transfer payment, will be transformed into a social cost of significant dimension. As Posner [17] has established, the social cost of monopoly usually will be higher the larger the industry's sales revenue at the competitive price and output and the greater the percentage price increase over the competitive level. They will always be higher the less price-elastic the demand for the product at the competitive price.

Nor should it be thought that the total costs of regulation are small in mixed economies like the USA and the United Kingdom. For

Posner has estimated that approximately 17 per cent of GNP in the USA originates in industries – such as agriculture, transportation, communications, power, banking, insurance, and medical services – that contain the sorts of controls over competition that might be expected to lead to supra-competitive prices. This estimate excludes those sectors affected by tariffs and similar restrictions. Calculations based on the estimated price increase due to regulation and the price-elasticities of demand within the regulated sector suggest that 19.8 per cent of the total revenues of the regulated sector are lost in social cost. In such circumstances, some 3.4 per cent of GNP would be wasted in that sector. Even halving the regulatory effect puts some 1.7 per cent of GNP as the (partial) cost of regulation. The overall figure must be higher since even regulators and their offices have an opportunity cost!

By contrast, if it is assumed that prices are 2 per cent above the competitive level and that demand elasticities average–1. 1607 at current prices, manufacturing and mining, in the USA, would appear to account for only 0.6 per cent of GNP as a social cost of monopoly despite the fact that this sector accounts for 30 per cent of GNP. For only one-fifth of the output in this sector arises in industries in which the largest four firms account for 60 per cent or more of sales, and Posner surmises realistically in the case of the USA that the Sherman Act, for the most part, offers effective protection against cartel activities. Such a comparison excludes, of course, the relative cost of regulation and of anti-trust enforcement and the relative benefit, if any, for example via scale economies, from monopoly in the two sectors. However, whereas scale economies may be responsible for concentration within the unregulated sector there is no body of evidence that ascribes similar social benefits to regulations that restrict entry and prohibit price competition.

The implications of rent seeking behaviour, as outlined here, for industrial policy in the mixed economies will be outlined in a subsequent section of this paper.

AGENCY THEORY AND CORPORATE ENTERPRISE

Economists for some time have been concerned with the incentive problems that arise when decision making in the corporation is the responsibility of managers who are not major security holders in the organisation that they govern. A large number of 'behavioural', 'managerial', and 'X-efficiency' theories of corporate motivation have been developed over the last twenty-five years, almost all of them replacing the classical notion of the profit maximising entrepreneur in favour of utility maximising management. Such theories, despite the stringent environmental assumptions on which they rest (viz. an inefficient capital market and a monopolistic product market) have provided considerable scope for those who are critical of unregulated capitalism as an instrument for allocating resources efficiently. However, recent developments in contract theory cast a very different impress upon this literature.

Specifically, the literature has moved toward theories that reject the classical and the behavioural models of the firm but which assume classical forms of economic behaviour on the part of agents within the firm. [1, 10, 13] The classical notion of the entrepreneur is laid to rest with the two functions usually attributed to the enterpreneur, management and risk bearing, treated as naturally separate factors within the set of contracts called a firm. The firm itself is disciplined by competition from other firms (to the extent allowed) and this forces the evolution of devices for efficiently monitoring the performance of the whole team and of its individual members. In addition, managers face the discipline and the opportunities provided by the markets for their services, both within and outside the firm.

Firstly, therefore, agency theory views the concept of firm ownership as irrelevant. In particular, ownership of capital is not to be confused with ownership of the firm. For each factor in a firm is owned by somebody, with the firm just a set of contracts covering the way in which inputs are joined to create outputs and the way in which receipts from outputs are shared among inputs. Dispelling the notion that firm ownership lies with the security holders is important as a first step toward understanding that control over a firm's decisions is not necessarily the province of security holders.

Secondly, agency theory dispels the role in the firm usually attributed to the entrepreneur even in such contractual theories as have been developed during the early 1970s by Alchian-Demsetz [1] and by Jensen-Meckling. Specifically, agency theory points out that if there is a part of the team with a special interest in viability, it is not necessarily the risk bearers. It is true that if the team should fail, factors like labour and management are protected by markets in which rights to their future services can be sold or rented to other teams, whereas the risk bearers, as residual claimants, appear to suffer the most direct consequences from the failure of the team. However, risk bearers in the modern corporation also have markets for their services – capital markets – which allow them to shift among teams at low cost and to hedge against the failure of any one team by diversifying their holdings across teams.

Indeed, portfolio theory suggests that the optimal portfolio for any investor is likely to be diversified across the securities of many firms. As such, an individual security holder generally has no special interest in overseeing the detailed activities of any firm. In contrast, managers rent a significant lump of wealth – their human capital – to the firm and the rental rates of such human capital are signalled in the managerial labour market in terms of success or failure of the firm. Thus, although a manager may not suffer immediate gain or loss in current wages from the current performance of his team, such performance impacts his future wages and thereby gives him a direct stake in the success of the team.

The security holders themselves assist indirectly in the evaluation of their management in the managerial labour market. For the signals provided by an efficient capital market concerning the value of a firm's securities will play a significant role in the managerial labour market's revaluation of a firm's management. The question thus is posed as to the extent to which the signals provided by managerial labour markets and by the capital market are able to discipline management. To a considerable extent, agency theory argues that such discipline can be imposed.

The outside managerial labour market exerts a number of direct pressures for the firm to compensate managers according to performance. One such pressure emanates from the fact that ongoing firms are always in the market for new managers. Potential new managers are directly concerned about performance criteria and its relationship with the reward structure. Furthermore, given a competitive managerial labour market, if a firm's reward structure is out of line with performance it will lose managers, the best being the first to leave.

In addition, of course, there is a great deal of internal monitoring of managers by managers themselves. The process of measuring the productivity of lower management is a natural function of higher management with clear returns in the outside managerial labour market and with likely returns within the internal market of the firm. Less well appreicated, however, is the monitoring that takes place from lower to higher levels of management. Three incentives exist for such monitoring. The first, competitive, reflects the gains perceived by lower management from superseding their less competent superiors.

The second, complementary, arises because the marginal product of lower management is likely to be a positive function of that of higher management. The third arises because all managers recognise that the managerial labour market uses the overall performance of a firm to determine each manager's opportunity wage.

All management below the very top level has a clear interest, therefore, in seeing that top managers select policies which provide the most positive signals to the managerial labour market. The crucial question concerns the mechanism whereby top management is appointed and then itself is disciplined. Agency theory offers no general view on this – indeed it cannot do so since so much depends on outside environmental factors, not the least important of which is industrial policy. A few aspects of the problem require consideration, nevertheless, at this stage in the analysis. First, a board dominated by security holders does not appear to be endowed with survival characteristics, since such holders are generally too widely diversified across the security market to take sufficient interest. Secondly, competition between top managers together with pressures from below will provide a modicum of discipline, especially when top managers are concerned about their own opportunity wages. Thus, there is a danger in packing a board with independently wealthy individuals if survival is desired. Thirdly, the threat of take-over by another corporation, though limited by the costly and regulated nature of such transactions, offers a last ditch method of ditching seriously substandard top management in cases where such management is not easily dislodged.

SOME IMPLICATIONS FOR EXISTING INDUSTRIAL POLICIES

THE MACRO-ECONOMIC ENVIRONMENT

All governments of mixed economies have assumed an increasing responsibility for macro-economic management during the period since the Second World War. Such macro-economic interventions, with few exceptions, have coincided with an ongoing relative rise in the size of the public sector at the expense of the private sector of the economy. Certainly, this is true in the USA and, to a spectacular extent of the United Kingdom. Ever since the election of the present Conservative Government in May 1979, real public expenditure has advanced in absolute terms despite the existence of a stagnant or even declining gross national product. Yet such advances contrast sharply with international experience over the period of 100 years prior to the First World War. For example, as a consequence of the Civil War, the US national debt in 1865 stood at $2.7 billion. By 1893, as a consequence of 28 years of continuous budget surpluses, the national debt had fallen to $961 million. During that period about 25 per cent of all public expenditure was devoted to debt amortization. The notion of the desirability of budget balance played a highly significant role in such accomplishments.

In the United Kingdom, the balanced budget principle was abandoned as early as 1945 by a Labour Government dedicated to Keynesian-type demand management through the business cycle. In the USA, the budget remained roughly in balance over the period 1947 until 1960, despite the high cost of the Korean War. Since 1960, budget deficits have become the established order in the USA as in the United Kingdom.

The shift from policies of approximate budget balance to the present policies of continuing budget deficits had two prime causes. The abandonment of the Gold Standard undoubtedly offered governments much great freedom to expand the money supply as one means of financing their deficits. For no longer was it the case that inflation automatically led to a drainage in gold and thence to a reduction in the stock of money. Although the relaxation was a gradual process, through the Gold Exchange Standard and fixed exchange rates, in 1971 President Nixon repudiated the gold convertibility of the dollar, offering a purely fiduciary standard. Thus was an unwritten element in the USA constitution and earlier in similar fashion a widely accepted constraint on the sovereignity of the United Kingdom Parliament eroded and finally eliminated.

The second, perhaps not entirely predictable cause of the shift to budget deficits was the Keynesian revolution in economic policy. [20, 21] This revolution created a view that budgetary imbalance was consistent with (indeed was required for) 'responsible' fiscal policy. In recession, a budget deficit would stimulate employment whilst if inflation occurred a budget surplus would reduce excessive expenditures. Thus policy was to shift (in principle at least) from one of budget balance to one of using budget imbalance to balance the economy.

What Keynes failed to recognise, but governments were quick to act upon, was a fundamental discrepancy between the requirements of efficient demand management (as then conceived) and the dictates of public choice. For in democracies, once the constraints are off, a political bias exists in favour of deficit finance. For budgetary policies are an important part of government economic policies which themselves usually are the central factor in the election process. Usually, tax reductions and increases in public expenditure both strengthen the governing party's base of support, because they offer immediate apparent benefits to voters in the form of real income increases and additional employment opportunities, whilst the associated detriments in terms of rising inflation, eroded real income, eroded employment opportunities are typically deferred until the election crisis is over. Policies designed to reduce expenditure and to increase taxes typically exert a contrary political effect. Only in the first year of a new government, in economies where the memory of the electorate is characterised by rapid decay is any attempt to obtain a budget surplus to be expected. Public choice theory, with its inference that all governments will attempt to woo the median voter, does not allow ideology much scope, and, therefore does not distinguish between political parties of left or right in this prediction.

The fundamental asymmetry of budgetary politics is accentuated by the inevitable growth in bureaucracy that budget deficits imply. For all members of bureaucracy stand to gain from further bureaucratic growth, since this tends to accentuate personal incomes, promotion prospects, power, patronage and (sometimes) public respect. Rent seeking typically is more effective in the public than in the private sector because the public sector is more monopolistic, tends to be less efficient, and information flows more easily are distorted. In the United Kingdom, for example, the unions and professional associations have developed highly skilled rent seeking techniques within the non-trading public sector, based upon the statutory monopolies accorded to them by the state. When such rents potentially are threatened as they are as of now by the Thatcher Government, they deploy sophisticated rent-maintenance policies which essentially involve distorting information to suggest that public expenditure cuts can only fall on highly valued services, rather than upon the (often) negatively valued bureaucracy which lives parasitically upon them. Thus is it that many areas of the non-trading sector are likely to be over-paid, under-worked and over manned by reference to their actual economic contribution.

The political and bureaucratic bias towards deficit finance in most mixed economies contributes both to capital consumption and to inflation, depending upon the relative extent to which deficits are financed by borrowing and by monetary expansion. When governments borrow, capital markets are disturbed, and interest rates *ceteris paribus* increase. To some extent, public borrowing crowds out private investment, with deleterious effects upon long-term living standards unless it can be assumed that public expenditures are deployed as efficiently as would have been the foregone private investment. Most studies in recent years suggest that the productivity of government investment generally is considerably below that of private expenditure in the USA and the United Kingdom. Moreover, government borrowing typically does not replace fully the private investment that is crowded out. For, while some private borrowing is for consumption, most of it is for investment. Whereas, while some government borrowing is for investment, most of it is for consumption. Thus, mixed economies in which the investment ratio is considered too low can ill afford continuous government deficits.

The reasons for the likely relatively low productivity of the non-trading public sector are to be divined to a considerable extent from the three perspectives whence this paper was introduced. In so far as politicians are vote conscious and detect short-term electoral returns from an increase in public expenditure, and in so far as their central bureaucracies consolidate them in this belief, the non-trading public sector will be over-expanded and will be demand rather than budget constrained in the sense of Niskanen. This implies that rents will be available within each bureau and that resources will be wasted in seeking such rents. In part, rents will be taken out, via union and professional association pressure, in excessively high personal incomes and manning levels, in part in the form of office and other perquisites inessential to the supply of output. But, overall, the cost of obtaining such rents at the margin will be equated to their *ex ante* expected value, with an overall efficiency loss, irrespective of distributional considerations.

The underlying loss of productivity to be expected from the above-mentioned factors will be accentuated by adverse environmental factors, if agency theory is given any credence. The non-trading public sector simply lacks the range of relevant signals to the managerial labour market that is available in the trading sector. In particular, there are no profit or other financial signals of commercial success. It is more difficult, therefore, for productivity conscious executives to work their way up the executive echelon by work performance alone. In addition, the policy objectives of top management are much less easy to formulate certainly than in the private sector of the mixed economy, and, indeed, to a considerable extent, are subject to the changing vote sensitivity of electorally conscious politicians. In such circumstances, inadequate top management may prove extremely difficult to remove. If the internal monitoring system fails – as is likely to be the case – there are no security holders and no possible take-over bids to offer a last-ditch alternative solution. Only *in extremis* are the politicans, central or local, likely to inform themselves sufficiently as to be in any position to intervene.

The industrial policy implications of the macro-economic environment in the mixed economy will be outlined in the final section of this paper.

REGULATION AND PUBLIC ENTERPRISE

Regulation is a concept capable of several alternative definitions and, as such, must be carefully employed. In the narrow sense employed by Posner [7], we noted that some 17 per cent of GNP in the USA originates within the regulated sector. Employing a similar definition with reference to the United Kingdom, the regulated sector would be significantly smaller, encompassing, for the most part, agriculture, the private transportation industry, banking, and parts of the pharmaceutical industry. Of course, if a wider definition of regulation is employed, almost all of USA and United Kingdom industry is the subject of regulation at the present time.

Public enterprise is a much less ambiguous concept, though not without its own nuances of interpretation. Viewed here as encompassing all trading enterprises whose capital is in public ownership, public enterprise, of course, is a much more pronounced feature of the United Kingdom than of the USA economy. Taken together, however, the regulated and publicly-owned trading sectors of both economies at the present time account approximately for 30 per cent of GNP in both economies.

If Posner's calculations of the welfare loss from regulation are extended (with a somewhat higher associated loss) to public enterprise, it would appear perhaps that some 5 per cent of USA GNP and some 8 per cent of United Kingdom GNP may be lost currently as a direct consequence of regulation and public enterprise (to say nothing about the dynamic loss in the underlying growth rates of both economies). In addition, there must be an unidentified but substantial secondary waste of resources in both economies in the regulatory machinery itself and in the bureaucrats associated with the various public enterprises in some attempt to monitor their performance.

The reasons why public enterprises have been entered with a greater associated welfare loss than the regulated enterprises are to be located in the different environmental conditions which confront them. Specifically, the regulated enterprise retains security holder influence, such as that is, and remains susceptible to bankruptcy pressures. Also, its protection against new entry in some cases will be less than absolute. None of these conditions apply in the case of most public enterprises. Specifically, public enterprise boards are subject to the control of Parliament and its bureaucracy, with almost all the implications discussed in the case of the non-trading public sector. There is no evidence, certainly in the whole of United Kingdom experience that public enterprises, however unprofitable, have been closed down, although periodically they may be required to contract, and in some but not in all cases there is a statutory ban on new entry. Such competition as exists, which in some cases is substantial, stems from substitute commodities and from imports.

In such differentiated circumstances, it is useful to return to agency theory to justify the different welfare losses associated with the two environments. In the case of regulation, its existence modifies the nature of the performance signals that reach the managerial labour market, raising question-marks as to how far a good or a poor commercial performance is the impact of specific regulations. The signal is not altogether destroyed, however, since comparisons may be drawn between regulated enterprises subjected to similar regulatory interventions. Nevertheless, the pressure exerted upon management by the outside labour market to a varying extent will be diminished with predictable consequences for managerial effort.

Internal monitoring undoubtedly will continue though in a more complex form than is the case with the unregulated sector. For private returns will now be perceived in manipulating the regulators as well as in supplying output. Top management will make fine decisions concerning how activities will be divided between the two processes. It may well be that those most successful in manipulating the regulators will proceed fastest through the managerial echelon. Certainly, much top management time in the USA is devoted to regulator dealings. Such resource allocations, for the most part, constitute a social loss. Moreover, the diversion of such resources from monitoring within the enterprise almost certainly involves losses in productive efficiency. Outside monitoring from the security holders, from the threat of bankruptcy and, where allowed, from the threat of take-over cannot be relied upon to make good the monitoring deficiency.

In the case of public enterprise, much will depend upon the political climate in which they operate, of which more anon. This is particularly so since the prime goal of wealth maximisation, which dominates the private sector may not be so strongly apparent in the case of public enterprise. If objectives are confused and conflicting, as has been the case, at least until the last few months, in the United Kingdom, the performance signals to the outside labour market to a substantial degree are destroyed. In consequence, outside pressures upon management to monitor effectively are almost eliminated. Furthermore, the internal monitoring process also is rendered extremely complex, since objectives are confused. Top management frequently do not attain their position as a consequence of the outside labour market signals but rather as a consequence of political patronage on the part of government. In some instances in the United Kingdom, politicians with no industrial experience have been placed in control of giant enterprises, with predictable consequences for productive efficiency.

Rent seeking also diverts resources within public enterprise, even though in some cases there are no apparent rents to be obtained. Rent seeking indeed is particularly attractive within public enterprise in the United Kingdom because the statutory obligation on public enterprise to cover its costs by its revenues is rarely enforced. Thus unions and management have been able (once again with a limited caveat as to the present) to combine in paying excessive wages and salaries by reference to marginal revenue products, to maintain excessive manning levels and to indulge themselves in excessive office perquisites, etc. The resources devoted to such rent seeking, which have been substantial in certain public enterprises, constitute a social waste. Moreover, the diversion of managerial effort must have a deleterious impact upon enterprise performance. There is no equivalent of the security holder, bankruptcy or take-over bid to counter-balance monitoring inefficiencies. Hence the welfare loss is more heavily weighted on public enterprise than on regulation within the context of postwar experience.

If governments are aware of the efficiency losses from regulation and public enterprise why is it that such activities have proliferated during the postwar period in the USA and in the United Kingdom? The answer is to be found in the lessons of public choice theory. Any political party, believing that a decisive voter group desires intervention will offer intervention in its election platform, whatever its ideological position unless it pines for long-term opposition (as indeed do certain parties of communist and fascist persuasion). In a political system certainly like that of the United Kingdom where the voting system tends to alternate in office parties of *slightly different* political persuasion (in reality rather than in ideology) – and this is true to a much lesser degree also in the USA – it is not surprising that interventionism is rife with decisive voter groups desiring to mete out penalties on those who previously had intervened against themselves. Thus, one ingredient for regulation exists.

This basic political ingredient for regulatory intervention is fuelled by a bureaucracy which obtains direct advantages from such a policy [15]. For, if governments are to intervene in the industrial sector much better that they should do so from the bureaucratic viewpoint via regulation than via tax-price/subsidy price techniques. For, with the former, the regulators are usually given wide discretionary powers which, optimistically, may be utilised to some degree to win friends within the industrial sector who, in return, may be willing to further the regulator's post regulatory career and which, pessimistically, may be utilised to expropriate illegal bribes and/or other (legal?) benefits. Thus is it, for example in the cases of environmental protection policy, that despite unusual agreement among the vast majority of economists that tax-price interventions are superior, in practice, consent restrictions are all but universal.

An additional factor favouring regulation is the rent seeking pressures of producers themselves in favour of such measures. Pressure groups are difficult to organise when, as is usual, the benefits obtained are available to firms or individuals who have not participated in the lobbying process. For, in such circumstances, the temptation to free-ride is considerable and the impact of the group, thereby, may be significantly diminished. In the case of firms (and unions) the benefits from successful pressure may be direct and significant. Free-riding, therefore, will be more easily controlled. In the case of consumers, however, any benefits are individually small and diffuse. Predictably, in consequence, the consumer case for tax-prices is overwhelmed typically by the producer case for regulation.

Thus is it that regulation and new regulatory legislation abounds in the mixed economies of the USA and the United Kingdom despite the significant welfare losses that are known to be imposed.

MONOPOLY

Most mixed economies – certainly the USA and to a lesser extent the UK – have developed policies which, at least in principle, are unfavourable towards monopoly. Nevertheless, monopoly, variously defined, remains a not insignificant feature of such economies. For example, Posner [17] uses a 60 per cent or more of sales accounted for by four firms measure to indicate that one-fifth of all output in US manufacturing and mining sectors is monopolised. He denies the possibility of effective collusion, given the effectiveness of anti-cartel policies in the USA. Even so, with output originating in this sector accounting for some 30 per cent of GNP, the monopoly problem within the USA cannot be ignored.

Similarly, a range of studies based upon recent UK census data [11, 12, 22] suggest that about 25 per cent of United Kingdom manufacturing output (private sector only) is characterised by monopoly in the approximate sense of Posner. The postwar period is evidenced by a persistent tendency for concentration to extend, in the case of the United Kingdom even when imports are allowed to enter the total market calculation, despite membership of the European Economic Community. Moreover, within the United Kingdom, collusion undoubtedly is more common than in the USA, despite the existence of restrictive practices legislation. Monopoly appears, therefore, to be a pervasive problem for the mixed economy.

We noted, in 'Some Recent Relevant Perspectives', that the welfare loss from monopoly is greater than conventionally has been assumed, as a consequence of resources wasted in rent seeking, which, otherwise might have represented just a transfer from consumers to producers. The costs involved in attempts to gain or to retain monopoly power may take many forms, including investment in excess production capacity, excessive accumulation of advertising goodwill stocks, excessive product differentiation, excessive research and development expenditures, efforts to obtain tariff protection, patent protection and other forms of preferential government treatment through campaign contributions, lobbying and bribery. In addition, management and unions will seek out their own rents, if any remain once monopoly is established. Of course not all such expenditures will represent a total loss to society, since beneficial by-products may result in some cases. Nevertheless, the effective loss may prove substantial.

Cowling and Mueller [7], employing an admittedly worst case methodology, obtained estimates of the welfare loss to monopoly in the USA, on various assumptions as to the pervasiveness of monopoly, ranging between 4 and 13 per cent of Gross Corporative Output, which is vastly in excess of Harberger's original measure of 0.1 per cent of US GNP. Perhaps most striking of all was their measure of the welfare loss from General Motors, which, at $1¾ billion per annum, accounted for 0.25 per cent of average GNP itself, exceeding Harberger's estimate for the entire USA economy. For the United Kingdom, using similar measurement procedures, aggregate estimates of welfare loss ranged between 3.9 and 7.2 per cent of Gross Corporate Output. The upper bound lies well below that for the USA principally as a consequence of much lower levels of advertising expenditures in concentrated markets by United Kingdom enterprises. In the United Kingdom, the two major oil companies, BP and Shell, dominated the welfare loss table with BP's welfare loss alone accounting for some 0.25 per cent of United Kingdom GNP in 1968/9 and in 1970/4.

These measures themselves may understate the overall welfare loss once agency theory is taken into account. For the existence of monopoly power within an enterprise undoubtedly distorts, though it does not entirely dispel, the signals concerning managerial performance to the outside labour market. In particular, it renders difficult the task of assessing the managerial contribution to an apparently successful financial performance. As with regulation, this distortion is likely to reduce the outside pressure upon the management of a successful enterprise to monitor efficiently. Unlike regulation, it should intensify outside pressure on the management of unsuccessful enterprises.

Internal monitoring will occur under monopoly conditions, although, as with regulation, the process is rendered more complex than under competitive conditions. For much of managerial effort, especially that of top management, will be diverted to monopoly creation and/or maintenace, involving decisions as to how much expenditure should be devoted to rent seeking and within that allocation where best it should be expended. As with regulation, it is not always clear that management who are well suited to rent seeking will prove equally successful in the internal monitoring process. Residual pressure via the security holders, potential take-overs and bankruptcy, of course, continue to play some role in monitoring monopoly management.

Although in some instances – now considered to be fewer than was the case during the 1960s – governments may legitimately take the view that monopoly is socially justified by scale economies, in the vast majority of cases they are aware of the social cost that is involved. Yet the movement against monopoly – indeed the movement against mergers from which monopoly must ensue – has been insufficient both in the USA and (especially) in the United Kingdom to prevent increasing industrial concentration throughout the postwar period. Reasons for such apparent inconsistency once again can be traced to the problems of public choice.

Firstly, the politicians themselves sense that votes are to be obtained – not least from the successful rent seekers, among whom are to be found many union members – from allowing monopoly to exist and from encouraging its extension. The loss of specific votes resulting from a withdrawal of such rents might not be counter-balanced as the early returns to competition policy would be slight given the costs of transition. In addition, some politicians may wish to curry favour with the top management of monopolistic enterprise, given the uncertainties of political life, in the expectation that future employment opportunities may be made available in their post-political careers.

Such a prejudice, should it exist, would tend to be accentuated by senior bureaucrats who themselves see advantage in retaining good relationships with large-scale enterprises, who find it easier to treat with few rather than many firms and whose task of statistical compilation and presentation thereby is much diminished. Part of the rent taking in bureaucracy undoubtedly is the quiet life and the senior bureaucrats are in a very powerful position to distort information concerning the costs and benefits of monopoly in presenting evidence to their governments.

Finally, of course, both politicians and their bureaucrats are susceptible to the rent maintenance and rent seeking expenditures of monopolists and potential monopolists. If they were not, such expenditures would quickly cease. Thus is it that monopoly retains its present grip even in such a reputedly pro-competitive economy as that of the USA.

Industrial Policy For The Future?

If the logic of first two sections of this essay is accepted, certain changes in the organisation of industry in the USA and in the United Kingdom would reduce existing welfare losses and might well be instrumental in raising the underlying rates of economic growth. In this section, a number of proposals briefly are specified and the contingent public choice difficulties of their implementation are evaluated.

The first, and arguably the most important, change required for an effective industrial performance in the USA and in the United Kingdom concerns the macro-economic environment provided by government. If the analysis in this paper appeals, it seems clear that industrial performance would be better with a government which balances its budget than with a government which budgets for a continuous and chronic deficit. Yet, there is a powerful bias in democracies in favour of deficit finance. Recognition of this discrepancy suggests the advantages of a fiscal constitution imposing explicitly the requirement of budget balance which was recognised implicitly for the most part of the nineteenth century in both countries and which was honoured, taking the period 1947–60 as a whole, by the USA until some twenty years ago.

Of course, constitutional constraints are more easily introduced in the USA with its written constitution, than in the United Kingdom, with its tradition of parliamentary sovereignty. Of course, there would be problems in defining 'crisis' situations, such as wars, when the fiscal constitution would be suspended. But, if public choice predictions are correct there are probably only two alternatives available which are capable of withstanding the spending propensities of democratic governments, both at central and at local level. The caveat is necessary because an alternative solution would be that of introducing a monetary constitution which controlled the monetary base, suitably defined, and through that the budget, given voter resistance to ever-rising real rates of interest. A second alternative, which would sacrifice all the advantages of flexible exchange rates, would be a return to a full Gold Standard in the form that it operated during the nineteenth century.

To those neo-Keynesians who would counter such a change in policy by suggesting that the government thereby would lose control over the management of the economy, the answer, in their own currency, lies in the existence of the balanced budget multiplier. By raising the total level of the budget, if Keynesian influences work, a multiplier of one should offer a degree of expansion to the macro-economy. To the scepticism of rational expectations monetarists such as Minford, who argue that the value of the balanced budget multiplier approaches zero, the answer, again in their own currency, is that the marginal propensity to save out of additional income is unlikely to be zero once inflation is controlled and interest rates become positive in real terms once again.

The implications of this analysis for regulation and for public enterprise for the most part are fairly clear. Regulation which provides monopoly power for its recipients – as does for example regulation of agriculture and private transportation – especially that protecting minimum prices or restricting new entry, should be dismantled. If residual protection is deemed necessary on crisis grounds it should be provided via non-discretionary subsidies resting on a clearly-based standard of evaluation. But such subsidies should be minimised in their extent. Similarly, the welfare destroying plethora of secondary regulations, of the kind outlined in the first section should be closely scrutinised. Where restrictions on output appear to be desirable, for example for environmental purposes, rights should be auctioned or tax-prices imposed rather than discretionary consents applied. For by so doing, welfare conserving transfers will replace welfare losses from rent seeking with all the additional distortions that the latter process implies.

Where other restrictions appear to be necessary, for example in health and safety at work, the vast bureaucratic organisations should be disbanded – in this field they are among the fastest growing of all – and should be replaced by a system of strict liability at law associated with a compulsory insurance scheme. Thus would a very considerable resource waste, and a serious diversion of managerial effort be minimised. In the case of other regulations, concerning minimum wages, employment protection, etc., the impact upon competition should be carefully evaluated, as a social cost, in determining whether or not they should be continued and in what form.

The public choice problems in introducing such changes are formidable. From the analysis earlier in this paper, there are no easy solutions, with consumers so evidently powerless against the combined self-interest of politicians, bureaucrats, industrialists and unions. Education, though slow, may prove helpful. Ingenuity in devising tax-price schemes (disliked by industrialists because (apparently) they cost them more) with subsidy attachments may help to break the solidarity of the pro-regulation conspiracy. At least if the public choice constraints are clearly recognised those who desire to increase welfare can set about the task of relaxing them. The present United Kingdom Government, with its policy of regulation-free industrial zones in inner cities, is offering an invaluable pilot study of the impact upon industrial performance.

The implications for public enterprise and for the non-trading bureaucracies equally are fairly evident. In both cases, all statutory monopolies should be withdrawn – if they are efficient presumably such restrictions are unnecessary – with potential new entry a device to curb wasteful rent seeking activity. In the case of public enterprise, the requirement to cover costs with revenues, or suitably higher financial conditions, should be rigorously imposed, with no additional support other than in the form of special subsidies to cover clearly identified externalities. Where trading losses are massive – as in a number of public enterprises in the UK at the present time – consideration should be given to handing over the assets to the work force on a suitably devised individual basis, accompanied by a withdrawal of ongoing deficit financing. At least in such circumstances, those so employed would be given a direct financial incentive to obtain a positive valuation on their shares.

Non-trading bureaux should be subjected – as to a degree they now are – to strict cash limits, perhaps with a more detailed ministerial directive than now occurs as to precisely where associated cuts should fall. For, in the absence of such directives, it is clear that a size conscious bureaucracy will seek to implement cuts where they hurt the consumer most as a means of limiting the power of vote conscious politicians to reduce the level of real public expenditure.

As with regulation, so with public expenditure, the public choice obstacles are formidable. Once again education and ingenuity are at a premium.

Finally, there is monopoly and the question of its control. The rent seeking and agency theory perspectives strengthen the case for anti-trust, if suitable control mechanisms can be devised. For, even if scale economies exist, the rents from monopoly will appear higher and will induce yet more socially wasteful expenditures in their competitive pursuit. The problem is that of devising a machinery of anti-trust that will itself not involve excessive wasteful bureaucracy and that will not induce excessive rent reduction avoidance expenditures on the part of those whose rents are threatened. For there is little point in replacing one socially inefficient system with another which is equally inefficient.

Evidence suggests that if anti-trust is to be socially advantageous it should take the form of clearly specified non-discretionary rules which are enforced via the courts. Administrative bodies with discretionary powers – like the Federal Trade Commission and the Monopolies Commission – are much more costly and subject to all of the regulatory limitations outlined above. The courts, though they too are not totally proof from pressure, are restricted by precedent from deviating too far from the rules as initially interpreted. As such, if UK experience with the Restrictive Practices Court is relevant, many rent holders abandon their rents fairly quickly once the initial cases have outlined the position of the court.

Because the politicans and the bureaucrats are less directly involved, anti-trust has a much better chance than any of the other proposals put forward in this paper. Hence, it exists, albeit in muted form both in the USA and in the United Kingdom. At least it provides a start – and if strengthened a testing ground – for the perspectives here outlined. If successful, it may strengthen the case for more radical reform.

President Pinochet is returning Chile to a competitive market economy unfettered by regulation and relieved of its public enterprise at the point of the dictatorial gun, which has emasculated the union movement. Can the USA and the United Kingdom achieve the same with at least in the case of the UK a willing government but one that suffers all the pressures of democratic public choice and faces a hostile trade union leadership? That is the unanswered – and as yet the unanswerable – question.

BIBLIOGRAPHY

1. Alchian, A. and Demsetz, H., 'Production, Information Costs and Economic Organisation', *American Economic Review* (Dec. 1972) pp. 777–95.
2. Allard, R., 'Expenditures on Monopoly Acquisition', *Queen Mary College Discussion Paper*, no. 65 (1980).
3. Breton, A., *The Economic Theory of Representative Government* (Macmillan, 1974).
4. Brozen, Y., *Is Government the Source of Monopoly*? (Cato Inst., 1980).
5. Buchanan, J., 'From Private Preferences to Public Philosophy: The Development of Public Choice', in *The Economics of Politics*, IEA Readings 18 (1978) pp. 1–20.
6. Buchanan, J., 'The Achievements and Limits of Public Choice in Diagnosing Government Failure and in Offering Bases for Constructive Reform', *Center for Study of Public Choice Working Paper* (1980).
7. Cowling, K. and Mueller, D., 'The Social Costs of Monopoly Power', *Economic Journal* (Dec. 1978) pp. 727–48.
8. Demsetz, H., 'Information and Efficiency: Another Viewpoint', *Journal of Law and Economics*, XI (Apr. 1969) pp. 1–22.
9. Downs, A., *An Economic Theory of Democracy* (Harper & Row, 1957).
10. Fama, E.F., 'Agency Problems and the Theory of the Firm',

Journal of Political Economy, vol. 88, no. 2, (Apr. 1980) pp. 288–307.
11. Hannah, L. and Kay, J.A., *Concentration in Modern Industry* (Macmillan, 1977).
12. Hart, P.E., Utton, M.A. and Walshe, G., *Mergers and Concentration in British Industry* (Cambridge University Press, 1973).
13. Hessen, R., 'Corporate Legitimacy and Social Responsibility', *Hastings Law Journal*, xxx (May, 1979) pp. 1327–50.
14. Kirzner, I., 'The Primacy of Entrepreneurial Discovery', in *Prime Mover of Progress*, IEA Readings 23 (Mar. 1980) pp. 3–30.
15. Niskanen, W.A., *Bureaucracy and Representative Government* (Aldine, 1971).
16. Olson, M., *The Logic of Collective Action* (Harvard University Press, 1965).
17. Posner, R.A., 'The Social Costs of Monopoly and Regulation', *Journal of Political Economy*, vol. 83, no. 4 (Aug. 1978) pp 807–28.
18. Rowley, C.K., 'Market "Failure" and Government "Failure"', in *The Economics of Politics*, IEA Readings 18, supra pp. 29–50.
19. Tullock, G., 'The Welfare Costs of Tariffs, Monopolies and Theft', *Western Econ. Journal* (5 June 1967) pp. 224–32.
20. Wagner, R.E. and Tollison, R.D., *Balanced Budgets, Fiscal Responsibility and the Constitution* (Cato Institute, 1980).
21. Buchanan, J.M. and Wagner, R.E., *Democracy in Deficit: The Political Legacy of Lord Keynes* (Academic Press, 1977).
22. Walshe, G., *Recent Trends in Monopoly in Great Britain* (Cambridge University Press, 1974).

4 The Comparative Performance of Public and Private Ownership

ROBERT MILLWARD
University of Salford

INTRODUCTION

At first blush it is remarkable how little work has been done by economists on a subject so popular and contentious in the political arena. At second blush there is perhaps little surprise given the huge pitfalls of a conceptual and measurement variety and the difficulty, at least in this country, of finding the two species in coexistence in the same product area. The recent surge of cost studies has, belatedly, drawn on the wide variety of institutional forms in certain industries in North America. Even so the coverage is patchy. Electricity has been well studied and there has been some work on water supply, railways, urban transport and airlines. In these areas output is generally subject to user charges. This paper therefore focuses on areas of a semi-commercial' nature so that health and education are not covered though the temptation could not not be resisted of including an area both fecund in its variety of institutional forms and one where economists seem to have found their true home, refuse collection. There is a problem in specifying what is meant by performance and how it is measured. There is, on the other side of the coin, a problem in knowing what can be deduced from those things that can sometimes be measured, that is relative costs and relative profitability. In addition this paper reconsiders some of the earlier comparative studies in the USA (cf. Peltzman 1971; De Alessi 1974) which carried conclusions about the relative inefficiency of public ownership in electricity and the claim of one writer (Spann 1977) that the relative inefficiency of public provision is reasonably well substantiated.

COMPARATIVE EFFICIENCY AND THE MODE OF OWNERSHIP

The behaviour of an enterprise, whether private or public, is a reflection of the behaviour of many groups, management, labour, owners, consumers, government. Part of the motivation behind studies of comparative costs and profitability and the one on which this paper focuses stems from an interest in management behaviour and, in particular, whether managerial efficiency is different under private and public ownership. Given the objectives of the enterprise how well does management allocate its time between various possible activities in achieving these objectives. Of two firms with the same objectives, does management in one firm so allocate its time between activities that the measured objective is higher, allowing always for matters beyond management control? Would we expect managerial efficiency, so defined, to be different in public and privately owned enterprise? In what measurable form will differences in managerial efficiency be manifest?

Ownership can be thought of as a set of rights or entitlements to the use of resources, rights which are delimited sometimes by law, sometimes by custom. Since the present focus is on activities involving the sale of outputs, then ownership in particular involves entitlements to the residual of revenue after inputs have been paid their contracted amounts; this residual is the owners' income. From the point of view of an individual or group of individuals within a community, private ownership involves the ability unilaterally to sell or exchange his share of these rights. In contrast, in public ownership the individual can exchange his set of rights only by changing his jurisdiction (migrating from one community to another) or by promoting a community decision to change the mode of the organisation.

It would be a working hypothesis of most economists that in the case of private ownership, the individual would seek to maximise the income from his set of rights. That is, he would seek to ensure that (a) management effort is directed to minimising the cost to the owner of producing any given level of output; (b) management effort is directed to choosing outputs which yield the biggest margin of revenue over such costs. How far the owner can and will do this will depend on the difficulty of acquiring information and of effecting changes. The self-employed man is hiring himself, has almost perfect information about the work setting and can monitor performance with ease. How far he will *wish* to raise his income, granted the economic environment will depend on how hard and long he wishes to work. This latter point applies at the opposite extreme to the shareholder of a large corporation, who, however, faces huge costs in acquiring information and effecting changes. Shares, however, can be bought and sold and take-overs take place; in so far as these dealings reflect, in the long-run, expectations about the future profitability of companies, then the expected gains or losses from current management action are capitalised in the share price. In this light the growth of specialised intermediate shareholders and institutional holders can be viewed as responses to the problems of information gathering and monitoring of management. Whether or not this is effective is an empirical matter.

In such a context, the criterion and measure of managerial efficiency would be, allowing if we can for factors beyond management control, profitability or, for some prescribed set of products, the level of costs. In the case of a public enterprise, the vested interests of an individual could, as an empirical point, lie as much in his possible role as consumer or employee as in his definite role as *citizen-owner*. Where the individual is in government or public service, his interests as politican or civil servant would likely override any role as citizen-owner. For example the public enterprise might then be seen as a vehicle for (a) the execution of the economic and social policies of the government; (b) the promotion of success in the next election. Hence cost minimisation and profitability can be used as criteria and measures of management efficiency *only when and where they are the avowed objectives of the enterprise*. To state the obvious, governments in this country played a major role in the 1950s and 1960s – rightly or wrongly, and for what ever reason – in the rate at which the declining railway and coal industries were contracted. The criterion of efficient management could not there be taken as cost levels or profitability.

Suppose one could, however, identify specific areas where cost minimisation and profitability were expected. Would one expect managerial efficiency, so measured, to be different in private and public enterprise, allowing in *both* cases for factors beyond management control? The expectations of some economists, even in such areas, is that managerial efficiency will be less in public firms. The arguments have been advanced and supported by Alchian, Demsetz, de Alessi, Furubotn, Pejovich, Davies, Peltzman, Crain, Rowley and Zardkoohi[1] and are based on

1. The inability of owners, except at prohibitive cost, to sell their rights in public enterprises thereby precluding (a) the pressure on management which comes from the share price capitalisation of the expected gain and losses from current management action; (b) pressure on management from specialisation in areas of ownership.
2. The control framework which is most successful in minimising costs and maximising profitability is that designed and exercised by people with direct economic interest in such items. Whatever are the political objectives of government, the associated control framework on public enterprises will have been designed and will be monitored by politicians and civil servants whose major interests are unlikely to be equivalent to a direct vested economic interest in minimising costs or maximising profits.

PROFITABILITY OF PUBLIC AND PRIVATE INDUSTRY IN THE UK

Let us now examine the cost and profitability studies in this light. Whilst differences in unit costs would appear to be more amenable than profitability to the isolation of managerial efficiency, it does require that similar outputs are being produced. The ratio measure of profitability suffers no such limitations. In that part of the American economy that has seen many comparative analyses of public and private, the electric power industry, analyses have suggested a wide variability across public firms in rates of return but an average public rate not widely different from the rates of return in private institutions. Indeed concern there has often been more about excess profit rates and the potential use of municipal enterprises as a source of local fiscal revenue.[2] In the UK, *Blue Book* data enable a comparison between the public corporation and company sectors, of gross trading profits, measured net of capital consumption, as a percentage of net fixed assets at current replacement cost. Rates of return in the private sector have been well above the public sector for all the post-war period. The private sector return has shown a consistent downward trend in the post-war period. By the end of the 1970s it was averaging

5 per cent but the highest level for the public corporation sector in the post-war period as a whole was 3 per cent at the end of the 1960s.

The tendency for post-war British governments to use the public corporations for objectives other than profitability and the inappropriateness of profit as the sole index of managerial efficiency would probably not be disputed. Moreoever the extent to which the low rates of return can be attributed to non-profit objectives cannot be readily calculated since the use of subsidies to compensate for non-commercial activites has not been consistent. The burden of price controls in the 1970s on the public sector, relative to the private sector, give, however, some glimpses of the sensitivity of profit rates to macroeconomic policies. The associated *initial* drop in profit rates in the early 1970s in the public sector, relative to the private sector, has already been well substantiated. The subsequent delays in the restoration of profit rates, despite some well-publicised price increases for the nationalised industries in 1974/5, is, however, worth pointing out. As the Annex to this paper shows,[3] in the 1960s unit labour costs were growing slower in public corporations than in the (private) manufacturing sector – a trend that, on average, continued in the 1970s, albeit with a smaller gap. Adding in the cost of bought-in materials, fuel etc., we find that (non-capital) unit costs were growing slightly slower in public corporations than in manufacturing in the 1960s and, on average, at about the same annual rate in both sectors in the 1970s. The movement of relative prices was such that rates of return in the public corporations rose gradually up to the 3 per cent figure mentioned above for the end of the 1960s. The period of severe discriminatory price restraint of 1970–2 saw a sharp fall in the rate of return – relative to the long-term decline in the private sector. The important point is that whilst the rate of return gross of subsidies fell relative to the private sector, 1970–2, it recovered thereafter. The rate of return net of subsidies also fell 1970–2 relative to the private sector, but never subsequently recovered; the restoration of gross profit rates took, in other words, the form of subsidies rather than price increases, which were never, subsequently, of sufficient size to put the net profit rate above its 1972 level; public sector prices, relative to manufacturers, at best tracked the movement in relative unit costs.

Since the capital/net output ratio does not tend to change dramatically in the short run, the best indication of the impact of price controls on profitability is the share of profits, net of subsidies, in net output. As the Annex shows, annual public corporation profits averaged zero in the 1950s. During the 1960s they rose, net of subsidies for mainly the railways to roughly 6 per cent of net output. This share then plunged down to (–) 20 per cent by 1974 and by 1978 was still substantially negative. Put otherwise, in the period 1970–8, annual revenue had not, on average, been covering even operating costs and the losses so defined averaged about 10 per cent of net output, a level still to be found in 1978.

RELATIVE COST EFFICIENCY

If we are to deduce anything about managerial efficiency from observations of differences in unit costs as between public and private firms, the crucial issue is knowing whether factors other than management efficiency are being held constant. There are three major issues:

1. In considering the costs of producing particular output levels or a constellation of different products, it is in the present context immaterial whether such output levels or some particular products are not worth producing by some other criterion such as profitability or social net benefit. If postal service to the Scottish Highlands is one of the activities of the public firm, it is immaterial whether this activity is profitable. What we want to know is whether a private firm can do this cheaper than a public firm. Similarly the cost studies treat the prices paid for inputs as the appropriate input cost rather than any shadow cost figure. If the ruling wage rate overstates the true cost of labour in some particular locale with high unemployment, where true cost is defined by some externally given social accounting method, this would be ignored unless both private and public firms in question had been explicitly subsidised to the precise amount. This clearly involves an assumption that an efficient management is one which treats the cost of an activity as the cash cost to the firm.

2. Both the quantitative and qualitative dimensions of output have to be carefully defined. Thus California private electric utilities have conceded that their costs are higher than publicly owned electric companies but argue that their territories are more difficult to serve.[4] Even so, the coexistence in the USA of large numbers of public and private firms in same industry in the same state clearly make comparisons rather easier than a comparison of CEGB with private electric companies in other countries. The procedure in the cost studies has been to estimate, across the sample of firms, the way in which costs vary with topography, volume of sales, number of

consumers, quality dimensions, etc., and then to estimate whether, allowing for the general movement of costs with these variables, it is still the case that observed unit costs in private firms differ significantly from public firms for example as a shift in the cost function.

3. The implications of the above two points for input prices need perhaps explicit mention. Since firms can face different fuel prices, wage rates, interest rates for reasons other than their being public or private, then input prices, when the data is available, are treated as additional variables in the cost function, separate from the mode of ownership. This approach is particularly useful when for example a public firm (like CEGB) is not allowed full choice in its source of fuel. On the other hand public firms might be paying higher prices for inputs precisely because they are public and some of the differential *may* be due to the absence of pressure on management to bargain. There is some evidence that in this country, allowing for normal cyclical movements, in the early 1970s wage inflation in public industry (cf. the Annex to this paper) rose significantly above that in manufacturing for the first time in the post-war period and that this also[5] manifested itself in wage levels. The particular reason for this movement has not yet been pinned down. Similarly, new evidence in Canada has pointed to significantly higher wage and salary levels in the public sector, after allowing for differences in grades, qualifications, sex, race etc.[6] Any tendency for public firms to employ, at high input prices, a larger volume of inputs than is typical in that industry, will be reflected in the cost function estimates for public firms, but whether this is due to weak management as opposed to say government policy, will not be reflected. Finally, there is the thorny question of capital costs. Where data have been available, annual capital costs have often been approximated as depreciation of the firm's capital stock plus a cost of capital times that depreciation. It is sometimes suggested that public firms have a lower cost of capital than the private sector and that the appropriate figure to use is the rate of profit earned in the private sector. Since however realised rates of profit in the public sector have been, at least in this country, affected by government policy, then the use of higher figures would overstate the cost of capital to the *enterprise*. If, again therefore, an efficient management is one which treats the cost of an activity as the cash cost to the firm, then, in cost studies purporting to reflect differences in managerial efficiency, the cost of capital should be treated like topography etc. – that is, exogenous to management. A remaining difficulty is that current differences be-

tween firms in cost of capital may not be the same as the differences in force in the past. Since in most of the cost studies, the data relates to a cross-section of firms for one year, any differences in unit costs may be reflecting in part differences in the cost of capital in earlier years.

THE COST OF ELECTRIC POWER IN THE USA

Adding the normal problems of data availability to the above requirements reinforces the difficulties of making efficiency comparisons between the UK public corporations, with virtually national monopolies of their products, and 'similar' private firms. Whilst the US electric utility industry has been described 'as close to perfection in public-private comparability as any other imagineable real world case',[7] it does contain problems arising from the size distribution of firms. Most of the research studies in this industry discussed in this paper were completed during the last five years and refer to cross-sections of data drawn from within the period 1964–72 and sampled from a basic population which included all but the smallest of firms.[8] Outside the basic population hundreds of municipal generating systems thrive on the low cost of capital afforded by preferential treatment with respect to corporate and bond holder liability for income taxes. The possible resource misallocation arising from this has been pointed out by Wallace and Junk (1970), but there is no question here necessarily of managerial inefficiency. Indeed in so far as there are public firms in the basic population with similar characteristics and in so far as the estimate of their cost capital includes before tax interest payments, the size of their capacity will look large relative to firms with the same apparent cost of capital; the results may to this extent be biased against management in public firms. A rather more difficult issue is that some municipals continue generating rather than buying in power simply because of the bitter rivalry between municipals and private wholesaling producers. In so far as management is not the driving force behind this rivalry the cost differences again cannot be attributed to them.

In this period there were 67 Federal projects, involving largely hydro-electricity, producing 12 per cent of the nation's power, wholesaling about half of this to other utilities. Of the 536 municipal firms in the basic population, slightly more than half were not involved in generation, 40 per cent generated less than 0.5 million mega-watt hours per firm per annum, 6 per cent generated between 0.5 and 4 million leaving 6 firms generating between 4 to 30 million. Municipal firms generated only 5 per cent of the nation's electricity though they purchased a similar amount for resale. The 210 private firms in the basic population produced 77 per cent of the nation's power and their distribution amongst the above size categories was 13 per cent, 20 per cent, 36 per cent with the remaining 3 per cent generating 30–50 million.

Yunker (1975) examined the allegation that public firms were inefficient by estimating costs as a function of output and the number of customers for 1969. Concerned at the different size distributions in the public and private industries, he restricted attention to private and municipal firms producing 0.5 to 4 million mega-watt hours per annum and further restricted to firms with at least 1000 customers since some firms sell to only a very small number of business or government users. Looking at the remaining 24 public and 49 private firms his equation suggested costs were lower in public firms but the results were not statistically significant. He concluded therefore that there was no evidence that private firm costs were lower than public firm costs. Yunker had not however controlled for input prices nor for the differing proportions of generation/transmission/distribution in each firm. Meyer (1975) also lacked data on input prices which he felt might vary regionally. He therefore attempted a partial offset by grouping the basic population geographically, excluded firms which were not engaged in all three functions and then random sampled 30 public and 30 private; a review of size of firms by volume of generation indicated that the composition of the public and private samples were quite similar. He found that from observations for each of the 3 years 1967, 1968, 1969 the cost structures of the two types of firm were significantly different in all the different functions. Generating costs per mega-watt hour declined with the number of mega-watt hours and were generally lower for public firms. Total transmission costs were primarily determined by the number of customers with the results pointing to lower costs for public firms. The percentage of sales to resale customers was not found to affect either transmission or distribution costs. Neither were distribution costs per mega-watt hour affected by the split of sales between residential and non-residential but they were affected in a complex way by both output and the number of customers, but Meyer did not identify the pattern of the difference between public and private. In each of the above estimates he excluded maintenance costs which were found, separately, to be primarily determined by plant size and maintenance costs per mega-watt of capacity[9] were significantly lower in public firms. Similar separate estimates of (a) sales and account expenses and (b) general and administration expenses, again pointed to lower costs in public firms.

The work of Yunker and Meyer was important in being the first[10] attempt to assess relative cost efficiency in electricity, but the estimates related simply to *operating costs* embracing therefore only labour, fuel and raw materials. Data deficiencies were the main problem but it does mean that, in addition to the problem of input prices, the results have significance only if the similar size composition of firms in the two samples controls precisely for differences in capacity and technology, that is for capital costs and Meyer's public sample included the Federal projects. Neuberg (1977) overcame some of these problems in his detailed study of distribution where he also argued that some of the complex features of customer characteristics and location could be picked up by allowing for miles of overhead distribution line (S_2) and the square mileage of the territory (S_3). From the basic population of firms he excluded the Federal projects and some 25 private firms not involved in distribution and then conducted a questionaire survey of the remaining private firms and a sample of the municipal firms, finishing up with data from 90 private firms and 75 municipal firms for the year 1972. Costs embraced distribution proper, sales, customer accounts and a proportion of general and administrative expenses. The main result for costs per ultimate customer was, in log form, and rounding out some of the figures,

$$\log.C_n = 6.1 - 0.40 \log.\gamma + 0.01 (\log.\gamma)^2 + 0.25 \log. \frac{S_1}{\gamma} - 0.09D + 0.92 \log. \frac{S_2}{\gamma} + 0.97 \log. \frac{S_3}{\gamma} + 0.30\, P_L$$

where γ is the number of ultimate customers, S_1 is mega-watt hours of electricity, P_L is the wage rate and D takes a value of 1 for public and 0 for private. The F and t tests were significant at the 0.01 level or better except for the coefficients on S_3 and the dummy variable.[11] Other models explored showed that when the last 3 variables are omitted and operating costs only considered (cf. Meyer) the dummy coefficient is significant at 0.01 level with the shift factor on costs per customer such that public firms are roughly 23 per cent cheaper. This figure falls to 15 per cent when capital costs are included. When S_2, S_3 and P_L are reintroduced the figure is 9 per cent as shown above and this is significant at the 0.09 level. Wage rate levels in public firms may therefore be different than private firms. On the other hand Neuberg's use of a common interest rate across all firms in his calculation of capital costs may work the other way if the public firms' actual cost of capital is–rightly or wrongly–lower than the private firms. Pescatrice and Trapani (1980) restricted themselves to generation data for the years 1965 and 1970. They were able to estimate a cost of capital[12] for each firm and in addition explored differences in generating technology. For the latter they argued that for two firms whose capacity was similar in age and broad technical method, the extent to which one firm had introduced newer vintages would be reflected in unit costs. From the basic population they therefore excluded firms for whom adequate data was not available and who were not generating exclusively by coal, gas, or oil. For each of the remaining 33 private firms and 23 municipal firms, they calculated a weighted average age of equipment (L). The basic approach allowed some flexibility in the form of the coefficients on output and on input prices. Since number of customers is not important in generation the rounded results, for 1965, may be shown in the form of (the log of) costs per million megawatt hours:

$$\log.\mathrm{Cp} = 1.43 - 0.01 \log.Q + 0.014 (\log.Q)^2 - \frac{1}{L} [0.01 + 0.002 \log. P_L + 0.001 \log.P_K - 0.0003 \log.P_F] + 0.25D + \log.P_L (0.05 \log.P_L + 0.04 \log.P_K - 0.16 \log. P_F - 0.02 \log.Q) + \log.P_K (0.07 \log.P_K - 0.20 \log.P_F - 0.01 \log.Q) - \log.P_F (0.03 \log.Q - 0.18 \log.P_F)$$

where Q is million mega-watt hours, L is the index of age of equipment, P_L is the wage rate, P_K the cost of capital, P_F the price of fuel and D takes a value of 1 for private firms and 0 for public firms. The U shape of the unit cost curve was found to be significant as it was in Neuberg's estimates of distribution cost per customer. The shift factor indicates that costs are roughly 25 per cent lower[13] in public firms with a t statistic of 1.86; for 1970 the results were 43 per cent (2.32). A potential source of this difference is the contents of the square brackets which is a measure of technical progress, comprising a neutral[14] technical change of 0.01 and price-induced changes which in the periods covered were fuel using. Measured at the mean prices in each sub-samples, the rate of technical progress in public firms was shown to be considerably higher than in private firms.

In summary then, and subject to the general problems of cross-section cost functions, the evidence is pointing to costs being lower, rather than higher, in public firms. Finally that part of De Alessi's study (1977) which related to the level of prices paid for wholesale electricity by distributing firms who bought in some of their supplies, has some bearing on the concern expressed earlier that standardising for input prices may obscure managerial inefficiency which manifests itself in bargaining. His data base was the selling price in 1969 of non-Federal wholesaling firms (145 private and 64 municipal) not financially associated with the buyers. De Alessi's hypothesis was that municipal buyers have less incentive to bargain and more incentive to conclude convenient agreements. Estimating the selling price as a function of the size and ownership mode of the selling firm, regional variables to pick up demand effects and input price variations, the number of customers and whether the buying firm had multiple sources and whether it was public or private, he found however that the prices paid by public firms were not *ceteris paribus*, significantly higher than those paid by private firms.

OVERMANNING IN WATER UTILITIES AND AIRLINES

Coverage of these areas is much less comprehensive than for electricity but the four pieces of work under review have a common thread in their authors' conclusions about excessive labour employed per unit of output. Crain and Zardkoohi initially (1978) examined data available from the American Water Works Association, on 1970 cost figures embracing operation, maintenance, administration and depreciation.[15] There were 24 private utilities left after those with inadequate data were excluded. Similar considerations restricted the public sample but the final number was limited to 88 firms because of difficulties of getting comparable data on cost of capital, and in addition any public firm larger than the largest firm in the private sample was excluded. All coefficients were significant on t and F tests at 5 per cent or better. On the pooled sample the shift factor on costs per million gallons of water (Y) per annum (C) was such that private firms had 25 per cent lower costs than public firms. The cost structures of the two separate samples were found to be significantly different and may be presented as follows:

$$\text{Public } \log.C = 0.93 - 0.24 \log.Y + 0.67 \log.P_L + 0.33P_K.$$
$$\text{Private } \log.C = -1.97 - 0.14 \log.Y + 0.84 \log.P_L + 0.16 \log.P_K$$

Thus returns to scale are such that a doubling of output reduces unit costs by 14 per cent in private firms but 24 per cent in public firms. However the output ranges in the sample of firms are never such that the absolute level of unit costs in public firms falls below that in private firms. Doubts about these results arise from the exclusion of the large public firms from the sample; if some of the smaller public firms have embryonic features of the large ones, results may be biased against public firms.

Setting this aside, what is the source of the unit cost differences in the above? Since a Cobb-Douglas production function was used, it can be shown[16] that these results imply that the elasticity of labour (capital) with respect to output is higher (lower) in public firms than private firms. Thus a given increase in output entails a proportionately larger (smaller) increase in labour (capital) in public firms. In a further exercise restricted to 78 of the above firms who could supply data on the value of capital stock, Crain and Zardkoohi (1980) estimated an equation for the capital labour ratio for the pooled sample as follows

$$\frac{K}{L} = 149.5 - 126.5D - \frac{P_L}{P_K}(59.3 - 6.7D) + Y(0.016 - 0.016D)$$

where D is equal to 1 in public firms and 0 in private firms and where only the coefficients on Y were significant and the one on DY was significant only at the 12 per cent level. That element in the capital–labour ratio which is independent of output is small and does not differ significantly as between public and private firms. Crain and Zardkoohi concluded that[17]that there is some suggestion that the capital–labour ratio responded more to output increases in private firms and whilst the private firms may be over-capitalised, the public firms are overmanned and the latter factor is the source of the relative cost inefficiencies.

Some further doubts about this result will be discussed in the section 'Competition and Regulation'. There can be no doubts however about the high manning levels in the public sector found in Davies's study (1971, updated in 1977) of employment, passenger and freight volumes and revenue in each of the years from 1958/9 to 1973/4 for publicly owned Trans Australian Airlines and the regulated private firm Ansett Australian National Airlines. The airlines operate on inter-state routes and government policy has been to equalise practically every aspect of their operation: viz. routes ports of call, frequency of stops, aircraft capacity and types, import licences for aircraft (there is no domestic aircraft production and aspirant carriers other than these two are refused import licences), take-off times, engineering and airport facilities, seating arrangements, fares, freight rates. There is of course a difference in mode of ownership and Davies expects this to lead to lower efficiency in the public firm. In 1958/9 the two airlines had about the same level of employment but the volume of freight was 139 per cent higher than in the private firm, passenger volume was 28 per cent higher and revenue was 16 per cent higher. By 1968/9 employment was 10 per cent higher in the private firm than in the public firm but the level of freight per man was 78 per cent higher, passengers per man 10 per cent and revenue per man 12 per cent higher. The private firm seems therefore to have excelled at low-valued freight traffic – which Davies does not discuss – and the public firm's improvement overtime (especially noticeable in passenger traffic) continued into 1973/4 when the measures of private firms superiority were 65 per cent, 7 per cent and 11 per cent respectively. Even so the differences are staggering and Davies's comment on the role of political factors warrants quotation: '... the Australian airline industry has been a political issue for over 25 years, and the current system partially appeases strong politically active minorites of the left and right, desirous of public and private enterprises respectively' (p. 165).

REFUSE COLLECTION IN CANADA, SWITZERLAND AND USA

Government ownership or regulation in electricity and water can sometimes be seen as a method of exploiting economies of scale and of contiguity without monopoly profits. Refuse collection has similar features, probably of a smaller magnitude, but in addition there is the concern to impose minimum despatching speeds for garbage to avoid public health danger, though the enforcement of minimum levels is by no means universal. The cost components would normally cover fuel, maintenance, labour and capital costs; the incidence of billing and disposal costs would vary with the institutional arrangement whilst the inclusion of taxes and licences varies across studies. Public provision is to be found in 37 per cent of USA communities in metropolitan areas (1977) Savas and is financed through municipal revenue with income from citizens taking the form usually of a local tax rather than a user charge. One result of this is that cost data has to be sought for services rather more integrated into general municipal costs than electricity and water and with varying accounting practices.

In studing the private sector, the focus is on the user charge levied or the contract price. In the USA at one extreme are areas where collection is completely unregulated firm/household agreements; then there are cities where user charges are regulated and/or hauling licences stipulated. Citizens can self-haul in such cities, as they can even in some cities where area franchises are granted to private firms, thereby allowing some exploitation of economies of contiguity. In the Edwards and Stevens (1978) study of private firm collection prices per household in 77 cities in the USA for 1975 no significant differences were found between these various agreements. The 318 cities initially contacted in a mail and telephone survey were reduced to the final sample on grounds of availability of data and to firms providing only once-a-week kerb-side service. The significant differences arose between the above group of arrangements and a further group which included franchise cities where self-hauling was not permitted and cities where households have no choice in service levels and are serviced by private firms with exclusive area contracts with the municipality paying the contractor. The lower prices found in this latter group were attributed to economies of contiguity and scale. Within this second group the contract cities were cheaper mainly due to the contractor not bearing billing costs; whether the contract was negotiated or determined by competitive bidding had no significant effect on prices.

The degree of detail of private sector arrangements in the Edwards and Stevens study has not often been matched in studies which compared private to public, where the latter, in the majority of cases, has been found to be more expensive. With exclusivities in area coverage associated with public provision, the various dimensions of 'output' become vital. Edwards and Stevens had controlled for frequency and location of service and included in their cost equations variables for household density, temperature, rainfall, average income levels and wage rates (but not for other input prices), but none of these variables proved significant. Other relevant variables would be the volume and type of garbage and how, if at all, it is separated, topographic variations, seasonal variations, the split between residential/commercial, households per pick-up point, distance from disposal site.

Thus the one US study which found public provision cheaper lacked much of the relevant information. Of the 63 collectors in Montana in the early 1970s,[18] there were 27 from whom Pier, Vernon and Wicks (1974) obtained data on costs, covering only however labour and capital. The only other variation across firms they could control for was number of pick-ups. More localised studies can sometimes implicitly standardise for several variables though obviously at a cost in terms of generality. Savas (1974) reports a comparison for 1968/9 between the New York Department of Sanitation and firms who were carrying similar garbage (putrescible waste and rubbish – Class I firms) and who were privately owned, levying user charges on contracted customers, the details of which were monitored by the Department of Consumer Affairs. The cost data for the public firm excluded taxes, licences, garage space, profit margin and an adjustment to reflect these items was made to the private sector quoted maximum charges. The costs per ton came out at $17 for the private sector (of which $10 was labour cost) and $40 for the Sanitation Department. The latter however serves residential users involving less volume per pick-up than the private firms serving commercial users – and this might partly, though certainly not wholly, explain the higher manning per truck and labour costs of $32 per ton. The private sector on the other hand has a more scattered population and despite this is able to get a better truck utilisation.

The problem of differing customer groups is not found in Savas's study (1977) of Minneapolis which, from 1971, for purposes of residential refuse collection, was served by the Sanitation Division in one area and in another area by a consortium of private firms on the basis of 5 five-year contracts. The latter spelt out frequencies and related service characteristics so that comparable requirements were made of both groups. Cost per ton for the Sanitation Department (overheads excluded) was some 10 per cent higher in 1971 than the contract income per ton (with monitoring costs not attributed) and costs expressed per household were 15 per cent higher (But see comments in the later part of this paper). A similar superiority of private producers appears in Bennett and Johnson's study (1979) of residential refuse collection in their home county of Fairfax, Virginia, one-third of which is serviced by the Solid Waste Division (SWD); in other areas householders must[19] contract individually with one of a set of 29 competing firms. The average user charge for the twice-weekly service came out at $85 per household per annum with all but 2 of the firms charging less than $100. Suspicious of cost data from municipal authorities, and knowing that households were charged for refuse collection on a fee basis (a flat amount plus a part related to property value), Bennett and Johnson based their cost estimates on the SWD's assertion that fee income covers their costs (excluding taxes but including disposal charges also levied on the public firms). The cost for households with average property values came out at $126 for a once-weekly collection, the difference with private firms being largely mitigated from the householders' point of view by the charge being allowable against state and federal taxes. What we do not know in this study is the significance of SWD serving the area at greatest distance from the disposal site.

Finally, two studies are of significance for their national coverage. From mail and telephone questionnaires Kitchen (1976) assembled data for forty-eight Canadian municipalities for 1971 on operating costs plus depreciation. He included most of the variables mentioned at the beginning of this section and found that costs were significantly higher in public provision though the varying private sector arrangements were not identified. As in other studies, economies of scale were found to exist once one got to the stage where larger equipment could be used. On the other hand increased population density actually raised costs, probably, Kitchen hypothesised, because of its association with multiple dwelling units and traffic congestion. For his key output variable population had to be used so that tonnages would only be picked up by the variable, persons per family. The cost of capital was not included on either side of the equation, thereby possibly under-estimating the efficiency of those firms with low costs of capital who took full advantage of this in their capacity plans. Furthermore the method of wage payment and the size of vehicle capacity *were* included which, from the point of view of public/private comparisons, are items which one would like to see reflected simply in the cost curve.

Pommerehne and Frey's sample of 103 Swiss cities embraced half the Swiss population. The costs (including all capital costs) of residential refuse collection were calculated for cities in 1970 who did not collect industrial and residential refuse jointly and also could supply, through questionnaires, necessary supplementary data to published sources. Forty eight of the firms were private and their costs were measured by the user charge or contract fee. A final form chosen for output was weight in 1000 tons (A), topography was controlled by a measure of height differences within each city (*C*) and distance of disposal site from the centre of the city (*E*) was included. One of their main results for (the log. of) costs per ton collected in francs, may be presented as follows:

$$\log.C_s = 1.03 - 0.82A + 0.31A^2\,10^{-6} + 0.10B + 0.49C - 0.19D + 0.30E + 0.05F - 0.07G + 0.05H - 0.36I - 0.03J + 0.12K$$

where the coefficients on G and H (seasonality variables for tourist traffic), I (the number of pick-ups per street kilometre, J (the number of households per picked-up point) and K (snowfall variable) were not statistically significant. F took a value of 1 if the service was largely financed by user charges (zero otherwise). The positive coefficient is suggestive of other indications[20] that user charge arrangements are more costly, including even public provision; the coefficient is not significant in this model but it is when costs are expressed per household. All other coefficients were significant. Unit costs are declining over a wide range; eventually economies disappear, a tendency often associated with the density of cities, a factor revealed in Pommerehne and Frey's other models of costs per household. B takes a value of 1 when collections are more than twice weekly (zero otherwise). Finally the coefficient on the dummy ($D = 1$ when private, 0 for government) indicates a shift factor on costs per ton such that private provision is some 20 per cent cheaper. The authors have in this model deducted from the private price an estimated 7 per cent profit margin (overall costs including interest charges). Whilst this can be defended, the more general problem is the lack of data on cost of capital and wage rates across firms. All the signs are however that private costs of refuse collection are lower than municipal costs

Tariff Structures in US Electricity

Some of the earliest work on public/private comparisons in the USA related to features of tariff structures but since they pre-dated the cost studies their results can now be viewed in a new light. Peltzman's approach (1971) was that the constellation of outputs and tariffs of public firms reflected political considerations. For a firm serving differing customer groups, he hypothesised there was one tariff structure which maximised profits but lower profit levels were consistent with varying combinations of prices to the different groups. He assumed that managers of public firms were interested in the continued existence of the enterprise and of their jobs, the vehicle for which was political support. *Ceteris paribus*, lower prices would raise votes. Moreover, though the cost of supplying group A might be greater than the cost of serving group B, price differences would not completely reflect this since a lower and lower price for group B might gain less votes than were being lost from group A. Thus Peltzman expected price differences between customer groups to be less than in private firms and also to be less closely related to cost differences.

His sample for 1966 was non-federal firms each serving at least 10,000 customers, excluding private firms serving more than one municipality–though the private firms remaining tended to operate in cities with larger populations. So far as the *level* of tariffs are concerned he found public to be significantly lower and asserted that this difference was due to their preferential tax treatment which was 'a manifestation of an overall political incentive to low rates'.[21] The possibility that public firms had lower costs was never mentioned. Meyer (1975) calculated for 1969 average revenue per kilowatt hour of residential, small commercial and 'other', where consumption levels per consumer were similar in private and public firms, and suggested that the lower price found for public firms was consistent with his cost estimates; for the resale group of customers the public price was only one-third of the private but part of this may have been due, given block tariffs, to considerably higher consumption levels for the public firm's customers. (For large commercial see later discussion.) Similarly some of De Alessi's results (1975, cf. above) take on a new light given the cost studies. He had hypothesised that management in public firms would not bargain hard in obtaining selling prices and found that, after standardising for other variables, the shift factor for the ownership dummy was such that public firm prices were some 30 per cent lower. This is however quite consistent with the cost differences revealed in other studies.

There is however rather more convincing evidence that the tariff structure of public firms is less differentiated with respect to customer groups and less reflective of differences in costs as between groups. Peltzman suggested that the cost per kilowatt hour for a firm, supplying a group of consumers with particular cost characteristics would be equal to the system-wide unit costs less amounts that get bigger the larger is the ratio of that group to the total customer population. He then regressed prices on system-wide unit, operating and capital costs and variables to reflect the varying proportions of residential/non-residential and, within each, high consumption/low consumption. For private firms he found that the prices of high consumption residential customers were significantly related to these variables whereas the public firm prices were not; a similar result emerged for non-residential customers. In confirmation of this De Alessi (1975) found that the 1966 selling prices of municipal wholesaling firms were less significantly related to regional variables than were the prices of private firms. Indeed by putting the price of one group as an independent variable in the price equation for the other group, Peltzman found that his residential and non-residential prices were highly and significantly inter-correlated for public firms but not for private firms. Thus costs of particular groups are reflecting themselves in the overall tariff structure rather than the price of particular groups. Suggestive evidence on the same lines can be found in Peltzman's other work[22] on liquor prices in state-owned and private stores.

Independently of cost differences, one might expect that, since electricity is non-storable and consumers can change monopoly area suppliers only inconveniently by shifting residence, firms will operate price discrimination. On the grounds that private firms are more geared to maximising their owners' wealth and less geared to the ballot box than public firms, more price discrimination might be expected in private firms.[23] Peltzman hypothesised that, given the same average price and standardising for differences in the number of customers and their income levels and any regional effects, a more enthusiastic execution of price discrimination would raise the volume of kilowatt hours sales per customer. The results indicated significantly higher volumes for private firms. He also found that private utilities tended to have a larger number of rate schedules but this result was not standardised for other variables. De Alessi's careful examination (1977) of rate schedules in 1970 involved allowing for regional differences in income and state regulation, for differences in city sizes, for the residental/non-residential mix and sources of power, by the selection of matching pairs of municipal and private firms. He finished up with twenty pairs and found that public firms had significantly lower numbers of peak schedules and of total schedules.

In summary, private utility tariff structures seem to be more profit orientated than those in public firms. There is however a problem in attributing this exclusively to political factors. Since the attenuation of property rights in public firms could lead to scope for more managerial discretion, then the results are consistent with the ease of managing simple tariff structures (De Alessi, autumn 1974). Alternatively, thinking of the British context, the fares and tariff structures of the UK nationalised industries were, historically, deeply influenced by the nationalisaton Acts which were consistently interpreted to require uniform fares and tariffs across different geographical areas and customer groups, to a large extent independently of cost characteristics. Whilst the short-run manipulation of these prices for electoral purposes does occur, the attribution of their long-run structure to similar electoral issues is to obscure their use as tools of wider economic and social policies – whatever views we, as economists, have about such policies. Some rather more discriminating tests of the electoral versus management inefficiency versus social welfare maximising models are required (cf. Millward 1978).

COMPETITION AND REGULATION

The performance of public firms may of course be affected by whether or not they face competition. The performance of private firms may be affected by the degree to which their prices and profit rates are regulated. Considering regulation first this carries the implication that cost differences between public and private may be reflecting inefficiences in private firms occasioned by regulation as much as any inefficiencies in public firms arising from the mode of ownership. Whether one would expect regulation of private firms to be active; whether, if active, it would be effective is still a matter of some dispute. Attention here is restricted to those few studies which have linked the question of regulation to private/public comparisons. De Alessi (1974, 1977) has argued that regulation of monopoly rents is likely to be active because regulators are under pressure from vested interests (buyers, consumers, potential entrants). In so far also as regulated firms can minimise interference by moderating prices and profit rates, then some of this intervention may be effective. He expects however it to be weak because regulated firms are well placed to collude and have an incentive to influence regulators, who in any case have little vested economic interest of their own in acquiring the full information needed for effect – the latter point being particularly apposite for regulation by independent commissioners each of whose job-related sources of income are usually equal.

To the extent that regulation prescribes a permitted average rate of return above the cost of capital and to the extent that this constraint bites in being lower than the unconstrained average rate profit, the Averch–Johnson effect involves an extension of the rate base.

Starting from an unconstrained profit maximising output and capital stock per man, the imposition of a prescibed lower rate of return will reduce actual profits and the latter can therefore be increased by raising the capital labour ratio (over capitalisation). It has already been recorded (cf. above) that in the Crain and Zardkoohi study, the capital/labour ratio in private water utilities was not significantly related to the relative prices of capital and labour. This, and its responsiveness to output increases, is suggestive of overcapitalisation. Since, however, overall unit costs were lower in private utilities than public firms they conclude that any inefficiencies due to private firm overcapitalisation are less than the overmanning inefficiencies associated with the mode of ownership. One doubt about these results has already been expressed arising from the exclusion of large public firms from the sample. A further query is that the coefficient for public firms linking changes in the capital/labour ratio to changes in output, is precisely zero – which certainly calls for, but does not get, any explanation.

In Pescatrice and Trapani's study (cf. above) of electricity generation, fuel, as well as as capital and labour was treated as an explicit input and some rather more complicated tests of regulation were required. The focus was that of the response of demand for inputs to changes in the prices of inputs. The standard response for a cost minimiser can be translated into a response measured in terms of an input's share of total cost. In particular the data enabled own and cross-price elasticities of demand for inputs to be calculated and the signs of these are the crucial guide. In a standard cost-minimising framework a rise in the price of a factor leads to reduced useage. Since, for public firms in the sample, the relevant elasticities were found to be negative in both 1965 and 1970 then in a comparative static sense the evidence is consistent with their being cost minimisers. On *a priori* grounds with three inputs, the signs of the cross-elasticities are not predictable so the finding that they were generally positive neither adds nor detracts from the result.

Similar signs emerged for the private utilities but this does not rule out the importance of regulation. Pescatrice and Trapani demonstrate that a firm for which the regulatory constraint (λ) is binding will so choose its inputs that their marginal rate of substitution is equal not to the normal input price ratio but to a ratio which replaces the cost of capital (P_K) by a lower shadow cost (P'_K). The regulated firm behaves as if it were minimising the cost of some given output using as the shadow cost of capital

$$P'_K = P_K - \frac{1}{1 - \lambda}(S - P_K)$$

measured as an average of actual rates earned by a firm during the current and previous two years and λ was allowed to take certain illustrative values between 0 and 1. A riso in P'_K would of course be expected to lead to reduced usage of capital and this is borne out in the results.[24] A rise in the price of labour will initially cut the profit margin and thereby reduce the firm's rate of profit below the permitted level. The firm would in such circumstances be permitted to raise prices and a restoration of the rate of return necessitates a contraction of capital as well. The impact on the usage of labour (contrast the standard case) and fuel is not known. Thus the prediction is that the cross-elasticity between capital usage and the price of labour will be negative. The results however for both 1965 and 1970 were a positive elasticity. A rise in the price of fuel would also be expected to lead to reduced usage of capital; for 1970 the elasticity was positive but for 1965 it *was* negative. Finally we should note that their general findings were not particularly sensitive to variations in the value of λ.

In summary, the evidence that some of the cost differences between public and private firms may be due to the effects of regulation on private firms is lacking substantial support at present. Another 'market structure' effect may however eventually prove more decisive. The cost efficiency of firms might be greater if they are facing competition. One would expect this for private firms; for public firms the *a priori* effect has not been explored in the literature in any depth. Where government has built comparative yardsticks into the supervisory process or where government is sensitive for other reasons to cost inflated prices then again one might expect some difference in performance when competition is present. Meyer's analysis (cf. above) of the degree to which lower public firm costs were reflected in lower prices stumbled over the problem that for large commercial users private and public average revenue per kilowatt hour was the same. Since sales per large commercial customer by private firms were double those of public firms, the block elements in tariff structures could thereby be offsetting the lower unit costs. The average revenue was however noticably lower than any other customer group (except resale) and Meyer felt that the large commercial customer's ability to set up his own generating capacity was a sizeable threat. Rather more pointedly Savas's report on refuse collection in Minneapolis, as we have already seen, showed the private firms with lower costs in the first year of a scheme of segregated areas – which had replaced a scheme where public and private dealt in different kinds of refuse. From 1971 the two sectors were performing similar functions and the City Sanitation Division's cost inefficiency, relative to the private sector, quickly diminished such that by 1975 costs per ton were only 1 per cent higher and costs per household were actually 1 per cent less. The city cost per ton had risen in constant 1967 dollars from 25 in 1966 to 32 in 1969 and then fell to 23 by 1975.

Finally there are Primeaux's more detailed findings which drew on 1964–8 data concerning municipal firms only. Addressed in part to the question of whether the conferment of area monopoly status on electricity suppliers (whether public or private) was necessary, he used an apparently not well known fact that there were a number of cities (49 in 1966 with a population exceeding 25,000) where competition between utilities existed – mainly municipal versus private. In some cases customers cannot switch after committing themselves to one firm; in others a switch at any time is possible. For each of the municipal firms so positioned he selected one other municipal in the same state, of the same size and with the same power source and excluded from the non-competitive group any firm which did not adequately match the competitive municipal firm for whom it was the nearest approximation. He then (1977) regressed costs (excluding taxes) per 1000 kilowatt-hours on sales, capacity, fuel costs, consumption per consumer by customer group, cost of purchased power, market density, a variable for firms using internal combustion and several regional dummies. From the use of a further dummy he concluded that competition significantly changed the unit cost curve from being downward sloping to upward sloping. In a further study (1978) he excluded firms which did not generate electricity and estimated an equation for capacity utilisation (actual annual kilowatt hours/maximum possible). The competition dummy did increase excess capacity but not by a statistically significant amount. Moreover and more importantly the 1977 study had showed that the whole unit cost curve though changing its slope was shifted downwards, by competition, by a factor of roughly 10 per cent.

There would seem to be some scope in the transport area for examining the performance of public firms relative to private firms and relative to the market structure. To date however there are no studies of which I am aware, controlling for both the mode of ownership and the type of market structure. The public firms within the sample of fifty-eight US urban bus transit systems examined by Pashigian (1976) had monopolies of their particular service. After controlling for total vehicle mileage travelled, he found that profit margins were less in publicly owned systems, a pattern consistent with the hypothesis that in such areas the systems are unattractive to unsubsidised private firms because they would be intolerably regulated, especially where marginal costs lay below average costs. As with most profit data, little can be deduced about managerial efficiency in publicly owned transit systems though Pashigian has some interesting points to make about the impact on routes, fares and profits of voters who are non-users. Whilst the study by Caves and Christensen (1978) of the experience of Canadian railways in the period 1956–75, does not allow an examination of performance with and without competition, the finding that the publicly owned Canadian National did not have higher unit costs than Canadian Pacific is supportive, now in a competitive context, of the broad pattern from electricity. The regulatory framework applies to both railroads and had become increasingly restricted to the transport of prairie grain and flour. The authors compared total factor productivity in the two firms for each year and since the two output categories of passenger and freight were weighted by cost elasticities and the different inputs were weighted by cost shares – revenue shares would have partly reflected the regulated fare structure – the comparison is, in principle, similar to a unit cost study. Canadian National factor productivity was some 10–15 per cent lower than Canadian Pacific in the period 1956–64. Canadian Pacific was experiencing however a substantial decline in passenger volumes. During the next two years CN productivity caught up and in the period 1967–75 its factor productivity was higher, the size of the superiority being bigger the more one allowed for differences in the composition of freight ton miles.

CONCLUSIONS

Many studies have to rely on cross-sections of firms for only one year, coverage of areas is patchy and in general the subject is in an embryonic state. One of the problems of using *ex post* data is that it tells us nothing about the way problems have to be faced *ex ante* with all its uncertainties. The *perception* of costs and revenue could be different in the two modes and this itself might be obscuring anything that can be deduced about managerial efficiency. Subject to these provisos the following conclusions seem warranted.

1. If managerial efficiency is higher in private firms, one would expect there was a good chance of this being revealed in unit cost studies. This paper has analysed the results emerging for firms in North America involved in 'semi-commercial' operations but finds, overall, no broad support for private enterprise superiority. In US electricity the evidence seems to suggest that unit costs are lower in public firms whether or not one controls for differences across firms in wage rates, cost of capital, area covered. The possibility that this difference is attributable to the effects of regulation of private utilities lacks substantial support. The Canadian railroad work found no significant differences in total factor productivity between public and private. A study of US water utilities found costs were lower in private firms after allowing for differences in input prices but the larger public projects were not embraced in the sample. The Australian airline case study indicates that the private airline with the same basic flying capacity carried larger volumes of passenger and especially freight per man but the significance of this industry as a political football needs to be gauged. In summary there seems no general ground for believing managerial efficiency is less in public firms.
2. The setting, by government, either explicitly or implicitly, of goals other than cost minimisation, would mean that costs could well be higher in public firms in such areas and whilst such a public/private comparison has not yet to my knowledge been documented it would be surprising if costs were not found to be lower in private firms – for example in the British steel industry. To isolate the role of managerial efficiency in such a context would not be an easy task. Moreover, government policy may or may not be misguided and *public enterprise* thereby inefficient by some different criterion of efficiency.
3. Similarly, low profitability is not inconsistent with an efficient management. The price controls on nationalised industries in the last decade are only one manifestation of 'interventionist' UK government policies. But public enterprise might be inefficient for those who wish to judge efficiency in terms of profitability. Indeed the studies of tariff setting in US electricity strongly suggest that such tariffs, in their discrimination between customer and cost groups, are more profit orientated in the private sector than the public sector. Urban bus transit systems in the USA seem to be put in public ownership and run at lower profit margins in cities where income levels and car ownership is lower than aver-

age. These results may be telling us something about vote-getting in the USA or about public enterprises as a tool of other policies. It is not yet clear that they are reflecting an inefficient management.

4. Many of the public firms in the cost samples are municipal rather than nationalised. It is not impossible that this puts more pressure on public enterprise managers. However refuse collection is also local and the evidence suggests that, subject to the absence of data on input prices, whilst public provision is less costly than an unfettered private user-charge system, private contract arrangements are even cheaper. It is not impossible that where public provision includes selling at a price, as in electricity, the associated financial controls are more effective in holding down costs than in areas financed from general tax revenue, but such a proposition needs further investigation.
5. Similarly the comparable cost performance of the Canadian publicly owned railway, *vis-à-vis* its privately owned rival and the evidence that unit electricity costs are lower in US municipal firms facing competition than in those municipal firms who are not, is suggestive of the importance of market structure but the interrelationship between mode of ownership and market structure is not yet clear.

ANNEX

Thanks are due to Mr R. Ward for the calculations associated with the attached charts. Figs 4A.1 and 4A.2 show the annual percentage rate of change of relative prices, relative wages, etc., public corporations/ manufacturing. Unit labour costs, unit inputs costs (fuel, raw materials, etc.) and the two combined (unit costs) are weighted by their proportion to price. Manufacturing data was taken from the Department of Employment gazette. The hourly wage rate data for public corporations was from the same gazette but the coverage is imprecise, viz. the industrial orders mining and quarrying, gas, electricity and water, transport and communications. For employment, unit labour costs, prices, earnings, special series were developed from data in the Annual Reports of British Rail, NCB, Post Office, British Gas, Electricity Boards in England and Wales, British Airways (domestic or BEA originally).

In Fig. 4A.3 and in contrast to the above, the *Blue Book* profits data on public corporations embraces, each year, all corporations who were public in that year, irrespective of whether they had been public throughout the post-war period. The subsidy figure for public corporations in the attached charts includes the amounts shown in British Rail annual reports on grants for unremunerative services and track maintenance. Stock appreciation has not been deducted from either the company sector or public corporations since its tax treatment has fluctuated considerably (cf. Bank of England, 1980).

The basic method in all the above is almost identical to that in Millward (1976). For full sources, methods and data, a statistical annex may be obtained from the author on request.

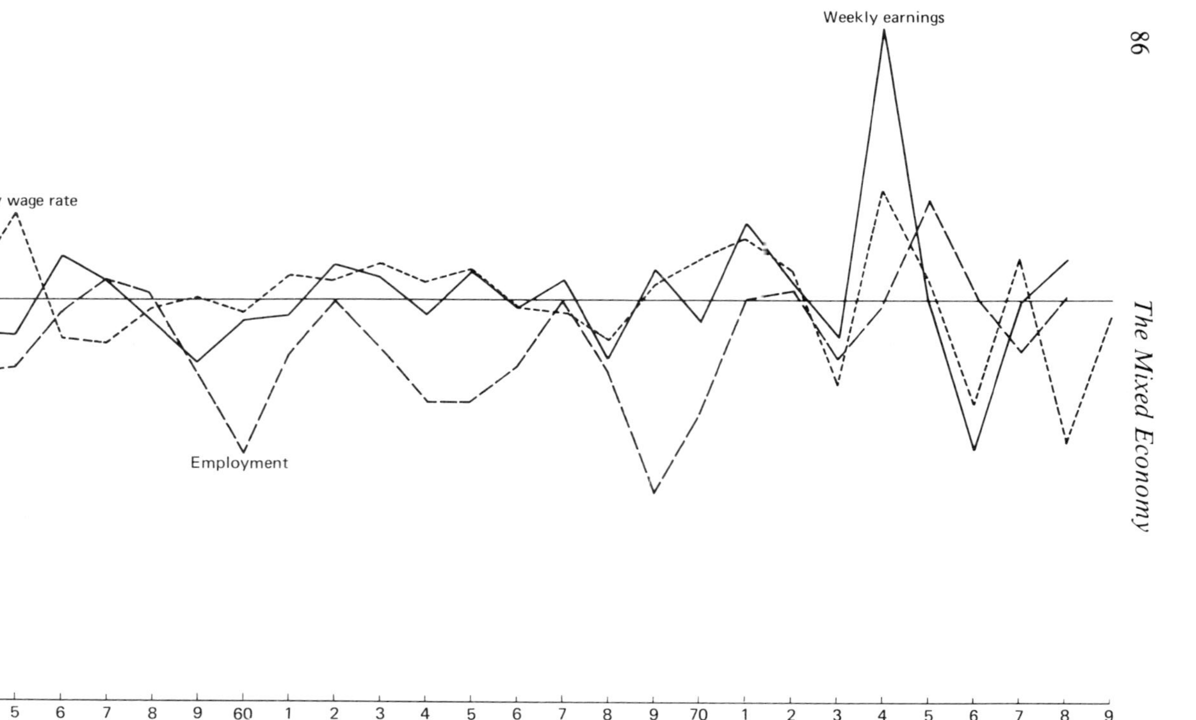

FIG. 4A.1 Growth rates of relative wages and employment in public and private industry in the UK (public corporations/manufacturing)

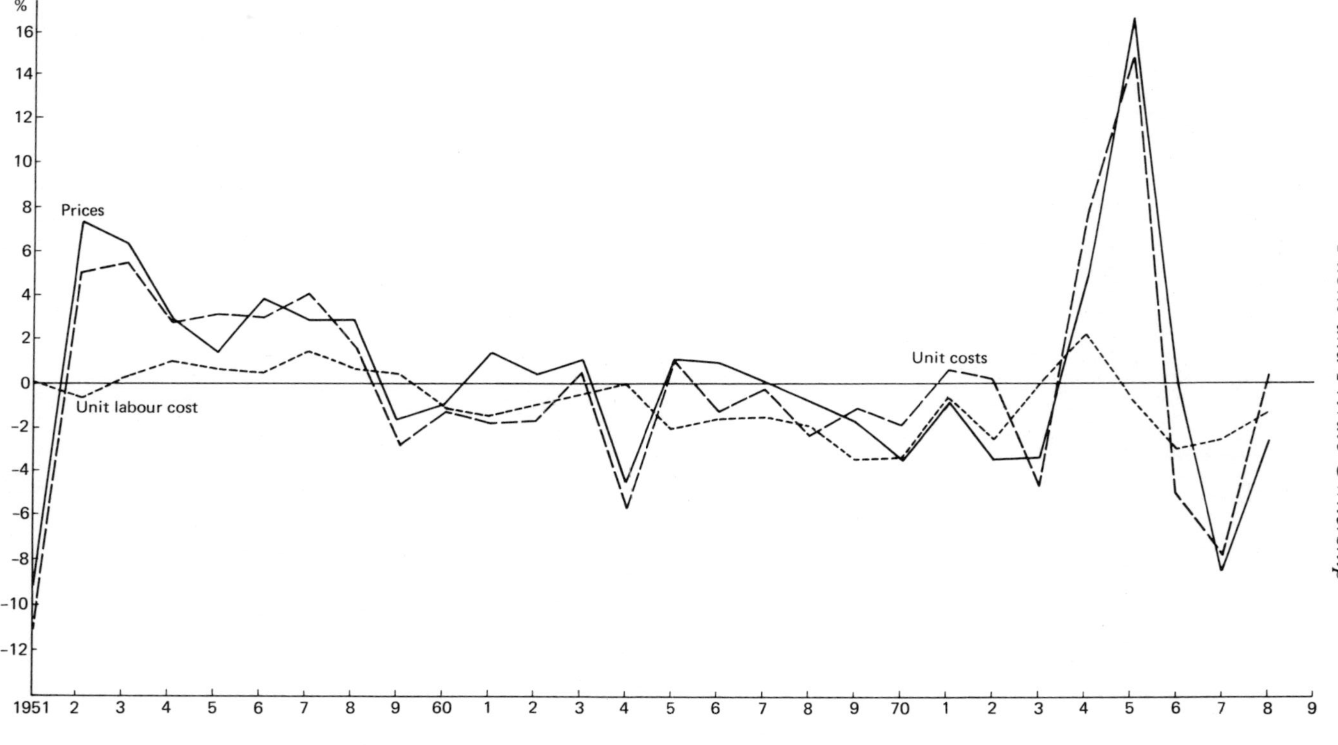

FIG. 4A.2 Growth rates of relative prices and weighted unit (non-capital) costs (public corporations UK/manufacturing UK)

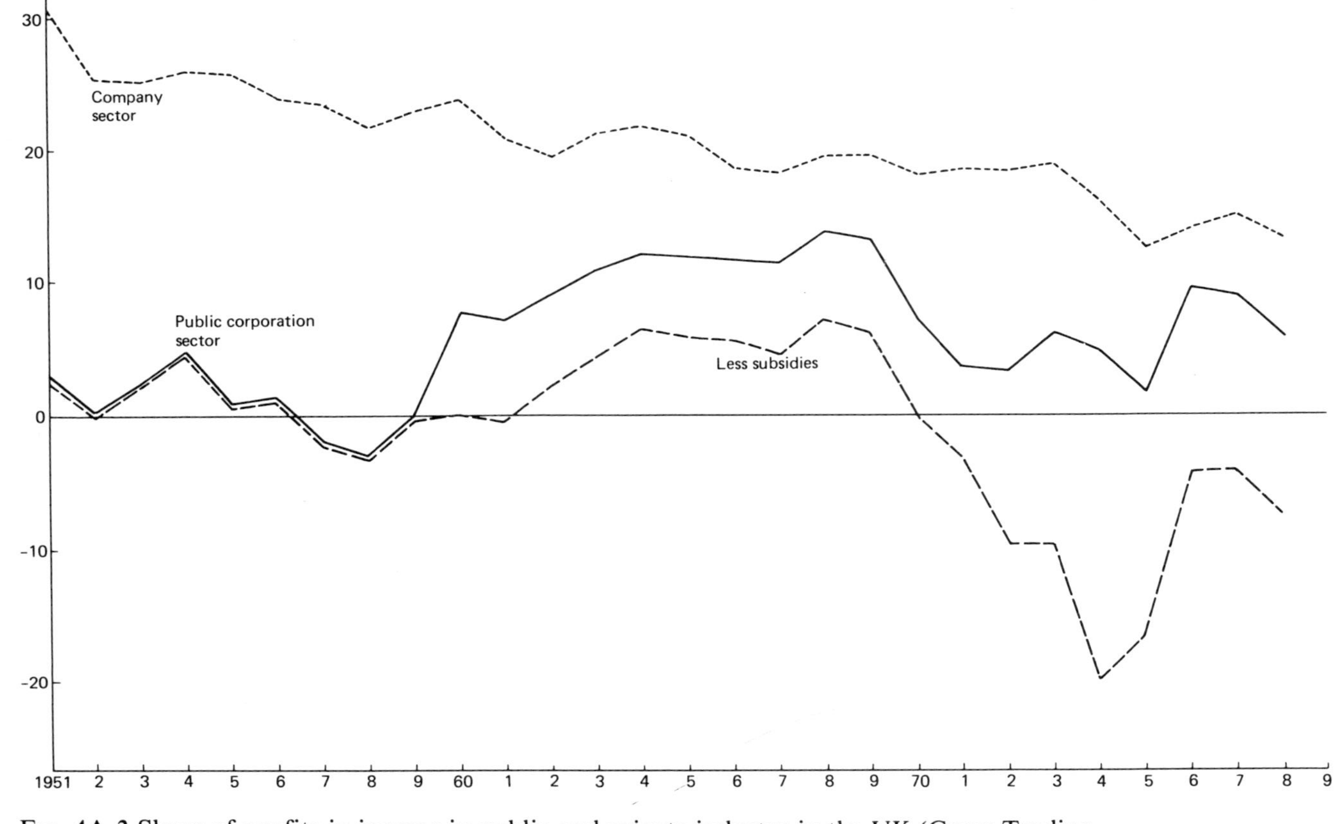

FIG. 4A.3 Share of profits in income in public and private industry in the UK (Gross Trading Surplus as a percentage of Domestic Value Added, both measured net of capital consumption)

NOTES

1. Thus Alchian: '... the evidence of poor management and the opportunity to capture wealth gains by eliminating it is revealed to outsiders by the selling price of the ownership rights' (p. 827). Rowley suggests that in public enterprise there 'is no takeover to pressure X-inefficient managers' (p. 13). For Davies the inability 'to exchange ownership claims along with lack of specialisation inhibits inexpensive detection and rectification of poor management in the case of public ownership' (1971, p. 150). Crain and Zardkoohi argue that in public firms 'entrepreneurial activities such as organisng, coordinating, and metering productive activity are predictably reduced in public enterprise' (1978, p. 398). Pommerehne and Frey suggest: 'Control of management behaviour is much weaker in public enterprises' (p. 223). 'With the higher costs of reshuffling ownership...' says Peltzman 'the management of the government enterprise will be enabled to trade more of the owners' wealth for objects of utility to the managers than will managers of private enterprises' (p. 111). For De Alessi 'managers of political firms have greater opportunity to increase their own welfare at the expense of their employers' wealth' (May/June 1974, p. 646) and such firms 'can survive for long periods in the presence of ... grossly inefficient management' (autumn 1974, p. 7). Moreover it is possible to 'mask bad management under the guise of fulfilling a variety of social goals' (1977, p. 9) Furubotn, Pejovich, Alchian with Demsetz do not comment explicitly on the Western-type public enterprise but their comments on the not for profit firm can be readily extended. For a wider discussion of the Chicago school and regulation, see Trebing (1976).
2. Cf. Neuberg, p. 303. Mann (1970) reports average electric utility operating income as a percentage of net electric plant 1966 for a sample of electric utilities as 7.14 per cent for public and 6.74 per cent for private; allowing for other plant and income or net asset base or deduction of interest charges pushes the public rate below the private. Yunker (1975) found for his sample of electric utilities an accounting rate of 4.3 per cent for public and 3.8 per cent for private but for operating income measures the public rates were lower. In both cases the dispersion of rates was bigger in the public sample. See also Pashigian (1976) on lower profit margins in publicly owned urban bus transit systems.
3. I am grateful to Mr R Ward for all the calculations associated with the charts in the Annex. For earlier work on price controls see Millward (1976) and NEDO (1976).
4. Neuberg 1977, p. 310, footnote.
5. Dean 1975, 1977.
6. See Gunderson (1979) but note also Hammermesh (1975).
7. Yunker (p. 66), also for data on the size distribution of firms. The problems of comparing British public firms with 'similar' private firms in other countries are well discussed in Pryke (1971).
8. Sales of less than $1 million in 1970 (De Alessi, autumn 1974, p. 11, footnote). Note that the remaining basic population includes firms involved in gas as well as electricity and Meyer (1975) excludes such multi-purpose firms from his sample.

9. He was forced to use net investment in plant as a proxy for capacity.
10. Note that Moore's (1970) main purpose was that of examining the effects of regulation but he did find that there was no significant difference between private and public firms in excess capacity (ratio of peak demand to total capacity), labour per plant and the cost of building plant, all of which are indirect indications that cost efficiency is not less in public firms.
11. Both Neuberg and Meyer found the cost equations for the two samples were significantly different using Chow tests.
12. The sum for each firm of interest and dividend payments divided by the sum of nominal debt and equity capital. Real capital employed was measured as the undepreciated value of the plant in 1958 dollars.
13. At the sample means private costs exceeded public costs by 23.5 per cent in 1965 and 32.9 per cent in 1970.
14. The coefficient was not significant.
15. The meaning of the depreciation figure and the size and structure of the basic population are not discussed in the article.
16. If a_1 and a_2 are the coefficients on capital and labour respectively in a Cobb-Douglas production function then the coefficient on the log of output with respect to the log of unit costs will be $\frac{1}{a_1 + a_2} - 1$, the coefficient on P_L will be $\frac{a_2}{a_1 + a_2}$ and the coefficient on P_K is $\frac{a_1}{a_1 + a_2}$. Hence $a_1 + a_2 = 0.76$ public and 0.86 for private. The elasticity of output with respect to labour is $a_2 = 0.88$ public and 0.97 private.
17. The authors assert but do not demonstrate that marginal costs and the marginal product of capital (labour) appear to be absolutely lower (higher) in public firms.
18. Pier *et al.* (1974) join Bennett and Johnson in not stating the date to which their data refer.
19. The authors do not clarify in what sense householders 'must' contract– nor under what regulatory framework, if at all, the private collectors operate.
20. Hirsch (1965), Savas (1976, 1977), Young (1974).
21. Peltzman 1971, p. 136.
22. Towards the end of the 1971 article
23. Mann and Siefried (1972) paradoxically treated evidence of public electric utility prices being affected by income levels, after standardising for costs and other variables, as indicative of inefficient non-profit tariff structures.
24. A rise in P_K, as opposed to P'_K, will have no effect for the regulated firm as long as P_K is less than S since the gross profit margin is unaffected. For other discussion of the regulated firm see Averch and Johson (1962), Courville (1974) and Spann (1974).

REFERENCES

Alchian, A.A. and Demsetz, H., (1974) 'Production, Information Costs and Economic Organisation', *American Economic Review*, vol. 62 (Dec.) reproduced in Furubotn and Pejovich (1974).

Alchian A.A., (1965) 'Some Economics of Property Rights', *Il Politico*.

Averch H. and Johnson, L.K. (1962), 'Behaviour of the Firm under Regulatory Constraint', *American Economic Review*, vol. 52 (Dec.).

Bank of England (1980), 'Profitability and Company Finance', *Quarterly Bulletin* (June).

Bennett, J.T. and Johnson, M.H. (1979), 'Public Versus Private Provision of Collective Goods and Services: Garbage Collection Revisited', *Public Choice*.

Caves, D.W. and Christensen, L.R. (1978), 'The Relative Efficiency of Public and Private Firms in a Competitive Environment: The Case of Canadian Railroads', Social Systems Research Institute, Workshop Series (Oct.).

Crain, W.M. and Zardkoohi, A. (1978), 'A Test of the Property Rights Theory of the Firm: Water Utilities in the United States', *Journal of Law and Economics*, vol. XXI, no. 2 (Oct.).

____, (1980), 'Public Sector Expansion: Stagnant Technology or Property Rights', *Southern Economic Journal*, vol. 46, no. 4 (Apr.).

Courville, L. (1974), 'Regulation and Efficiency in the Electric Utility Industry', *Bell Journal of Economics and Management Science*, vol. 5 (Spring).

Davies, D.D., 'The Efficiency of Public Versus Private Firms: the Case of Australias Two Airlines', *Journal of Law and Economics*, 1971.

Dean, A.J.H. (1975), 'Earnings in the Public and Private Sectors', *National Institute Economic Review*, No. 74 (Nov.).

____ (1977), 'Public and Private Sector Manual Workers' Pay 1970–77', *National Institute Economic Review* (Nov.).

De Alessi, L. (1969), 'Implications of Property Rights for Government Investment Choices', *American Economic Review*, vol. 59 (Mar.).

____ (1974), 'Management Tenure under Private and Government Ownership in the Electric Power Industry', *Journal of Political Economy*, vol. 82 (May/June).

____ (1974), 'An Economic Analysis of Government Ownership and Regulation: Theory and Evidence from the Electric Power Industry', *Public Choice*, vol. 19 (autumn).

____ (1975), 'Some effects of Ownership on the Wholesale Prices of Electric Power', *Economic Inquiry*, vol. 13 (Dec.).

____ (1977), 'Ownership and Peak Load Pricing in the Electric Power Industry', *Quarterly Review of Economics and Business*, vol. 17 (Winter).

Edwards, F.R. and Stevens, B.J. (1978), 'The provision of Municipal Sanitation Services by Private Firms: An Empirical Analysis of the Efficiency of Alternative Market Structures and Institutional Arrangements', *Journal of Industrial Economics*, vol. 27 (Dec.).

Furubotn, E. and Pejovitch. S. (1972) 'Property Rights and Economic Theory: A Survey of Recent Literature', *Journal of Economic Literature*, vol. 10 (Dec.) reproduced in Furubotn, E. and Pejovitch, S., *The Economics of Poverty Rights* (Ballinger Press, 1974).

Gunderson, M. (1979) 'Earnings Differentials between Public and Private Sectors', *Canadian Journal of Economics* (May).

Hammermesh, D.S. (1975), 'The Effect of Government Ownership on Union Wages', in D.S. Hammermesh (ed.), *Labour in the Profit and Non-Profit Sectors* (Princeton).

Hirsch, W.Z. (1965) 'Cost Functions of an Urban Government Service: Refuse Collection', *Review of Economics and Statistics*, vol. 47 (Feb.).

Kitchen, H.M. (1976), 'A Statistical Estimation of an Operating Cost Function for Municipal Refuse Collection', *Public Finance Quarterly*, vol. 4, no. 1 (Jan.).

Mann, P.C. (1976), 'Publicly Owned Electric Utility Profits and Resource Allocation', *Land Economics*, vol. 46 (Nov.).

____ (1974), 'User Power and Electricity Rates', *Journal of Law and Economics*, vol. 17 (Oct.).

____ and Siefried, E.J. (1972), 'Pricing in the Case of Publicly Owned Electric Utilities', *Quarterly Review of Economics and Business*, vol. 12 (Summer).

Meyer, R.A. (1975), 'Publicly Owned Versus Privately Owned Utilities: A Policy Choice', *Review of Economics and Statistics* (Nov.).

Millward, R. (1976), 'Price Restraint, Anti-Inflation Policy and Public and Private Industry in the UK', *Economic Journal*, vol. 86 (June).

____ (1978), 'Public Ownership, the Theory of Property Rights and the Public Corporation in the UK', Salford Papers in Economics, 78-I.

Moore, T.G. (1970), 'The Effectiveness of Regulation of Electric Utility Prices', *Southern Economic Journal*, vol. 36 (Apr.).

National Economic Development Office (1976), 'A Study of UK Nationalised Industries'.

Neuberg, L.G. (1977), 'Two Issues in the Municipal Ownership of Electric Power Distribution Systems', *Bell Journal of Economics*, vol. 8, no. 1 (Spring).

Pashigan, B.P. 'Consequences and Causes of Public Ownership of Urban Transit', *Journal of Political Economy*, vol. 84.

Peltzman, S. (1971), 'Pricing in Public and Private Enterprises and Electric Utilities in the United States', *Journal of Law and Economics*, vol. 14, (Apr.).

Pescatrice, D.R., and Trapani, J.M. III (1978), 'The Performance and Objectives of Public and Private Utilities Operating in the United States', *Journal of Public Economics*, vol. 13.

Pier, W.J., Vernon, R.B. and Wicks, J.H. (1974). 'An Empirical Comparison of Government and Private Production Efficiency', *National Tax Journal*, vol. 27 (Dec.).

Pommerehne, W.W. and Frey, B.S. (1977), 'Public Versus Private Production Efficiency in Switzerland: A theoretical and Empirical Comparison', *Urban Affairs Annual Review*.

Primeaux, W.J. (1977), 'An Assessment of X-Efficiency gained through Competition', *Review of Economics and Statistics* (Feb.).

____ (1978), 'The Effect of Competition on Capacity Utilisation in the Electric Utility Industry', *Economic Inquiry* (Apr.).

Pryke, R. (1971), *Public Enterprise in Practice* (MacGibbon and Kee).

Rowley, C. (1977), 'Efficiency in the Public Sector', in C. Rowe (ed.), *Industrial Efficiency and the Role of Government*' (Dept. of Industry, HMSO).

Savas, E.S. (1974), 'Municipal Monopolies Versus Competition in the Delivery of Urban Services', *Urban Affairs Annual Review.*

____ (1976), 'Policy Analysis for Local Government: The Private Delivery of a Public Service', *Policy Analysis.*

____ (1977), 'An Empirical Study of Competition in Municipal Service Delivery', *Public Administration Review* (Nov/Dec).

____ (1977), 'Policy Analysis for Local Government: Public Versus Private Refuse Collection', *Policy Analysis*, no. 3.

Spann, R.M. (1974), 'Rate of Return Regulation and Efficiency in Production: An Empirical Test of the Averch-Johnson Thesis', *Bell Journal of Economics and Management Sciences*, vol. 5 (Spring).

____ (1977), 'Public Versus Private Provision of Government Services', in T. Borcheding (ed.), *Budgets and Bureaucrats: The Sources of Government Growth*' (Duke University Press).

Trebing, H.M. (1976), 'The Chicago School Versus Public Utility Regulation', *Journal of Economic Issues*, vol. 10, pt. I.

Wallace, R.L. and Junk, P.E. (1970), 'Economic Efficiency of Small Municipal Electricity Generating Systems', *Land Economics*, (Nov.).

Young, D.R. (1974), 'The Economic Organisation of Refuse Collection', *Public Finance Quarterly*, (Jan.).

Yunker, J.A. (1975), 'The Economic Performance of Public and Private Enterprise: The Case of US Electric Utilities', *Journal of Economics and Business*, vol. 28, pt. I.

5 Steel in a Mixed Economy

AUBREY SILBERSTON
University of London

INTRODUCTION

It is perhaps natural to think of the British steel industry as being more or less wholly nationalised. In fact the whole of the steel industry was not nationalised in 1967. The private sector was powerful then, and is even more powerful today, especially in the wake of the strike in the British Steel Corporation (the nationalised sector) in the first three months of 1980. In addition, imports of steel have never been controlled, so that both public and private steel-makers have been subject to foreign competition. Controls have been placed only on foreign trade in steel scrap, and these controls (when in force) affect both sectors of the steel industry. The steel sector is as mixed in nature, therefore, as the economy as a whole.

The approach of this paper will be to consider the relative roles of the public and private sectors of the British steel industry, and then the overall trends in steel consumption and trade since 1967. The British Steel Corporation itself will then be considered, with particular reference to the way in which it has performed its role. Its relationship with government has been and is important, and this will be discussed also. Finally, consideration will be given to whether the present structure of the steel industry in Britain needs to be modified in order to improve the performance of the industry. This needs to be thought of both in relation to the effieiency of the industry itself and to its role in contributing to the efficiency of the British economy as a whole.

PUBLIC AND PRIVATE STEEL

The British Steel Corporation (BSC) was established in July 1967 by the Iron and Steel Act of that year. It became the sole owner of the shares of fourteen companies which had each produced, in the year ended 30 June 1964 475,000 gross tonnes or more of steel (including alloy steel). The formation of the BSC represented the largest industrial merger ever to have occurred in the United Kingdom.

The effect of nationalisation was that the BSC took over all the bulk steel-making companies, plus their subsidiaries. These included nearly 200 companies, of which 40 were overseas. Several subsidiaries were producers of special steels. In 1967/8 BSC produced some 23 million tonnes of crude steel. It was the largest steel producer in Europe and the second largest in the world. Employment in the UK was 254,000.

The private sector, following the formation of the BSC, accounted for some 25 per cent by weight of finished steel deliveries to the UK market and for rather less than 10 per cent of exports. By value, the private sector's share was considerably higher than these figures suggest, since the private sector's output was very much concentrated on high-value special steels. Much of the crude steel used by the private sector came from the BSC, which accounted in 1967/8 for some 90 per cent of crude steel output. The private sector has always been predominantly based on electric arc furnaces: this route has traditionally been used for special steels. Its usual raw material is steel scrap. The BSC inherited some electric arc works for making high carbon special steels. It therefore competed directly with the private sector in many outlets, but for some products, in particular high value alloy and stainless steels, the independent sector accounted for the bulk of final output, and was in some cases the only supplier. The BSC was at the same time a major competitor of the private sector in some sectors and its major source of supply of crude steel.

Broadly speaking, this situation has continued throughout the period since 1967. Both sectors have been affected by changes in the British steel market, and especially by the depression of the last few years. A recent development in the private sector has been the establishment of low output electric arc 'mini-mills' making general carbon steels. These steels are suitable for continuous casting and subsequent rolling into light products such as bars and rods, and more recently into wide strip. There have been several entrants into the private sector making this type of steel, including three multinational firms. They have built electric arc plants on green-field sites to use locally arising supplies of scrap and to sell to local markets. In this way they have competed directly with the BSC in its bulk steel business, in the same way as mini-mills in such countries as the USA and Germany. They have captured virtually the whole of the reinforcing bar business, and are now going up-market into strip. Some have also become successful exporters. They have benefited from the low price of scrap that has resulted from depression conditions, and provide serious competition for the BSC in their chosen field.

The BSC has invested heavily in the period since nationalisation, but has shut down a lot of old capacity in the last few years. The result has been a net reduction in BSC capacity as compared with the situation in 1967. At the end of 1979, the BSC had a liquid steel capacity of some 22 m. tonnes, while the private sector's capacity had grown to nearly 6 m. tonnes. The BSC therefore accounted for some 80 per cent of crude steel capacity as compared with 90 per cent at the time of nationalisation. Sales in the calendar year[1] 1979 were approximately as follows:

Sales 1979 (calendar year), m. tonnes finished steel

BSC	8.7	Consumers and stockholders
	1.7	Private sector
	3.1	Exports
	13.5	(= 18 m. tonnes liquid)
Private	4.0	Home sales
	1.0	Exports
	5.0	(= 6.6 m. tonnes liquid)
Imports	*3.3*	

Sales, private sector 1979 (calendar year), m. liquid tonnes

3.7	Based on own output of steel
1.9	Based on BSC steel
1.0	Based on steel from imports and stockholders
6.6	Total sales

In 1979 the BSC was producing at under 80 per cent of its much reduced capacity, while the private sector's output of liquid steel was at about 65 per cent of its capacity – not a healthy situation for either sector.

PRODUCTION, CONSUMPTION AND FUTURE CAPACITY

In the period since 1967, real consumption of steel in the UK has been subject to marked cycles. The Appendix gives the figures (in terms of deliveries of finished steel). From a level of 16.4 m. finished tonnes in 1967/8, consumption increased to a peak of 18.7 m. tonnes in 1970/71, but then fell markedly. Consumption rose to a new peak in 1973/74, but fell with the recession to below the 1967/68 level in 1975/76. By 1978/79 it had fallen even further, to its lowest level since 1962/63. This was partly on account of the hauliers' strike in January/February 1979, but the primary reason was the world depression in steel demand. In EEC countries as a whole steel consumption in 1978/79 was about 15 per cent below the 1973 peak and steel production was at about 65 per cent of rated capacity. EEC figures for 1979/80 are not yet available, but UK consumption fell even further in that year, and was 4 per cent below the depressed 1978/79 figure.

Crude steel production in the UK has fluctuated more sharply than consumption, partly because of movements of stocks during the steel cycle. Output has been exceptionally depressed in recent years. Already by 1975/76 it was at its lowest level for sixteen years. There was some recovery in 1976/77, but a fall again in 1977/78. BSC output in 1975/76 was the lowest since its formation, and output in 1977/78 and 1978/79 was at virtually the same level. In 1979/80, a year which included the 1980 steel strike, BSC production, at 14.1 liquid tonnes, was almost 20 per cent below the previous year's level.

Imports, on the other hand, have shown a marked rise over the period since steel was nationalised. In 1967/8 some 1.9 m. tonnes of finished steel was imported, or about 12 per cent of real consumption. By 1974/75 the comparable figure was more than 3 m. tonnes. Imports remained at much the same level in the following four years, but rose to 20 per cent of consumption as the latter declined. In 1979–80 imports were 3.6 m. tonnes, or 25 per cent of total UK demand. The majority of imports come from other members of the EEC. It is interesting that, despite the increase, import penetration is still low in the UK in comparison with most other EEC countries, although the position may change following the 1980 BSC strike.

Export performance has not kept pace with the increase of imports. In 1967/68 exports represented over 20 per cent of production. They rose until 1972/73, but subsequently fell. From a trade surplus in 1967/68 of some 2 m. tonnes, the UK became a net importer of steel for the first time in 1974/75. Exports have done better since then, and by 1976/77 there was a small surplus of exports over imports, but the strike turned the balance the other way again in 1979/80.

The depressing figures for recent years contrast not only with those for previous years but also with what had been expected when the BSC was drawing up its future plans in the early 1970s. Indeed, at that time, the prospect seemed to be for continued expansion of demand for UK steel. It was recognised that demand for steel in developed countries rose rather more slowly than the rate at which GNP increased. For example, between 1955 and 1970 the trend growth in UK steel demand averaged 1.7 per cent annum, while the rate of growth of GNP was 2.5 per cent. Nevertheless, it was believed – at least by the BSC – that prospects for national economic growth in the 1970s indicated a rate of growth of steel demand of some 2.5 per cent annum. Rising demand was expected for investment goods, consumer durables, motor cars and equipment for North Sea exploration. World steel demand was expected to rise at double the UK rate, and the prospects for steel exports from the UK were considered to be good. In the light of these forecasts, the BSC drew up an investment programme which was designed to take the Corporation's capacity from 27 m. tonnes of liquid steel at the end of 1972 to 33–5 m. tonnes by the late 1970s and to 36–8 m. tonnes during the first half of the 1980s. It was recognised that these figures might need to be revised as time went on, and the programme was therefore conceived as a flexible one. Nevertheless, these orders of magnitude were considered about right and they gained the support of the (Conservative) government of the day.

Today these figures seem to be absurdly optimistic. The BSC has incurred catastrophic losses over the last few years. It has closed works and shed labour on a considerable scale. It now plans to have a liquid steel capacity of a mere 15 million tonnes, plus a standby capacity of 5–6 million tonnes. Even these figures may be revised downwards when the new chairman of BSC (appointed from July 1980) has had time to consider how best to stem BSC's losses. At the same time the private sector has been in trouble and there have been closures there.

What has gone wrong? Has the BSC management been incompetent? Has the management been good, but prevented by government interference from running the industry efficiently? What about the private sector? Has that done better, and if so why? How far has the poor performance of the BSC in particular been due to the poor performance of the UK economy? How far has it been the result of the worst world depression since the 1930s, which has brought severe price cutting in markets throughout the world? What about the new steel producers like Mexico, Korea and Brazil? How far is it their fault?

These are a lot of questions, and there are many more that could be asked. I will do my best to answer briefly those I have posed, particularly those which throw light on the working of the mixed economy.

INVESTMENT PLANNING AND PERFORMANCE IN THE BSC

Investment in the British steel industry during the mid-1960s was low compared with that of its international competitors. Many of the companies from which the BSC was formed were financially weak. The BSC inherited a large number of works – most of them small in relation to the minimum optimum scale – with obsolete technology and low productivity. No doubt the low level of investment prior to nationalisation was casued partly by fears that the industry would be nationalised. Possibly also a number of inefficient works had survived because of the control exercised over the industry from 1951 to 1967 by the (government imposed) Iron and Steel Board. In practice, this control probably tended to confirm the *status quo*. Whatever the reasons, there was no doubt that in 1967 much needed to be done to render the UK steel industry efficient.

The BSC's first development strategy concentrated on exploiting the potential of five major steelworks – the 'heritage' works of Port Talbot, Llanwern, Scunthorpe, Lackenby and Ravenscraig. Its ten-year development strategy, outlined in the White Paper of February 1973 (HMSO, 1973), proposed that each of these five plants should be brought up to its optimum capacity and modernised, that a start should be made on a new steel complex on the south bank of the Tees and that perhaps two new smaller electric arc steelworks should be built, one of them in Scotland. This would take the BSC's capacity to a maximum of 36–8 million tons in the first half of the 1980s.

It will be seen that no major 'greenfield site' steelworks was proposed: even the plant on Teesside was to be based on an existing works. Politics were probably the main reason for the proposed new electric arc plant in Scotland, but a proposal to build a major new works at Hunterston was not accepted, although a new deep water port was to be developed there. By concentrating on improvements and expansion of existing works, the BSC was giving itself a degree of flexibility it would not have had if major new works had been envisaged.

These plans brought with them the need to close the whole or part of many existing works. The White Paper was a little reticent about what was intended, partly in order not to stir up a hornet's nest. It did however mention plans for Wales, for example, to end iron and steel-making at Ebbw Vale and Shotton, and it foreshadowed the total closure of East Moors. The labour force of the BSC would be correspondingly reduced, from some 250,000 on nationalisation (230,000 in 1972) to 200,000 by the end of the period of the strategy. Labour productivity was expected to rise considerably. In the new Teesside works it was expected to be about 800 tonnes a man-year, as against 250 tonnes in the best existing works.

The huge new investment programme was expected to cost over £3000 million (at 1972 prices) in ten years. Once the strategy got under way, capital expenditure reached high figures, although inflation accounted for a good deal of the increase. The Appendix shows investment expenditure. It will be seen that this reached a peak in 1976/77, and then fell. According to the Report of the Select Committee (HMSO 1977), capital expenditure between 1968 and 1976 could be allocated between modernisation and expansion (77 per cent), replacement (19 per cent), and statutory obligations (4 per cent). The programme involved the replacement of obsolete open-hearth steel-making by basic oxygen steel making, the erection of large new blast furnaces and the modernisation of others, the introduction of continuous casting on a large scale, and some investment at the rolling and finishing stages. It involved a radical change in the whole pattern of the British steel industry.

Not surprisingly, the progress of the development programme was slower than expected. Difficulties were encountered in the rate at which new plant could be designed, built and commissioned, and there were industrial relations problems on sites involving a number of different contractors. More important than this, the depression following the energy crisis of October 1973, with its accompanying problems of inflation, followed by contractionary government policies, reduced the rate at which new steel capacity was required. Plans for an expansion of Port Talbot to a total crude steel capacity of 6 million tons were abandoned, as were plans for a wide plate mill at Redcar with a capacity of 2 million tonnes per year. Nevertheless, although in many respects the BSC is not as technically up-to-date as several of its main competitors (Aylen 1980b), that part of the UK steel industry for which BSC was responsible was by 1980 far better equipped, in fewer larger plants, than had been the case in 1967.

A dramatic development at the end of 1979 was a decision by the BSC to revise downwards its capacity requirements to under half of what had been envisaged in the heady days of 1972–73. Capacity was to be cut to 15 million tonnes, plus a standby capacity of 5–6 m. tonnes. Manpower was to be run down to 100,000. More than 6 m. tonnes of capacity were to be closed, with a loss of over 50,000 jobs. This action followed extremely heavy losses by BSC (although not as high per ton as several foreign competitors) – losses which were aggravated by high loan interest repayments arising from the expensive development programme. When Sir Charles Villiers came to the end of his term as chairman of the BSC in July 1980, to be succeeded by Mr Ian MacGregor, the widespread view was that the BSC had turned out to be a disastrous failure. Its story seemed to be an indictment both of nationalisation and of the men who had been in charge of the Corporation. How justified is this view?

BSC, THE GOVERNMENT AND THE UNIONS[2]

All nationalised industries, by virtue of the relevant nationalisation Acts, have to obtain government permission before they can take certain actions. In particular, they have to gain approval for their investment programmes and for the methods by which outside finance is raised to pay for these. In addition to the controls derived from the nationalisation acts, the government may place other obligations on boards, although these are not always derived from specific legal powers. The control of price increases is a case in point, since this has often been done when no specific legislation controlling prices has been in force.

Until the UK's entry into the EEC in 1973, the BSC was subject to price control by the responsible minister. Proposed price increases were reduced in 1969 and 1971, and throughout the period from its creation the BSC has been subject to continuing pressure to hold back prices. The BSC has estimated that if, between 1967 and March 1975, prices had been set at a level comparable with those prevailing in the EEC, an additional £783 m. of revenue would have been generated. This figure has been subject to criticism, but it is likely that the figure would be a large one even if some alternative basis of calculation were used.

Another form of government interference has affected the closure programme, and through this the investment programme. Following the election of 1974, the Labour Government began a review of the BSC's closure programme under Lord Beswick. The effect of the Beswick review was that in some cases the closure proposals were confirmed, while in others they were either reversed or deferred until the early 1980s. In general the decisions confirmed the 1973 White Paper strategy, but slowed down its implementation considerably. The Select Committee quote a BSC estimate that the net cost of maintaining the 'Beswick' works was at least £65 m. during 1976/77. The Select Committee itself estimated that further costs of government decisions, e.g. in connection with Port Talbot and Shotton, may have exceeded this total by more than as much again.

It is ironic that, in the desperate rush to close plants that occurred in late 1979 and early 1980, closures of all the Beswick plants were confirmed, plus several more that had not been scheduled for closure at the time of the Beswick Review, such as those at Corby (steel-making only) and Consett. This was at a time when general unemployment was much higher than when the Beswick review was taking place.

In addition to the holding back of price increases and of closures, the government has undoubtedly taken up an enormous amount of BSC top management time, thus diverting attention that might have been given to pressing day-to-day problems. The Beswick Review is one such example. Another is the time taken up by the Joint Steering Group, which was set up by the Heath Government in 1970 and did not report until May 1972. It is clear that, in one way and another, BSC's performance has been hampered very considerably by government intervention.

The BSC's relations with the trades unions have been affected by the fact of nationalisation in rather less obvious ways. The main trade union, the Iron and Steel Trades Confederation, was on the whole very co-operative with the BSC until the strike of January–March 1980. The National Union of Blastfurnacemen was less co-operative, and its dispute with the BSC over manning and pay on the large modern Llanwern blast furnace kept the new furnace standing idle for over a year, and was only settled after a court of enquiry had met. The industrial relations record of the iron and steel industry during the 1970s has been considerably worse than that of manufacturing industry as a whole. At the same time, both the BSC and the unions have given much time and thought to the improvement of industrial relations procedures. The 'Heathrow conferences' of 1974 and 1975 resulted in a number of joint working parties and reports. In January 1976 a joint statement was issued by the BSC and the steel unions, making provision for negotiations on job restructuring aimed at a big improvement in labour productivity. Progress was slow following this agreement, however, partly because of the recession in steel demand.

Although this is very much a matter of judgement, it seems to me likely that the delays over the commissioning of new equipment, and the reluctance to negotiate genuine demanning agreements – at least until comparatively recently – were influenced by the fact that the BSC was a nationalised concern. In spite of heavy losses at times by the BSC, the unions knew that nationalised industries are not normally allowed to go bankrupt. They therefore felt able to hold out for conditions which would not have been obtainable from private firms at comparable times. Similarly, the unions put on pressure for delays in closures, in spite of the cost to BSC of this policy. Recently, the unions have opposed closures, although in practice these have been accepted by their members on account of high redundancy payments. The strike of 1980 is perhaps the major example in recent years of union pressure for a settlement that no private firm would have found it possible to make.

Private industry is not of course immune from trade disputes which seem to go against reason, as was seen in the case of *The Times*, when it closed for nearly a year in 1978/79. But it is perhaps fair to conclude that if the BSC had not been nationalised it would have found it easier to improve its efficiency in the use of labour, and to economise on resources generally, than has actually proved to be the case.

THE BSC'S OWN RESPONSIBILITY

It is very easy, when discussing a nationalised industry, to fall into the habit of placing all the blame for its failure on factors connected with nationalisation, and particularly with government interference. This is seldom likely to be the whole truth. It is difficult, however, to separate out those failures which are in some sense a consequence of nationalisation and those which are not. After all, the very structure of the BSC was a consequence of nationalisation, and it could be argued that those put in charge of this vast organisation were given an impossible task. They had to run the BSC as it was, and could only dispose of parts of it, or acquire new parts, with government consent. Similarly, they had to be particularly sensitive to industrial relations and human problems, and act as a good employer in every sense. Nevertheless, the BSC was effectively in charge of its own planning and its own operations, and had a wide measure of discretion open to it.

The present author was a part-time member of the BSC board from 1967 to 1976, and therefore jointly responsible for the decisions made during that period. This should be remembered in what follows.

Perhaps the severest criticism of the BSC is that its development plans, as outlined in the 1973 White Paper, were wildly optimistic. So much was this so, that the capacity now aimed at is only about half of what was envisaged in the plan. If one goes back to the time when the plan was prepared, however, the picture looked very different. There had been a sustained rise in steel demand throughout more or less the whole of the post-war period. The British economy had grown at a faster rate than ever before, and was expected to continue to grow. Concern was being expressed, especially by the Labour Party in opposition, about the ability of the UK steel industry to cope with cyclical peaks of demand. They suggested a capacity of 40 m. tonnes by the early 1980s. The BSC development plan was based on government forecasts for the economy, interpreted cautiously. It was the result of one of the most sophisticated planning exercises ever carried out in British industry. It was the subject of much criticism within the BSC, and it had to go through prolonged (and hostile) investigation in the Joint Steering Group. This Group did succeed in reducing the scale of the plan somewhat, but its main outlines–the decision to concentrate bulk steel-making on a small number of large coastal sites, and to move towards the new technologies – were questioned by none at the time, and by few since. Indeed, as regards modernisation, the pace has been criticised as being too slow rather than too fast.

Having said this, it must be admitted that within the BSC there were several doubters. They were criticial of the high export forecasts, and they thought that the home market forecasts were also high. There was however pressure from the chairman, Lord Melchett, towards an expansionary industry, and his views carried great weight, especially as he was so admired and respected. Where the doubters got their way was in seeing that caveats were made about flexibility. In practice, partly on account of government action, the capacity achieved by 1980 was much nearer to the conservative than the optimistic levels set in the plan.

What nobody foresaw was the oil crisis of late 1973. Nor did they foresee the decline of the British motor industry and the malaise in mechanical engineering and manufacturing generally. They certainly did not anticipate what has happened to the exchange rate. Recessions were expected, but there was no reason then to expect as deep a depression as that which has actually occurred. A growth in steel output in new countries was anticipated, however, and in this the forecasts were not bad. All in all, I do not think that the BSC can be accused of more than optimism, but optimism which could be tempered as time went on and the level of demand assessed more accurately.

In any event, the present configuration of the BSC is that envisaged by the development plan, and is accepted as being appropriate today. The main departure from the plan is that Llanwern and Port Talbot, both heavily dependent on the motor industry, are being demanned in order to run at half capacity. There are even suggestions that one of these plants should be permanently closed. If that were to occur, that would be a most serious step and a major departure from the plan. My own view, for what it is worth, is that the BSC, under pressure from the Conservative government to eliminate its losses, over-reacted at the end of 1979, and that the scorn then poured on past decisions was overdone. Short-term pressures may have influenced long-term decisions. It is true that many steel-using industries in Britain appear to have a bleak future, but even so, gloom about the future may be excessive. Depressions do not last for ever, and it is hard to believe that the demand for British steel will not revive appreciably during the 1980s.

Another criticism of the BSC, on rather the opposite tack, has been that the Corporation was unable to meet demand at times of boom, especially in the early 1970s. Its share of the UK market declined from 70 per cent of deliveries in 1970 to 53 per cent by 1975, its place in the market being taken by imports. The private sector has kept its share. The BSC has explained its poor performance by plant inadequacies, shortages of skilled manpower, labour disputes and raw material problems. One cannot help feeling, however, that production problems sometimes arose which should have been foreseen, and that these criticisms of BSC's production performance have a good deal of substance.

A further area of criticism has concerned BSC's productivity performance. The productivity of the BSC compares poorly with that of its major overseas competitors. The BSC attributes this partly to old equipment and a multiplicity of small plants, at least in the past. It also gives union-induced overmanning as a reason. Detailed studies of very similar plants in the UK and Europe have certainly shown labour productivity at two or three times the UK level (Aylen, 1980b). Overmanning among maintenance workers, lack of flexibility between different groups of employees, and below-capacity operation have been cited as reasons.

Clearly the BSC cannot be blamed entirely for its productivity record, since for many years it has been negotiating with the unions on these issues. Possibly however the BSC was slow to grasp the importance of high labour productivity, especially in its early years, when it was keen above all to formulate and implement its development plans. Its development was, however, an important route to higher productivity.

Has the BSC been quick enough in developing new products as market needs have arisen? Criticism has been directed, for example, at BSC's slowness in providing pipe for natural gas and for North Sea oil distribution. It is true that in cases such as these imports have been necessary before the BSC's own production has come on stream, but the BSC has had to have regard to the prospective profitability of new developments when Japan, for example, was already in the market on a large scale. Where the BSC has been ahead of the market – for example with the two direct reduction plants at Hunterston – this has sometimes led to large losses. The BSC's success or failure in producing products for new markets is not therefore as easy to judge as might appear.

A more general criticism has been that BSC management has been poor. This is one of those charges that is difficult to prove or deny. One encouraging sign is that the BSC has gained contracts to design steelworks overseas, for example in Mexico, which seem to have been efficiently carried out. The execution of some investment schemes at home, for example the Anchor scheme at Scunthorpe, has also clearly been successful. It is probably true, however, that sufficient detailed supervision of day-to-day operations has not always occurred. Justified criticism has also been made of the BSC's commercial performance.

Several major reorganisations of the internal structure of the BSC have taken place since 1967. One may question how necessary all these were. They certainly caused much disruption, and diverted much top management time from other matters. The BSC can therefore perhaps be criticised on this ground also.

It should not be forgotten however that a very high proportion of BSC top management time has been taken up by the demands of government. The chairman in particular has been continually called upon, and attempts to confine certain contacts with government to lower levels (although still high levels) have often failed.

The BSC has been by no means blameless, therefore. But it has had a hard row to hoe, as the recent difficulty in finding a suitable chairman has illustrated.

THE PRIVATE SECTOR

The most marked development here has been the growth of minimills, which have successfully competed with the BSC in certain bulk steel items and are now starting to move up-market. Their growth is the main reason why the private sector has kept its share of the British steel market. It is not clear how these mills will perform at a time when scrap prices reach boom levels, although they are probably small enough and sufficiently well-managed to survive even in these circumstances.

The special steels sector has done less well on the whole. Many of the firms are small and technically backward, with a poor level of investment. Even the new Alpha Steel hot wide strip mill at Cardiff – in the basic steel sector – incorporates few technical innovations. The private sector remains highly fragmented, despite recent mergers, and economies of scale are hard to grasp. Very few of the private sector producers are large enough to maintain an independent research and development capability, although here they suffered from the suppression of the British Iron and Steel Research Association after the formation of the BSC. The most technically advanced plants making special steels in the UK are the new stainless steel plants put up by the BSC at Tinsley Park and Shepcote Lane, near Sheffield.

It has been argued that rationalisation among the small special steel producers is long overdue, and has been hampered by their independent spirit. UK private sector steel producers have however received no special grants or loans from the British Government. Certainly the private firms have suffered severely from the recession as well as the BSC. Patent Shaft has recently gone out of business, and further bankruptcies are on the cards. It cannot be said that the performance of the private sector is in marked contrast to that of the BSC, with the exception of the new mini-mills making basic steel. Indeed, the special steels sector of the BSC has been its best performer and is its brightest prospect. BSC research facilities and access to investment funds, together with high quality engineering, have put its special steel plants in a strong competitive position.

CONCLUSION

This has necessarily been a rapid and somewhat superficial survey of the British steel industry. It has concentrated above all on the BSC and its performance. It has noted the impact of economic conditions, of government controls and intervention, and of the performance of BSC's own management. A good deal of criticism has been directed at government intervention, although it has been seen that the BSC itself has not been blameless.

What of the future? The issue of how large BSC capacity should be has been discussed briefly, and it has been suggested that present plans may be too pessimistic and too dominated by the present deep recession. In any event, investment expenditure has now slowed down very greatly, and no major new developments are planned. Yet the BSC is by no means unique at present among European and US steel producers in making heavy losses, and cutbacks in these overseas countries do not seem to be envisaged on the BSC scale. In France, for example, the steel industry was virtually nationalised in 1979, and in Italy there is predominant state ownership. Neither country is taking the same view on steel as the British Government, and in Italy a new strip mill is being planned for the Naples area. The British steel-using sector is doing badly, but there is a danger that, if present trends continue, potentially efficient British plants will be shut down, while imports from European and other overseas plants take their place.

Would matters be improved if the structure of the BSC were altered in some way? The more profitable sectors might of course be sold off – for example, the special steel plants – but this would do little to improve the basic steel sectors, except to reduce the load on top management a little, while it would deprive the Corporation of profits. The serious question, when future efficiency is considered, is whether the bulk steel-making part of the BSC should be split into two or more nationalised sectors. This would give the advantage of smaller and more manageable units, and would introduce competition between them. But competition in major investment would not make sense in an industry where economies of scale are so important and the overall market relatively small. Price competition would be ruinous, and would be unlikely anyway in so closely knit an industry, with a long history of open or tacit price agreements. On balance, the disruption that would be caused by splitting the BSC would scarcely seem to be counterbalanced by the likely benefits.

Steel has not fared well in our mixed economy, although its future may not be as bleak as it is now painted. It has suffered because of the overall poor performance of the British economy, and the high exchange rate of recent years, as well as because of excessive government intervention. In any event, the British steel industry must clearly continue to remain largely in public ownership. Let us hope that, in the future, we shall be able to mix, more successfully than in the past, public ownership of steel with freedom for its managers to be enterprising. I confess, however, that I am not optimistic.

APPENDIX

UK and BSC steel statistics 1967–1980

	1967/68	*1968/69*	*1969/70*	*1970/71*	*1971/72*	*1972/73*	*1973/74*
BSC liquid steel production (m. tonnes)	23.0	25.4	25.3	25.5	21.4	25.1	23.0
BSC total finished steel deliveries, (m. tonnes)[a]	17.1	18.8	19.2	19.4	16.3	18.0	18.1
Private sector finished steel deliveries to home market (m. tonnes)	4.3	4.3	4.5	4.4	3.7	4.3	4.9
Total exports by steel producers of finished steel (m. tonnes)	3.9	3.3	3.4	3.3	4.1	4.1	3.2
Total Imports by consumers and stockholders of finished steel (m. tonnes)	1.9	2.0	1.0	1.0	1.5	2.2	2.5
Deliveries of finished steel (m. tonnes)[b]	16.4	18.0	18.4	18.7	15.6	17.8	19.6
No. of BSC employees at end of year (000)	254	254	255	252	230	227	220
BSC profits before tax (£ m.)	−11.1	−21.9	10.2[c]	7.4	−44.7	9.1	55.8
BSC capital investment (£ m.)		74	39[c]	143	237	198	187

UK and BSC steel statistics 1967–1980

	1974/5	*1975/6*	*1976/7*	*1977/8*	*1978/9*	*1979/80*
BSC liquid steel production (m. tonnes)	20.8	17.2	19.7	17.4	17.3	14.1
BSC total finished steel deliveries, (tonnes m.)[a]	15.0	12.7	13.7	13.4	12.5	10.5
Private sector finished steel deliveries to home market (m. tonnes)	4.6	3.9	4.1	3.8	3.9	3.8
Total exports by steel producers of finished steel (m. tonnes)	2.7	2.8	3.4	4.1	3.9	3.4

Total imports by consumers and stockholders of finished steel (m. tonnes)	3.1	2.9	3.0	3.1	2.9	3.6
Deliveries of finished steel (tonnes m.)[b]	18.0	15.0	15.9	15.3	14.8	14.2
No. of BSC employees at end of year (000)	228	210	208	197	186	166
BSC profits before tax (£ m.)	89.3	−246	−69	−455	−327	−544
BSC capital investment (£ m.)	311	530	579	476	318	282

NOTES

1967/68 and 1968/69 are for years ending 30 September, 1969/70 and subsequent years are for years ending 30 March.

a. Includes deliveries to UK private sector, and exports.

b. Net deliveries from BSC and private sector, plus imports to consumers and stockholders (N.B. figures include stock gains and draws).

c. Six months ending 30 March.

SOURCE

Mainly from British Steel Corporation Annual Reports.

NOTES

1. The BSC's financial year ends on 31 March, but the 1979/80 figures were distorted by the steel strike in the first three months of 1980. The calendar year 1979 gives a more normal picture.
2. See Silberston (1978) for a further discussion of these issues.

REFERENCES

Aylen, Jonathan (1980a), 'Innovation in the British Steel Industry', in K. Pavitt (ed.), *Technical Change and British Economic Performance*, (London: Macmillan).

____ (1980b), 'Britain's Steelyard Blues', *New Scientist*, 26 June.

British Steel Corporation, *Annual Report and Accounts* (London: BSC).

HMSO (1973), 'Steel. British Steel Corporation: Ten Year Development Strategy' Cmnd. 5226 (London: HMSO, February).

____ (1977), 'First Report from the Select Committee on Nationalised Industries', Session 1977–8, 'The British Steel Corporation', vol. 1 (London: HMSO, 9 Nov.).

Silberston, Aubrey (1978), 'Nationalised Industry, Government Intervention, and Industrial Efficiency', in D. Butler and A.H. Halsey (eds.), *Policy and Politics* (London: Macmillan).

6 Politics And The Mixed Economy

ROY HATTERSLEY
Member of Parliament for Sparkbrook

Robust assertions of belief in the mixed economy are becoming fashionable again within some sections of the Labour Party. Simple statements of conviction made by sophisticated politicans are usually coded messages which, when they are deciphered, turn out to have complicated meanings. Thus generalised support for the mixed economy can veer between

(1) indications of proper impatience with the view that an extension of public enterprise will, in itself, create a more equal or more prosperous society;
(2) an attempt to express, in ideologically acceptable language, the passionate belief that freedom only flourishes and resources are only effectively employed if private capital is allowed to dominate the economy and, therefore, influence the life of the whole nation.

In fact, a simple statement of support for the mixed economy, whatever its underlying intention, is meaningless. No politician of any consequence really contemplates the total abolition of either the public or the private sector. Party rhetoric aside, the real argument is not about the existence of the mixed economy but the relative size of its constituent parts – and, perhaps equally important, how to induce a better social performance from both sectors.

Within the Labour Party the argument has been enormously complicated by two errors. The first is the conviction that grew up with the 1918 Manifesto and the 1919 Constitution that socialism and public ownership are synonymous. That is clearly not so. The percentage of national resources owned and controlled by the state is an absurd way to measure equality and freedom – socialism's central characteristics.

That is particularly true if equality is properly measured in terms of power as well as wealth and if public ownership is wrongly regarded as no more than state monopoly. Both post-war Russia and pre-war Italy demonstrated that state capitalism, by concentrating power in the hands of a central bureaucracy, makes society less equal as well as less free. The workers at Gdansk and Stettin do not seem to hold the view that the central ownership of the means of production and distribution guarantees either liberty or equality.

The second, more recent, error is the heresy into which the modern revisionists fell. In part, it is also the product of the confusion of the public sector with a state sector, owned and controlled by central government. Revisionists have argued – and no doubt argue still – that the extension of *nationalisation* is a threat to both personal liberty and industrial efficiency. To that assertion they add the related, but not wholly consistent contention that more nationalisation is unnecessary as well as undesirable. Control, they argue, is more important than ownership and modern governments possess the ability to control industrial behaviour without owning whole industries.

Once again the real issues are obscured by confusion about what public ownership really means. It may mean a state corporation that provides national ownership of a public utility. It may mean a single publicly owned company set up to compete with private sector rivals. It may – as it has come to be understood by both the Labour Party and its opponents – mean worker or consumer co-operatives which, in a strict sense, are not *publicly* owned at all. Clause 4 of the Labour Party Constitution embraces all these forms of organisation within the title 'common ownership'. All those enterprises within the mixed economy which are not privately owned are best described by the comprehensive title 'social ownership'. And thinking of 'social ownership' not 'nationalisation' helps to put the call for an extension of the public sector in proper political and economic perspective.

If a call for an enlargement of the public sector was no more than a demand for the creation of more state monopolies, fears about both limitations on freedom and reductions in efficiency might well be justified. A soceity in which working men and women have only one potential employer is not a free society. An economy in which prices are set by edict and the government decides which goods are manufactured and which are imported is unlikely to maximise its productive potential. But then, nobody I know is advocating the command economy of Soviet centralism.

On the other hand, the ownership by the Government of a substantial proportion of a nation's productive capacity does allow a degree of national economic planning. A point may come when the advantages of a national plan are vitiated by the inefficiency of state monopolies. But it is indisputable that a government anxious (say) to stimulate investment and employment in certain areas of the country would perform that task more easily if a number of manufacturing industries were dominated by state near-monopolies that can be instructed to move from Basingstoke to Billingham.

At least that is the theory. In practice the planning objective of nationalisation has rarely been realised except on those occasions when 'rationalisation' and 'the elimination of wasteful competition' has been interpreted as the need for closure, retrenchment and redundancy. Unfortunately the fulfilment of the planning function is better typified by the 1948 Transport Act which enjoined the Commission it created 'to serve and promote the provision of an efficient, adequate, economical and properly integrated transport system'. Thirty-two years on we still do not have an integrated transport system. But we have had the closure of a large number of branch railway lines.

The problem assumes an extra dimension when social ownership is extended to manufacturing industry. The managements of the public utilities at least partly accept that they were created to behave in a way which distinguishes them from the private gas works and the London and Midland Railway. British Steel and BL on the other hand seem (particularly though not uniquely under the pressures created by the present Government) to long for nothing more than to operate in the way they would behave if they were privately owned and subjected to the normal commercial constraints.

The causes of that compulsion are many and various – cash limits, the Davignon Plan, the psychology of management. But whatever the reason, that desire raises a major problem for a publicly owned company – particularly in conditions of structural decline. It produces a reaction in the workers which is at once complacent and antagonistic. They believe that the Government will always protect them from ultimate collapse. But they feel none of the enthusiasm for the company's fortunes which ought to be one of the major advantages of social ownership.

Where nationalised industries fail to take proper account of considerations other than their own short-term return on capital investment it is usually the fault of the Government which forces them or allows them to take a narrow view. Indeed, the 1977 Nationalised

Industries White Paper, which was originally meant to encourage estimates of the social cost of nationalised industry investment programmes, became an instrument for enforcing narrow concentration on 'commercial behaviour' defined by arbitrarily selected accounting targets. But, potentially, state ownership allows a detailed Government control of large sections of the economy that is difficult to obtain without full-blooded nationalisation. That is simultaneously the strength and the weakness of a state monopoly.

The revisionists recognised the weakness but refused to acknowledge the strength. Yet socialist government cannot operate all of the levers of control it needs by the application of the techniques of Keynesian demand management – prime interest rates, levels of public spending and the rest. The British economy is certainly in need of a massive increase in effective demand. But that alone will not defeat the institutional and structural (or even the psychological) problems faced by a chronically sluggish economy. It is no betrayal of my unrepentently Keynesian position to argue that a socialist government needs to control and stimulate the long-run supply side response of the economy in a more detailed and specific way than macro-economic management of short-run demand will allow. That is true for any economy composed of autonomous enterprises, whatever the balance between private and social ownership.

In short, if we accept that the paradigm of social ownership is not a state-owned gas monopoly, largely insulated from the dissatisfaction of its customers, incapable of taking wholly independent decisions about investment or location and forced to adopt price policies which have little to do with marginal cost and everything to do with the Government's monetary targets, two conclusions follow. An extension of social ownership need not strengthen the power of the state. But equally it will not necessarily increase a government's ability to plan the whole economy and subvert sectional interests to wider obligations.

On the basis of these contentions, I assert

1. That a substantial increase in social ownership is desirable, not least because it is likely to improve our overall industrial performance.
2. That such an extension of social ownership is not a threat to liberty – even when conventionally defined as the absence of restraint.
3. That a growth of the socially owned sector still requires the de-

velopment of techniques by which the national interest can be properly represented when individual industrial decisions are taken.

Central to those assertions is, of course, the belief that independent managements of socially owned companies will pursue the interests of those companies in much the same way as private managements pursue the interests of their firms. In the narrow context of mangerial behaviour and incentives I do not dissent from John Stuart Mill's judgement that 'there is no one so fit to conduct any business or determine how it should be conducted as those who are personally interested in it'. My objection to the conventional interpretation of that opinion is the implication that it is a justification for private enterprise. Nobody is more 'personally interested' in a company than the workers whose livelihood depends upon its commercial success.

These 'interests'–real though they are–are unlikely to be perceived within the present structure of public ownership Few BL workers feel any more commitment to the success of their publicly owned company than they did to the success of Austin, Morris, or MG. Indeed, because of the size structure, constant reorganisation and changing systems of payment at what successively became BMC, British Leyland and BL their commitment and identification has diminished. It will only be resuscitated by a reorganisation of the company that makes its employees feel that BL belongs to them. Today the identification of workers and company interests always appears in newspapers as the need for the worker to accept redundancies and agree new working practices. We need to convince BL workers that public ownership offers them more than state-controlled short time. If we succeed in this, I suspect that they will pursue the coincidental interests of themselves and their company with a zest which, although not without problems of its own, is wholly to be welcomed.

Indeed, the creation of autonomous and socially owned companies will offer a major advantage to the nation. The involvement of their work people in their management – increased by a genuine and effective system of industrial democracy – is more likely to bring a new spirit to British industry than a titillation of directors' bored palates by cutting the standard rate of income tax. Let me give a simple example–the motor cycle industry. Much has been said in criticism of the Meriden Motor Cycle Co-operative. I was myself deeply opposed to the way in which it was set up and the damage done by the method of its creation to other motor-cycle firms–the largest of which was in my constituency. But if you compare the spirit and determination of the workers who ran Meriden with the incompetence and sloth of the directors who let BSA Small Heath dwindle and die, there is only one possible judgement to be made. The British economy needs more of the spirit of Meriden because initiative has been stifled by the attitudes of Small Heath. The extension of autonomous socially owned companies that I advocate will, I believe, bring a new vitality to British industry. Workers will have, and will recognise, the strongest vested interest in the success of their companies. Professional managers will know that the mood is for growth and expansion. Ideology aside, an injection of enthusiasm is what the British economy most needs. Social ownership can provide it.

But the extension of independent, enthusiastically managed, socially owned enterprises in no way absolves the government from the need to create a system of selective and specific intervention in the economy. Government intervention is necessary in an economy made up of autonomous firms – whatever their form of ownership.

That requires an extension of what I shall call the horizontal rather than the vertical division of the mixed economy. The vertical division accepts the existence of a public and private sector, but leaves the private element to take its own decisions and regulate its own behaviour. Indeed, wherever possible it allows the public sector to act according to its own judgement – a permissiveness that usually results in public enterprises behaving as if they were private. The only decision governments and political parties who support the vertical division have to take concerns the place at which the boundary between the sectors should be drawn. Governments working the system have normally claimed to apply R.H. Tawney's dictum

> 'Whether, in any particular instance [social ownership] is desirable or not is a question to be deciced in the light, not of resounding affirmation of the virtues of either free enterprise or of socialism, but on the facts of the case.'

Naturally the 'facts of the case' have been interpreted according to their prejudices.

The horizontal division of the mixed economy also accepts that it has two distinct parts, but observes common characteristics in both sectors. In the context of today's discussion the most important is the tendency to maximise sectional interest – sometimes to the detriment of wider obligations. A government which accepts a horizontal division is obliged to decide by how much, and in what way, both private and public enterprise should be required to respect the national interest.

Conflicts between individual and national interest will take two forms and require two distinct techniques of government intervention. The government needs powers to *control*; the ability to prevent undesirable practices. It also needs powers to *stimulate*; the opportunity to encourage desirable practices which would not be adopted by companies acting on their own volition. I turn first to negative controls–the power to prevent.

This area of intervention should be based on the general rule that competition both preserves individual freedom and maximises industrial efficiency. Despite much loose thinking that confuses competition with private enterprise, there is nothing strange in socialists supporting the consumer sovereignty that comes from real competition. I offer two impeccable socialist authorities

> Now that a socialist government is in power our task is to organise competition.

> ... the public must be the master of industry. This condition is sufficiently satisfied in trades in which free competition is maintained.

I quote from Gaitskell and Lenin. For those of you who remain uncertain I ought to explain, the first was Lenin and the second Gaitskell.

Our system of detailed intervention should begin with the control of both private and public monopolies by

(1) limiting their creation by a stronger anti-merger policy;
(2) limiting their existence by the assumption of power to break up existing monopolies;
(3) limiting their freedom of action in those cases where monopoly is adjudged desirable in the national interest.

The United Kingdom has the weakest mergers policy in the western industrial world and, as a result, the most concentrated economy. Our hundred largest firms account for 42 per cent of net manufacturing output. In America, the comparable figure is 32 per cent. In Germany 22 per cent. Most British mergers failed to produce the results their progenitors promised. Many of them proved less productive and less profitable after amalgamation than their constituent parts had been before the take-over. Some were created with the specific intention of entrenching inefficiency and maintaining the security of failed management.

Most mergers in Britain are not carefully planned acts of industrial integration aimed at creating the most efficient size of operating unit. They are financial devices aimed at making money, not goods. They conferred riches and status on their new companies' directors. But they inhibited the natural growth of small- and medium-sized firms – one of the principal engines of expansion in a dynamic economy.

Nobody should be surprised by that. It is the nature of private companies to protect themselves against the bracing wind of competition. It is an impertinence to quote to this audience a paragraph from Adam Smith which is, no doubt, hung in pokerwork and embroidered texts over your beds – 'People of the same trade seldom meet together, even for merriment and diversion, but the conversation ends in a conspiracy against the public or in some contrivance to raise prices.' I refer to it only because of the tendency of some of Adam Smith's most devoted supporters to talk and act as if competition is a natural condition that operates in the absence of government action.

It is not, and the 'natural' tendency to merge, monopolise and create agreements in restraint of trade requires us to create a mechanism by which undesirable mergers are prevented, undesirable monopolies broken up and desirable monopolies prevented from exploiting their monopoly position. The agency which performs that task will have to operate selectively. It cannot enforce *general* rules based on a formula concerning size of enterprise or market share and applied mechanically and automatically. General rules which aim at a universal prescription of proper industrial behaviour are by their nature indiscriminate and are, therefore, largely ineffective. They are either drawn so tightly that they catch companies that should be exempt or constructed so loosely that companies which should be included escape.

Whilst it is difficult adequately to construct rules about company behaviour, it is possible to make judgements about industrial structure. For example, I hoped, when at the Department of Prices, to establish a presumption that a firm which controlled more than a fixed percentage of any market was operating against the public interest – unless it could demonstrate the desirability of its dominant position.

No doubt some companies would have been able to demonstrate that the optimum size of an efficient company within their particular industry was an enterprise which wholly dominated its market. So even with a policy that allows the creation of only those monopolies that, through their size and efficiency, operate at optimum levels of output, some control of monopoly behaviour remains absolutely essential. Some monopolies may be adjudged desirable. But, unrestrained, they will still be capable of exercising undesirable monopoly power.

That rule – allow but restrain – applies to nationalised public utilities. There is no national argument for breaking up what amount of service industries created, at least in part, to provide energy and transport on relatively equal terms all over the country. In most cases the public utilities enjoy genuine economies of scale and the national corporations (sometimes broken down into regional distribution organisations) are generally the optimum size for the highly capitalised mass production of coal, gas and electricity. But whilst I regard talk of breaking up the public utilities as foolish and the sale of their related profitable assets as vindictive, I do not pretend that they are not monopolies.

I regard them as neither the model for future public ownership nor the paragons of socialist virtue. They need the same sort of supervision as that which is applied to private monopolies, save for one provision. The exception is important. The Government may wish, legitimately, to use nationalised industry as the instrument of economic policy and must possess the power to do so. But those powers must be used openly. There should be no covert Treasury pressure to relieve the PSBR by unnecssary price increases when the Government is afraid openly to impose to fuel tax.

In both the public and private sectors, the principal manifestation of monopoly power is, of course, the charging of prices higher than those which would apply in a genuinely free market. That is why prices policy – again a *selective* prices policy – cannot be separated from competition policy and why, if we are adequately to manage the mixed economy, the Government needs the power to control prices. Again, universal rules applied whenever a company stumbles over some tripwire hung between the historic profit and current price levels are obvious nonsense – as the Heath/Barber/Cockfield Price Code demonstrated. Nor should we delude ourselves (or attempt to deceive others) by pretending that a prices policy can, in itself, make a material contribution to the inflation level. Inflation cannot be legislated out of existence. But a prices policy, used as a weapon against unjustified price increases and all the other excesses that companies which dominate their markets are heir to, can help to create a climate in which an adequate counter-inflation policy can be organised.

The controls that prices policy can exercise must be used against more than unreasonably high prices alone. 'The best monopoly profit', said John Hicks, 'is a quiet life.' And certainly the reports of the Price Commission demonstrate that firms which dominate their markets accept unreasonably high costs, fail to innovate and postpone new investment. Price intervention can be used to stimulate innovation, investment and cost consciousness.

Let me make emphatically plain that I am not suggesting price intervention as a public relations exercise to coax trade unions into the acceptance of wage restraint. I certainly believe that our long-term economic interests demand the organisation of an effective and permanent incomes policy. But the sort of incomes policy I want to see will protect rather than diminish the value of real wages. It is not a bitter pill that has to be sweetened by price control. It can be justified on its own merits. So can a prices policy as a surrogate for competition.

If Adam Smith's invisible hand really prevented the slothful undesirable practices that sprang up in less than perfect markets, a price policy would not be necessary. If we could, by Government intervention, immediately create genuinely competitive markets when thrusting entrepreneurs hold each other's prices down, oblige the timid to innovate and force the cautious to invest, a prices policy would have no purpose. But since we do not have, and cannot create sufficiently quickly, an effectively competitive market, we need an institution that can bring the same pressures to bear. Very largely they will be negative pressures to prevent

- prices above the competitive level
- protection of market shares by other means than reduction in price and improvement in quality and the consequences of that artificial protection of market shares
- inadequate levels of new investment
- neglect of innovation and product improvement

To promote more competition, where that is possible, and to produce the same stimuli and restraints through the action of a government agency where competition cannot be created is more than an argument about industrial efficiency. In the competitive condition individual companies compete for the consumer's favour and custom. That makes the consumer, if not the master of the company, at least an influential voice in a wide range of commercial decisions. It shifts some of the power from the board room and the annual meeting into the hands of the purchasers of goods and services. Those needs will not be met simply by involving trades unions in company management. An extension of industrial democracy – desirable though it is – will not necessarily make companies more sensitive to the demands of their specific consumers or of a whole nation. It is easy to imagine collusion between workers and owners which would be directly against both interests – the continuation of venerable inefficiency, the artificial protection of prices and therefore wages, the refusal to introduce new technology. Only competition, or in its absence state intervention, can prevent that from happening.

I have argued, so far, that the national interest is best served by the creation of companies which – either from the operation of a competitive market or as a result of government action that simulates market pressures – respond to the demands of their customers. I have described the powers which enforce or imitate competition as 'negative powers' because I see them as preventing industry's natural tendency to combine and make collusive agrements. But governments also need 'positive powers' to induce or persuade companies to take action that they would not otherwise take *even if they were fully competitive* – indeed in some instances because they are fully competitive.

The obvious examples are taken from regional policy. It may be wholly reasonable from its own point of view for a company to expand its operations or set up a new plant in Chingford or Bromley. Indeed, to oblige it to expand in County Durham or on the Clyde may require it to lose some of the competitive edge that the negative powers are supposed to encourage. Yet few people would argue that a government should not, on occasions, require the national interest of employing unused resources in an area of high unemployment to take precedence over the real advantage or imagined convenience of setting up the new plant in exactly the spot management would have chosen. Indeed, in terms of the productivity and efficiency of the whole economy the balance of advantage may well lie in establishing a new firm in areas of high unemployment.

Even in a competitive market, companies may neglect both research and innovation becasue they fear that a first in the field will pay all the costs, whilst the dilatory benefit. They may pollute the environment because reducing pollution also reduces profit. The result may well involve the whole community in social costs far greater than the companies' savings.

A similar conflict may exist between the individual and national interests when investment decisions have to be taken – or timid managers may imagine that it exists. I take my example once more from BMC/British Leyland. For a decade people outside the company thought the need to modernise and extend Land Rover production was obvious and overwhelming. For years the company provided persuasive reasons why it was not in their interest to do what was transparently necessary. The mood, the attitude, that results in the failure to take advantage of the Land Rover's success has to be changed.

The next Labour Government must develop techniques for encouraging new investment. As we slide into deeper slump, it is easy to slip into the comfortable conviction that as long as we stimulate demand, abandon our obsession with the Public Sector Borrowing Requirement, reduce prime interest rates to a reasonable level and maintain the exchange rate at a sensible figure, investment will naturally follow. The record of the last decade does not support that optimism. Recall the days when Lord Barber was at the Treasury. Every other economic objective was abandoned in the interests of creating an 'investment climate'. But the investment was not made.

Our failure to invest is as much a psychological phenomenon as a rational response to market conditions and the prospect of reasonable return. Nevertheless a return to rational demand management and a credible prices and incomes policy will create the conditions in which growth is feasible again and some entrepreneurs will respond. However, their response is unlikely to be big enough, quick enough or sufficiently sustained to ensure that the economy moves forward at the speed we need.

To get the sort of investment levels that we need private investment requires to be augmented in ways we have been too timid to develop in the past.

1. A re-invigorated National Enterprise Board must be provided, with the power and the money both to set up new companies and to invest in existing profitable enterprises. Of course, the public investment will carry with it the normal equity right over the appointment of directors and policy.
2. The present Co-operative Development Agency should be given extended powers to help in the formation and finance of both workers' and consumers' cooperatives. That power should apply both to the creation of new enterprises and the conversion of existing private companies.

Once set up, those enterprises will inevitably and properly operate independently of the Government and the agencies which financed their creation. They will of course be subject to the policies of intervention that the Government has created for the whole economy.

I accept that such policies will make it difficult to recreate the form of partnership that was central to the Labour Government's industrial strategy. But during the years I spent on the National Economic Development Council (NEDC) I grew increasingly sceptical about the merits of that sort of formal institutionalised partnership. It is a policy for observers but not participants. Thirty influential men and women, sitting round a table, can identify industrial and economic problems. But identifying the problems is not the same as solving them. Perhaps the Sector Working Parties – the sub-committees of the NEDC – working with individual industries, were able to act more dramatically on a smaller stage. But the whole operation was too cosy, confidential and comfortable. British industry is not likely to be talked into improvement. Indeed, on the evidence of the NEDC talk inhibits action – particularly action of which industry disapproves.

I recall the collapse of Spillers – the direct consequence of the management's determination to protect future profits from the consequences of past incompetence. I remember the big brewers reluctantly accepting a dilution in the monopoly arrangements that enabled them to survive despite growing consumer dissatisfaction, diminishing returns on capital and manifest inefficiency. I am unlikely to forget the Ford Motor Company's total unwillingness to co-operate with the Government's incomes policy and the clear view that it had done Britain a favour by establishing an engine plant in South Wales. I cannot recall a single occasion when industry and government disagreed and industry was 'talked' into accepting the Government's view. When the government view prevailed, it was because of the strength of its powers, not the persuasiveness of its argument.

That is hardly surprising. The arrangement through which government and private industry meet to find voluntary agreement about industrial policy is not a partnership of equals. Private companies – answerable to shareholders and under the control of professional managers whose position and prospects depend on short-term success – will never willingly accept policies which appear to be against the specific interests of their individual firms. Certainly the CBI saw the 'industrial strategy' as an opportunity for private industry to make demands on government. If the CBI ever saw it as a chance mutually to determine the national interest which was then elevated above the pretences of its members, I do not recall the occasion.

It is doubtful if the industrial strategy, in its original form, would have survived the election of a majority Labour Government. The Prime Minister had already told the NEDC Council – to the visible consternation of its employer members – that a new administration would expect the general acceptance of planning agreements and introduce legislation promoting the extension of industrial democracy. The partnership which was almost dissolved over the 1976 Budget strategy seemed unlikely to survive the introduction of policies so passionately rejected by the CBI.

Nothing essential would have been lost. Of course, the next Labour Government will want to establish a permanent dialogue with industry. And the hard fact of that dialogue will be that the CBI in particular and private industry in general will co-operate with the Government when it is in their interest to do so. For the rest of the time they will act as a sheet anchor, slowing down, if not actively preventing, the change and progress that a Labour Government wants to make.

If we are to get the economy moving again, we cannot afford a mechanism that allows industry to protect its old practices or an institution that encourages procrastination and delay. That is why I want the next Labour Government to adopt an attitude to the mixed economy which is at once more positive, more active and more radical. You will, I hope, recall that by more radical and more positive I mean

1. A substantial increase in social ownership is likely to improve the performance of British industry – if it takes the form of autonomous companies under the control, not of the state, but of their employees.
2. An extension of socially owned companies, which are largely independent of the state (as distinct from the creation of new state monopolies) is neither a threat to personal liberty nor economic efficiency.
3. A growth in the socially owned sector still requires the development of techniques by which the Government can intervene in the individual decisions of both socially and privately owned companies as both forms of enterprise will, from time to time, wish to pursue policies which are against the national interest.
4. The system of selective government intervention must
   (a) prohibit undesirable monopolistic and anti-competitive practices;
   (b) encourage new industrial investment.

5. Such a policy may prevent the creation of a permanent formal relationship between a Labour Government and private industry, but a worthwhile dialogue (based on mutual self interest) will still be possible.

For a more positive, active and radical policy requires the careful construction and determined application of a system of detailed, specific and selective government intervention in the economy.

7 Health Services in the Mixed Economy

A.J. CULYER
University of York

Although the continuing existence of the National Health Service is not, and is not likely to become, seriously questioned in any practical options put before the country, there is today a growing scepticism about the appropriateness of the NHS as a way of organising the nation's health care that is particularly evinced by recent ministerial predictions about the likely growth of private relative to NHS practice over the next decade. After a period of quiescence, it seems that an old argument about the rival merits of state and market provision of health services is in the process of resurrection. It may therefore be timely to review some of the arguments that have been made in earlier rounds of this controversy, and to ask whether there is reason to suppose that the balance between the public and the private sectors has become out of tune with today's needs.

The arguments that have most commonly been adduced for or against the provision of health services in the public sector rather than the private may be divided into two broad categories: questions of political philosophy concerning personal responsibility, equality and freedom; and questions of political economy concerning the efficiency of market or public agencies in the provision of health care. I shall take each in turn.

QUESTIONS OF POLITICAL PHILOSOPHY

There are sincere and probably irreconcilable differences between those on the one hand who see medical services as part of those good things of life to which the personal accumulation of earnings entitles one, and those who regard good health as a fundamental right of all – a right, moreover, that is not merely a basic human right to which each is equally entitled but is itself a necessary condition for the productive activity that generates earnings. There are probably few today who would emphasise personal responsibility for conducting one's affairs so strongly, and regard economic incentives for productive work as so uniquely important, that they would consider the withdrawal of medical services from the system of commodity rewards for productivity as an irrevocably damaging blow to that system. Nonetheless, the removal of any service from the set that are purchasable only from one's own income clearly weakens incentives for productivity and, while few today would be prepared to rely solely on private charity for the truly indigent, it is obvious that not all have such a view of the desirability of equality that they would draw the line between 'acceptable' and 'unacceptable' reductions in economic incentives at the same point.

A strong emphasis on personal responsibility and the need for economic incentives is often coupled with the argument that high earners *deserve* their income and also, of course, the things that high incomes can buy. This argument, however, is not impressive because desert, as a justification for someone's moral entitlement to his income, must relate to that person's efforts in producing a valued output. It is an elementary proposition in economics, however, that the value of a person's contribution to output (the value of his marginal product) depends not only on his own effort but also the effort of his fellow workers, the available machines embodying available technologies, chance, the output and quality of substitute products, and a host of other factors. Even if one restricted the set of factors affecting a worker's output to those tending to enhance it, it is clear that his own effort is but one of these, so if he is to be held to deserve his income by virtue of his contribution then the other factors can be held also to deserve his income by virtue of the fact that without their contribution he would have no contribution to make. Neoclassical marginal productivity theory is really very destructive of desert justifications of the income distribution.

While it is unwise to place too great an emphasis on personal responsibility and desert it is, however, also unwise to over-emphasise the 'basic human right' argument. Even if we were to grant that such a right exists, it is commonly argued as a right to *health* rather than as a right to health *services*. And there is a good reason for this – health services are but one means of affecting health status. Many epidemiologists and experts in social aspects of medicine would today emphasise the importance of life-style and preventive measures rather than the personal health services in maintaining and improving the health of the nation. Indeed a number would go a good deal further and argue that for a good deal of conventional medicine (including surgery) there is no evidence of any benefit in terms of health to the patient. Thus the 'human rights' approach needs to be advanced with no less caution than its principal rival. The moral case for equality of access to ineffective – or cost-ineffective – care is not at all appealing.

In North America there is a good deal more suspicion than in Britain that *compulsory* health insurance, whether provided via private agencies or, as in Britain, publicly, does irreparable damage to freedom. Britain has preserved all the traditional medical freedoms as well as safe-guarding the patient's right to choose his first-line doctor in the NHS or, if he so wishes, to 'go private'. It is true that private patients receive no compensation for their tax contribution to the NHS but this would be exceedingly difficult to arrange since very few indeed are privately insured against the expenses of treating most catastrophic or chronic disease; nor could they afford treatment out of their own wealth. Effectively the private sector exists to treat 'cold surgical' cases – the sort that make up most of our hospital waiting lists. When it comes to the really serious diseases that kill, the cancers, circulatory diseases and head injuries, we are all NHS patients. There is, therefore, a problem of determing that part of a private patient's tax contribution to which he may be thought to have a right of reimbursement. Actuarially, it would doubtless be possible to make a calculation. Administratively, the costs would doubtless outweigh the benefits.

Given this exceeding summary treatment of some of the political concerns in health service provision, I want to make only two general conclusions. First, the position of those who advance a single societal objective like 'freedom' or 'equality' or 'to each according to his deserts' is rarely appealing simply by virtue of the fact that so few of us hold values that can be succinctly summarised in a simple rousing slogan. Most of us hold multiple objectives, for example, regarding freedom *and* equality *and* self-dependence as *all* being of value and hence, since some may be attained only at the cost of a reduction in others, the problem is one of striking a balance rather than maintaining any single value inviolate. This focuses attention more on questions like 'how can we guarantee a more-or-less equal access to health services for each person with the minimum reduction in personal freedom?' than on questions like 'how can one justify any sacrifice of freedom at all?'

The second general point is that the nature of modern medicine itself must be taken into account when considering these questions. Health services are instrumental in enhancing health; they are a means to an end. Since only the end can justify the means, before one tackles political philosophical questions concerning individual access to these means one must investigate the technical relationship between the means and the ends: between health services (and other means) and health. On the one hand this type of consideration is likely to modify at least some of the objects one seeks: for example, to seek equality of access to *ineffective* health services would seem to pursue the object of equality beyond reason. On the other hand this type of consideration is likely to raise basic questions about the kind of political rights one is considering. The consumer of medical care is not in the same position as the consumer of other goods: he is in receipt not only of a highly technical service about whose technical side he typically knows little and of which the competent delivery is hard to evaluate; but he is also placed in a highly personal relationship with his physician, bringing to him his fears – real or imagined – and placing considerable trust in his physician's ability to interpret his needs. In large part, the agency role of the physician necessarily requires the surrendering by the patient of much of his freedom of choice: the physician to whom much choice is delegated becomes the agent of the consumer. He must be free to choose his physician (as he is in Britain) but he is never the sovereign consumer that he sometimes is in other aspects of economic life.

QUESTIONS OF POLITICAL ECONOMY

It is convenient to divide questions in the political economy of health services into two sets: those concerning demand and those concerning supply. I shall take them in that order. Whereas the central questions for the political philosophy of health service delivery are to do with equality, personal responsibility and freedom, the central questions of the political economy of health service delivery are to do with efficiency. I shall follow a pattern that is long-established in the literature by considering a set of issues each of which suggests that the market is inadequate. In each case I shall consider what merit lies in the argument. At the end I shall consider whether the sets of arguments taken together on both the demand side and the supply side have any collective force in arguing for or against the market provision of health services.

DEMAND SIDE

Individuals are Irrational in Health Matters

Although this argument has often been put in the literature against the market, I do not intend to devote much attention to it. My reason for this is that, regardless of any merit it may have (and in evaluating its merit we would, of course, have to consider what was meant by 'rational' and 'irrational') it does not have any obvious bearing on whether health services would be more efficient if organised in the market or by the state. If individuals are *irrational*, then the efficiency of *any* system in satisfying their preferences is scarcely worth enquiring about. If they are rational then we can use the language of efficiency, but we have no information relating to the ability of the one type of system or the other to satisfy such rational wants. In short, the rationality or irrationality of medical care consumers is completely irrelevant in discriminating between the degrees of efficiency of the market and the state in medicine.

Individuals are Ignorant about Their Health and Its Likely Future Trend

Since there is no evidence I know of that individuals are better informed about these matters in (say) Britain than (say) the USA, I take it that this argument is not so much directed to the point that the state more effectively removes ignorance than the market as to the point that in the one the consumer may be better protected from the unfortunate consequences of ignorance than in the other. The main issue here seems to be avoiding any impediment in the system to the early investigation, detection, and treatment of disease. The most obvious impediment of this kind is financial – the fear is that financial charges will deter patients from a consultation, with the consequential possibility of an irreversible (or expensively or painfully reversible) deterioration in health. In so far as individuals see it as being in their own interest to protect themselves from this risk, some form of insurance would seem the appropriate solution. The risk can be removed or reduced in *both* the market and the state-run systems. The problem does not enable us to discriminate between them.

Individuals Are Ignorant about the Quality of Care They Receive

This argument is usually put in rebuttal of the common economic assumption that rational individuals will 'shop around' and thus activate the beneficial forces of competition. It is difficult to see what point is really being made: if it is a characteristic of medical markets that consumer ignorance makes them uncompetitive and inefficient (as indeed it may!) is it being suggested that competition will be the greater, or ignorance the lesser, if the market is swept away and a state-operated system set in its place? That hardly seems likely. If anything, it would seem to me that the sensible way to overcome or mitigate this particular problem would be to tackle it directly: by providing the necessary information to consumers on the one hand and requiring the professionals to submit to scrutiny and review of their training programmes and the quality of the care they provide. In so far as one would wish to proceed along either of these two routes one can do so (and one does) in either the state-run system or in the market. The difficulty that has been raised does not, yet again, really help us to discriminate between the two alternatives.

The Incidence of Medical Expenses Is Unpredictable and Can Be Crippling

This argument is not a telling one against the market since the market itself generates a means of turning high unpredictable expenditures into smaller certain ones: insurance. More significant is a set of problems arising from private insurance that I shall discuss in a moment, and the fact that many of the most spectacular problems of medical indigence arise not from the *un*predictability of expense but its very *predictability*: either because an individual already has a disease, which makes him uninsurable, or because his expectations of sickness are such that the premiums are 'excessively' high. How high 'excessively' high is, must remain a matter for the judgement of others, for the problem of an individual's ability to meet actual or expected medical costs must be seen in its essentials as a distributional problem. In summary, in so far as there is merit in this argument against the market, it lies not in the failures of insurance to deal with uncertainty, but in the market's inability to generate family incomes related to what may loosely be described as family needs. A market supporter thus has his defence to hand–if you don't like the present distribution of income, give some to whomsoever in your judgement needs it–but do not destroy the market in the process.

Insurance problems

But there are problems with private and voluntary insurance arrangements in the market. One is that since insurance companies incur costs, and may enjoy a monopoly position, premiums will inevitably be set on average at a rate higher than that which is actuarially fair: in the jargon, they are 'loaded'. Thus, if you have a 10 per cent chance of having to spend £500 this year, the actuarially fair premium would evidently be £50. The closer the actual premiums charged by insurance agencies can be brought to this fair premium, the more people will be able to avoid the financial risks of ill-health. To the extent that a public insurance scheme can, through economies of scale, more closely approach the actuarially fair premium it has an advantage over private systems. In my judgement the balance of evidence supports the view that a public system is usually administratively cheaper to run. The evidence is, however, by no means agreed by all.

Another insurance problem goes by the name 'adverse selection'. This is a tendency – which is greater the more competitive the insurance market is – for the best risks to be driven out of the system leaving it to cope with only the worst. Adverse selection occurs in the following manner: suppose in a population of 1000 people 500 expect their medical expenditures in the next year to be £100 each while 500 except theirs to be £900. Suppose that insurance companies cannot discriminate between the two groups but can make a judgement about overall expected expenditure per person. If the individual expectations are fulfilled, there will be an overall expenditure of £500,000 and an insurance premium per person in excess (due to loading) of £500, the fair premium. But even if only the fair premium were charged, it can readily be seen that cover for expected expenses of £100 at a premium of £500 will seem a poor deal for the best risks, though possibly acceptable to those expecting to pay £900. The consequence is, of course, that the best risks drop out, leaving the worst risks in the scheme – and premiums even higher. The most obvious way of avoiding this problem is to make health insurance compulsory, so that the best risks cannot drop out. If, therefore, the loading problem can be best minimised by a public system, and the adverse selection problem by compulsory insurance, we have two arguments that offer a putative case for government-run compulsory health insurance. To be sure, if you regard all government activity as an unacceptable threat to liberty, and compulsory insurance represents an unquestionable additional infringement of liberty, then you will not accept this conclusion. If, on the other hand, empirical evidence suggests that the gains from lower loadings and no adverse selection are sufficiently large, many would find them acceptable compensation for the loss of liberty inherent in the solution to these problems.

Yet another common difficulty with all insurance systems goes by the quaint name 'moral hazard'. This is a two-fold phenomenon. On the one hand it refers to the tendency for insured persons to take less care in avoiding those eventualities that cause expenditures to be incurred. Of course, few individuals would actively pursue a life-style with the intention of bringing about ill-health. However, to the extent that insurance removes the financial disadvantages of sickness, and individuals are aware of the connection between life-style and health, they are more likely to drive motorcycles, smoke, eat and drink to excess, take little physical exercise, and so on. The second aspect of moral hazard arises from the the fact that insurance encourages the consumption of discretionary parts of medical care (an internationally known surgeon, famous alike for his skill and his fees, rather than the local man; more lavish hotel facilities in hospital; longer convalescence, etc). This drives expenditure, and hence premiums, up to levels that again begin to deter those who would wish otherwise to insure, and to levels at which those who continue to insure may have had the benefit of their insurance substantially eroded. Both kinds of moral hazard can be reduced in the market by having fixed indemnities, making the patient bear some of the cost of care at the time of use, and by other financial penalties, but it is a feature of all these mechanisms – which are widely used in the USA – that they tend to detract from the advantage of being insured in the first place. In the British type of system, moral hazard is complete since all care is virtually free. The problem is solved here by medical judgements about the patient's needs. In effect the doctors, through the exercise of their judgement, replace the workings of the price mechanism.

Distributional Problems

At various points we have already touched on the problem of the distribution of medical expenditures. To the extent either that one cares about other people's health, and is therefore reluctant to see charges asked of them that may deter utilisation, or that one cares about their incomes, and is reluctant to see expenses that may be extremely burdensome or simply not manageable, one will seek a method of replacing or modifying the market. In general, only modification is really required, particularly in the form of subsidised premiums. Depending on the nature of the concern one has for the health and wealth of others, these subsidies may be related to the income levels of the recipients. The general conclusion, however, is that subsidies ought to be given in a form specific to medical care, rather than in the form of general income supplements.

Conclusions

We may now review these demand side arguments to see where they have got us in considering the relative roles of the market and the state in the finance and provision of medical care. I shall be summary:

1. There is a case for regulating the quality of care given the difficulty the patient has in evaluating it and given also the highly personal nature of the doctor-patient relationship. Such regulation would be no less desirable in a publicly operated system than in a market.
2. There is a strong case for insurance against medical care costs.
3. Public insurance *may* be less costly than private, but a hidden cost may be some loss of freedom of choice.
4. Compulsory insurance may also be less costly than voluntary – but not, of course, to those who would under no circumstances choose to insure themselves.
5. A public system is more able to apply medical criteria in dealing with moral hazard, whereas a private system tends to apply financial criteria. However, there must be constraints on any public system offering free care, or the moral hazard problem will cause it to suck in very large, and wholly unwarranted, amounts of the nation's resources. So there still is an ultimately financial constraint even in the NHS, but it is one that applies to the system: the resources of the patient himself are not the constraint. Whether resource constraints of this sort, imposed by the government, are preferable to those imposed by insurance agencies is not a question to which I think political economy has a ready answer.

I detect in all this a presumption that some regulation of the medical and or allied professions is desirable. I also take the view that the sacrifices of freedom inherent in compulsory public health insurance are trivial in comparison to the gains. It is to be noted, however, that all the arguments adduced thus far have implications, aside from those dealing with quality of care, only for the *finance* of medical care. Not one of the considerations thus far has really suggested that the market in the provision of medical care itself, as distinct from the market for insurance, needs any substantial interference. Perhaps such an inference can be drawn from considering supply side aspects of the political economy of health services.

SUPPLY SIDE

I want to discuss four characteristic features of medical practice in this section: medical effectiveness, medical monopoly, non-profit institutions and, finally, the agency role (again) of doctors.

Medical Effectiveness

I mentioned earlier that many experts believe that medical care has become more marginal in protecting man from disease and its consequences. I also mentioned ineffective care. You may be shocked at the assertion that many treatments are ineffective. Yet it is true. According to the US National Institutes of Health's Clinical Trials Committee many treatments remained in medical practice too long and often at very high cost and to the detriment of patients. The list includes gastric freezing for peptic ulcer, colectomy for epilepsy, potassium arsenite for treatment of leukaemia, bilateral hypogastric artery ligation for pelvic haemorrhage, mercury for the treatment of syphilis, portacaval shunt for hepatic cirrhosis, renal-capsule stripping for acute renal failure, sympathectomy for asthma, internal mammary artery ligation for coronary artery disease, the 'button' operation for ascites, adrenalectomy for essential hypertension, complete dental extraction for a variety of complaints thought to be the result of focal sepsis, and wiring for aortic aneurysm. Amongst apparently ineffective procedures still used (not to mention many unproven ones) – using drugs to reduce blood cholesterol to prolong life after recovery from heart attack, treatment of older coronary victims in intensive care units, treatment of severe viral hepatitis with corticosteroids, cervical smear tests for the presymptomatic diagnosis of cancer in women, tonsillectomy, lengthy bed rest in treating tuberculosis. (Cochrane 1972; Ederer 1977).

There is also variation and uncertainty in diagnosis and treatment. It is now increasingly difficult to distinguish unambiguously between a healthy and a diseased state using technological measurements. For haemoglobin levels, blood pressure, blood sugar levels, and several other testable indicators, a decision has to be taken as to how far above or below average a measure must read before action is warranted. Observer error exists, notably in the reading of X-ray photographs, but also in the measurement of blood pressure. Even among the most experienced hospital doctors, diagnoses can vary quite markedly. One study compared the diagnoses made by consultants in a major hospital with the final diagnosis reached, usually after surgery had taken place. For one common condition, appendicitis, only 75 of the 85 cases were correctly diagnosed by the most experienced men in the hospital. Overall, they were 80 per cent correct in their diagnoses.

Appropriate treatment is likewise far from being as easy and unambiguous to identify as may be popularly thought. There is generally a choice of treatment. In an appendix to the Sainsbury Committee's report on the pharmaceutical industry it was reported that 455 general practitioners prescribed over 30 different prescriptions for each of 5 common illnesses. Only 8 out of a total of 2275 prescriptions were found to be unacceptably toxic or ineffectual, but the cost variation was substantial. For painful osteo-arthritis, for example, 11 per cent of GP's recommended Indocid at a prescription of 180 old pence, while 10 per cent recommended Aspirin at a cost of 2d.

Hospital practices can also vary widely. For example, despite strong evidence that hospital bed rest is unimportant in the treatment of pulmonary tuberculosis, the mean length of stay in hospital is falling only slowly and is very variable from specialist to specialist. (In one case nearly 20 per cent of male patients were discharged in under a month and all within three months. In another 10 per cent were discharged in under a month and over 20 per cent were still in hospital after a year).

The effects of several standard treatments on the normal course of disease is unknown or in dispute. Tonsillectomy, for example, is the commonest cause for the admission of children to hospital and the operation has a positive (if small) mortality. Yet there is evidence to suggest that the best medical treatment may be superior, or not inferior, to surgery. Certainly, admissions for tonsillectomy vary enormously per head of population from region to region in Britan (from 234 per 100,000 population in Sheffield to 410 in Oxford in 1971, of which 18 per cent of the cases were aged 14 or less). Need can often be a matter of fashion. Some years ago in the USA, 389 11-year old children with intact tonsils were examined by a group of physicians and 45 per cent (174) were recommended for tonsillectomy. The remaining 215 were recycled past a second, similar, set of physicians and 46 per cent (99) were recommended for tonsillectomy. The remaining 116, who had received a clear bill of health from the first and second group of doctors, were then recycled past a third and 44 per cent (51) were recommended for tonsillectomy. After three examinations only 65 children (17 per cent) had not had a tonsillectomy recommended! One of the most striking areas of doubt is the field of mental health. A doctor at Stanford recently managed to plant eight 'normal' people in mental hospitals where they remained undetected for as long as they could endure it. Further, within a mental hospital warned of impending planted normal patients, one consultant detected 41 and another 23 out of a population of 193 entirely 'genuine' patients already diagnosed elsewhere as being mentally sick.

The production of *health* by health services is, for so important an area in terms both of cost and potential consequence, remarkably under-researched. While this poses problems for economists seeking efficient ways of allocating the nation's resources, it is not of course particularly their role to remedy the deficiencies. Epidemiological research into these questions is fortunately growing apace and beginning to provide some of the answers. But while it is important not to be starry-eyed about the accomplishments of modern medicine, just what flows from its successes and failures for the organisation of the 'industry' (if I may so describe it)? I think just one thing: much of the evidence now points to the importance of considering health policy in a wider context than that of the institutional health services: prevention, life-style adjustments, community care outside institutions, integration with other domiciliary caring services for families and people living alone. My own suspicion is that it may be easier to get this overall policy perspective within a unified set of public services than by attempting co-ordination between private services (who would do the co-ordinating?). There is, of course, a tradition of co-operation between private voluntary agencies in Britain and the public authorities, and so too much should not be made of this point. However, I find it hard to see how an effective *health* policy could be evolved in a setting where there was a very high degree of decentralisation both of ownership and control.

Medical Monopoly

Doctors are always and everywhere joined in a strong professional association that combines the functions of a professional association (running conferences, publishing journals, etc.) and a trade union. In Britain, hospital doctors are salaried and GPs are paid basically according to the number of patients registered with them (with various add-ons according to age, specific services provided, and so on). Although GPs are independent contractors, their customer is the same as the hospital doctors' employer: it is the NHS, which thus has a powerful countervailing power (technically termed monopsony power) to offset the monopoly represented by the trade union. Pay is, in fact, determined periodically by a review body. Quite what the doctors' living standards would be without the countervailing power of the state is impossible, of course, to say. It must, however, operate to reduce the extent to which medical monopoly can push up pay. To that extent the state as a single customer/employer reduces the financial cost of medical services. Even the staunchest critics of the NHS grant that its financial cost is remarkably low.

Non-Profit Motivation

The traditional argument for the efficiency of market-based producers derives from the proposition that competition both in the capital market for the ownership of the enterprise and in the product market between rival producers, will ensure that tendencies exist both to ensure that what is produced is what the consumers prefer and that it is produced as cheaply as possible.

In medicine, unfortunately, neither of these two elements is present: in the USA, which probably most closely approaches the market model, only a small proportion of the agencies providing medical care are for profit; in Britain the fraction is minute. In the market for services, while competition is doubtless possible, it is assiduously limited even in the USA by bans on advertising, agreed fee schedules and the like.

To the extent, then, that there may sometimes be a general presumption that market institutions may, through competition, be conducive to efficiency we have to acknowledge that medical care is not an example where such a presumption may be made. To be sure, this argument does nothing to weaken the position of those who believe that *public* monopolies may be ridden with inefficiencies, but it seriously damages the position of those who argue that the medical market – or at least markets of the sort we have seen exist – is *superior* to public monopoly.

The Agency Role of Doctors

The function of the doctor in interpreting a patient's needs is often termed an 'agency' role, since the doctor acts as an agent for his patient. It is notable that the vocabulary of clinical practice is adapted in accordance with the agency relationship: doctors have neither customers nor clients; they have patients. Patients do not 'demand' or 'instruct' as with lawyers; they consult. The paternalism of the role is also revealed in professional discussion of the problem of 'compliance': getting the patient to do as he is told.

One consequence of all this is that, as we have already noted, the patient (voluntarily) sacrifices some freedom to his doctor. Another consequence, this time for the efficient operation of markets, is that it becomes difficult to keep separate the two categories of demand and supply: the doctor as agent not only supplies services and recommends other service suppliers, he also acts largely as demander.

It is at this point that many would argue medicine's most crucial special feature of all comes in: how can one best prevent the agency role from becoming contaminated by considerations related to the doctor's interests as a supplier of service. Thus, there is, for example, evidence that under fee-per-service systems of remuneration, usually found in market systems, demand has been manipulated in the interests of doctors – though not necessarily to the medical detriment of patients. In Canada, for example, when fee schedules have altered, more services whose fees have risen (relative to others) are demanded (and supplied). It is my belief, therefore, that the agency role of the doctor, if it is to operate most perfectly in accord with the health interests of patients, requires the clear separation of the exercise of professional judgement from the earning of the professional's income. Once again, this point is not *decisive* against the market or the state, for market systems throw up salaried employees in the USA and state systems throw up fee-per-service systems (as in Canada). Only in the state system, however, is it possible to remove completely the fee-per-service element that can distort the agency relationship. And that tips, I think, the balance of the argument in favour of the state.

CONCLUSIONS

It will be plain that on balance I tend to favour the NHS-type solution to the problem of how to run health services over more decentralised market systems. I should emphasise the 'on balance'. Most of the arguments considered on the demand side have implications at best for financing by the state rather than the direct supply of service. Taken with the supply side arguments, however, the sum of the separate arguments adds up to an argument that I find strongly supportive of the NHS: when so many features suggest the desirability of subsidy, universality and compulsory insurance; when the agency role suggests that movement away from the market involves no great loss of freedom and may even remove some distortions; when the monopsony power of a single employer can be thrown against the monopoly power of the most skilled of health manpower; when, in any case, the competitive preconditions for an efficient market are absent–all these features suggest not only that the NHS-type structure may be particularly suitable, but that the relative disadvantages commonly associated with state enterprise are absent: the combined bureaucracies of private hospitals, clinics, insurance firms, etc. in the USA, are larger than Britain's; the absence of a profit motive in the public sector is perfectly matched in the private, and so on.

Indeed, I would go rather further. I believe that people are increasingly going to demand that their health services promote, and are seen to promote, *health*. In promoting the health of the nation in an efficient and equitable way we are engaging in what, in large part, is a *technical* exercise of so organising things that effective services–and only effective services–go to those who need them–and only these–and that the most effective balances be struck between institutional and community care; prevention, care, and cure; medicine and environment; and, moreover, that the system be capable of being monitored effectively for its success (or lack of it), to indicate emerging needs as they arise, and to enable an overall comparison to be made between the potential claims made on the nation's resources by health affairs and the other good things in life whether produced privately or publicly.

The basic market-oriented vision seems defective in this context: large numbers of separate suppliers each competing to meet the demands of demanders. This is not to say, I should hasten to add, that all is well with the planning structure of the NHS. Nothing could be further from the truth. The details are for another occasion. What I hope to have done here is to have pinpointed some of the main issues that seem to me to have a bearing on whether the market or the state is likely to be the best method of organising health services. I pronounce in favour of the state not because the removal of the plain deficiencies of the market is *sufficient* to ensure the success of the state. That, alas, cannot be so. Rather, I pronounce in favour of the state because the removal of the plain deficiencies of the market is *necessary* to ensure the success of the state. The NHS structure, in short, is essentially *enabling*. The market must be judged, on balance, to be *disabling*.

There remains a role for a small private sector alongside the NHS. It is a safety-valve. It can respond more readily perhaps to demands for luxury hotel-type facilities in hospital. It preserves an important element of freedom. But I would be sorry to see it treating many more than the 7–8 per cent of patients in Britain it currently caters for. If, for example, it were to treat 25 per cent, as some have suggested would be desirable, that would have a 'creaming-off' effect, leaving the NHS with the geriatric, mental, chronic and costliest cases. It would remove most of the articulate and critical middle-class clientele from the NHS. It would also make the planning of an overall effective health care system a good deal more hard. In short, the market for health care in Britain performs a useful function so long as it is small. Were it to grow too much, it would have the disabling effect I mentioned earlier.

Should we conclude, therefore, that the balance between the public and private sectors of Britain's health services has become out of tune with today's needs? I think not. The privatised medical services elsewhere are among the costliest in the world. The evidence suggests they are *less*, rather than *more*, effective at extending life expectation and improving health. The arguments for the relative efficiency of the NHS-type structure are as strong today as they were ten or twenty years ago. Moreover, we increasingly have the medical knowledge and financial and planning mechanisms to make the NHS even stronger.

In the mixed economy, I should say the right mix between private and public health services would be about 5 : 95, give or take 3 percentage points on either side.

BIBLIOGRAPHY

This list is intended as a guide to those wishing to explore the literature in greater detail. The first three items provide an introduction to the results of recent research in epidemiology and the social history of medicine. The rest are more-or-less economic or political.

Cochrane, A.L. (1972), *Effectiveness and Efficiency: Random Reflections on Health Services* (London: Nuffield Provincial Hospitals Trust).
Ederer, F. (1977), 'The Randomized Clinical Trial', in C.I. Phillips and J.N. Wolfe, *Clinical Practice and Economics* (London: Pitman Medical).
Mckeown, T. (1976) *The Modern Rise of Population* (London: Arnold).

Barer, M.L., Evans, R.G. and Stoddart, G.L. (1979), *Controlling Health Care Costs by Direct Charges to Patients: Snare or Delusion*? (Toronto: Ontario Economic Council).
Boulding, K.E. (1966), 'The Concept of Need for Health Services', *Milbank Memorial Fund Quarterly*, vol. 64, pp. 202–21.
Buchanan, J.M. (1965), *The Inconsistencies of the National Health Service* (London: Institute of Economic Affairs).
Cooper, M.H. (1974), *Rationing Health Care* (London: Croom Helm).
Culyer, A.J. (1971), 'The Nature of the Commodity "Health Care" and Its Efficient Allocation', *Oxford Economic Papers*, vol. 23, pp. 189–211.
____ (1972), 'On the Relative Efficiency of the National Health Service', *Kyklos*, vol. 25, pp. 266–87.
____ (1976), *Need and the National Health Service* (London: Martin Robertson).
____ and Wright, K.G. (1978), *Economic Aspects of Health Services* (London: Martin Robertson).
____ (1979), *Expenditure on Real Services: Health* (Milton Keynes: Open University Press).
____ (1980), *The Political Economy of Social Policy* (London: Martin Robertson) ch. 8.
Donabedian, A. (1971), 'Social Responsibility for Personal Health Services: An Examination of Basic Values', *Enquiry*, vol. 8, pp. 3–19.
Jewkes, J. *et al.* (1963), 'Ethics and Economics of Medical Care–Discussion', *Medical Care*, 1, 234–44.
Klarman, H.E. (1963), 'The Distinctive Economic Characteristics of Health Services', *Journal of Health and Human Behaviour*, vol. 4, pp. 44–9.
____ (1965), 'The Case for Public Intervention in Financing Health and Medical Services', *Medical Care*, vol. 3, pp. 59–62.
Lees, D.S. (1961) *Health Through Choice* (London: Institute of Economic Affairs).
____ (1975), 'The Political Economy of Health services: A Liberal's Protest', discussion paper, no. 21, Department of Industrial Economics, University of Nottingham.
Seldon, A. (1968), *After the NHS* (London: Institute of Economic Affairs).
Titmuss, R.M. (1963), 'Ethics and Economics of Medical Care', *Medical Care*, vol. 1, pp. 16–22.
____ (1968), *Choice and the Welfare State* (London: Fabian Society).
Weisbrod, B.A. (1961), *Economics of Public Health*, (Philadelphia: University of Pennsylvania Press).

8 Education And Society: Old Myths versus New Facts

GEORGE PSACHAROPOULOS
University of London

INTRODUCTION

The role of education is extremely complex in modern society. The large involvement of the public sector raises issues of finance and accountability. Budgetary cuts are the order of the day. Voices on the existence of an educational crisis are heard the world over.[1] And more than once scientific investigations purport to have demonstrated that, after all, schools do not matter.[2]

In this paper I argue from different premises. It is my thesis that the present depressed budgetary condition of school systems in many countries is due to some major misconceptions on what education exactly does in our society. These misconceptions arise from an asymmetry between the costs and benefits of education, and also from the involvement of the public sector. In short, whereas educational costs are fully visible and tangible, educational benefits are extremely elusive, thus weakening the position of education *vis-à-vis* other 'hard benefit' sectors, such as steel or civil aviation. On the other hand, there exists a gap between research results pertaining to education and their assimilation by policy makers, who are as a rule, public administrators in a bureaucratic machine that has to rely on doubtful, slow-acting political or accountability incentives.[3]

In what follows I provide a review of the most often heard myths or slogans pertaining to the role of education in modern society along with the latest empirical facts on the issues at stake.

ON MYTHS AND FACTS

There exists a wide range of debated issues in the area of education which one could classify under efficiency, equity and finance headings. In what follows I have adopted a slightly expanded taxonomy within the same framework as to explicity address the most often cited issues and concerns regarding the role of education in our society.

THE ECONOMIC PROFITABILITY OF EDUCATION

This issue is of cardinal importance in deciding (or *ex post* rationalising, or evaluating) budgetary allocations to education. For if the socalled 'returns to education' are 'high', this is equivalent to a go-ahead signal for spending more on education. Conversely, if the returns are 'low', the evidence can be used as a rationale for financial cuts.

Unfortunately, actual decisions in education are not made this way, the governing criteria being bureaucratic inertia or political expediency. But the recent financial squeeze witnessed by educational systems in many countries must be based on the tacit assumption or belief that the economic profitability of spending on education is low. As shown below, this is a myth. In the first place, it is possible to estimate the yield per pound, dollar or rupee spent on education using a similar methodology as that in computing the yield of any other asset like building a bridge or a motorway. (See Appendix.) There certainly exist conceptual differences between costs and benefits that form the ingredients of the yield calculation in the two types of projects. However, by concentrating on the monetary benefits and rewards, the rate of return to investment in human capital is likely to be underestimated bearing in mind the consumption and spill-over effects of education.

Next, it is essential to make a distinction between who bears the costs and who reaps the benefits of educational investment. From the private point of view the yield of investing in education must be well in excess of 20 per cent whereas the social yield is of the order of 15 per cent.[4] These are world-wide averages pertaining to all countries without reference to a particular educational level. But there exist interesting differences in the returns to education by country type, as shown below:[5]

Country Type	Social Rate of Return
Developing	20 per cent
Advanced	8 per cent

The declining structure of the returns to education by the level of economic development makes full economic sense given the relative scarcities of human to physical capital in the two types of countries.

Also, when one disaggregates the overall rate of return to education by the level it refers to, another interesting structure emerges that again makes economic sense.[6]

Education Level	Rate of Return (per cent) Social	Private
Primary	> 25	> 50
Secondary	14	16
Higher	11	18

Namely, the returns to education decline at the margin in exactly the same way as the returns to any other investment project. Yet their overall level is such as to pass any usual alternative discount criterion.

By way of summary, educational investment is both privately and socially profitable.[7]

THE PRODUCTIVITY ENHANCING ROLE OF EDUCATION

The estimates presented above have not remained without challenge. The major objections pertain to the social rates of return and take different labels such as the screening hypothesis, the qualifications syndrome and labour market duality. All these are highly plausible and intuitive hypotheses, hence their popularity. However, they are all found wanting when put to a test.

What the screening (or certification) hypothesis says, is that employers use educational qualifications as evidence for pre-existing ability differences between prospective employees. Hence, whereas the acquisition of a degree is privately advantageous, the educational expenditure represents a waste from the social point of view as pre-existing abilities could be identified by a cheaper intelligence test.[8] Of course nobody could deny the fact that those of higher ability continue to further education. But the proposition that graduates have acquired nothing else than a 'sheepskin' (which is an alternative name for the screening hypothesis) is a completely different matter. Employers do value education certificates not only at the hiring point (something that they have to do anyway in view of imperfect information on the employee's productive characteristics) but increasingly *after* the employee has been with them under observation for some time. This distinction between initial and permanent screening provides one (but not the only) evidence against the certification hypothesis.[9]

The job competition or educational inflation model is very similar in character, stipulating that the more qualified bump out of the labour queue the less qualified and get the advertised job.[10] The problem with this model, however, is its extreme reliance on the exact correspondence between education and a particular occupational title, e.g. a typist should only have a secondary school qualification, anything beyond that level (say a university degree) being a social waste. What this model fails to take into account is the fact that an allegedly over-educated typist might be more productive in her job. There exists plenty of evidence that, even standardising for occupation, the more qualified earn higher rewards in the labour market, presumably because they are more productive in whatever job they are doing.[11]

Then there was the dual labour market hypothesis, stipulating that in our society in fact there exist two (or, perhaps no more than four) separate labour markets with insurmountable barriers between them. One group of workers belongs to the secondary segment characterised by bad working conditions and low pay, whereas another group of workers belongs to the primary segment of the market characterised by good working conditions and high pay.[12] Hence, giving more education to the low-pay, secondary-segment workers would be of little use since they will not be able to reap the rewards on the educational investment because they are trapped in the low segment of the labour market.

Empirical analyses, however, in the United States, the United Kingdom and other countries have shown that this first-hand plausible view is not backed by the data. The labour market is in fact a near continuum and the provision of education to an otherwise low-paid worker would help him to cross the (never documented) barrier between the two alleged labour market 'segments' and receive higher pay. At least this is what the statistics show.[13]

What the screening, job competition and dual labour market models have in common, is that they all challenge the *social* productivity of education. However, recent work on the production yields of educated versus non-educated farmers, the self-employed in general and public versus private pay (a theme to be elaborated below) all point to the fact that the positive correlation between education and earnings could well be a causation, and that differential monetary rewards in the labour market by level of schooling reflect to a great extent the value of the social product of education.[14]

EDUCATION AND UNEMPLOYMENT

Perhaps a more serious and often repeated contemporary myth, is that education produces unemployed graduates. To the extent this proposition is true, it constitutes a challenge to both the social and private educational calculus, for the individual will not be able to reap any benefits in any case, let alone the issue on whether these private benefits would correspond to the social ones. Although casual empiricism suggests this proposition is true, it fails the test when a distinction is made between the incidence and the duration of unemployment.

The incidence of unemployment is indeed high amongst the young educated. However, the duration of such unemployment is short, nearly every graduate finding a niche in a matter of weeks, at most in a few months, but certainly not in a matter of years. Bearing in mind the lifetime durability of the 'product' of education (say, over forty years in the case of university graduates), the early loss of earnings because of unemployment becomes trivial.[15]

Another common fallacy in this area is the belief that a general economic recession and the associated depression of earnings, lowers the social profitability of investment in education. However, exactly the opposite is likely to be the case. Namely, an economic recession, by virtue of lowering the earnings (perhaps to zero because of unemployment) of, say, secondary school graduates, reduces the opportunity cost of staying in school. However, economic recessions never last long enough to invalidate the lifetime differential of graduate to non-graduate earnings. This asymmetry (i.e. reduction in costs but validity of lifetime benefits) *increases* the rate of return to investment in education during a recession.[16]

Similarly, fear has been expressed that the continuous 'over' production of graduates would lead to a lower rate of return to education, not only by increased unemployment, but also because of a squeeze of the earnings differential between graduates and non-graduates. This prima facie plausible view is extremely exaggerated when looking at the facts.

Educational expansion in all kinds of countries has taken place at a phenomenal rate in the last two decades, especially during the sixties. Yet labour markets in these countries seem to have absorbed the increase with ease, and certainly without a drastic fall in the skilled differential.[17] Several explanations have been given to this phenomenon running from high elasticity of substitution in production between educated and other labour or the race between education (supply) and technology, the latter creating demand shifts to the right for educated manpower maintaining a near constant differential over time.[18]

EDUCATION AND EQUITY

Another contemporary belief espoused in many quarters is that education has little to do with income distribution and that demand-side policies might be more appropriate for the alleviation of poverty.[19] It has also been claimed that education might in fact make things worse as it perpetuates the *status quo* from generation to generation.[20] This is a multifaceted myth we will have to consider in stages in this and in the ultimate subsection.

There exist at least three ways in which education links to equity issues in our society. First, education affects people's income, hence it has an impact on income distribution. Second, and given the fact that education is largely state financed, questions are raised as to who is actually paying and who benefits from public educational expenditure. Thirdly, education may compensate for an adverse socioeconomic background and hence open up better career opportunities to children of low social origins.

That education links to income distribution is best demonstrated by the fact that every extra year of schooling is associated with an increment of earnings. This proposition is universally valid. For example, the mean annual earnings by single year of schooling in the 1975 UK General Household Survey are as follows:[21]

Years of Schooling	Annual Earnings (£)
9	2844
10	3002
11	3780
...	...
15	4171
16	6129
17	8261

It must be remembered that income distribution is a private issue and hence one is not concerned whether the above figures correspond to marginal products. All one is interested in for equity purposes is that the provision of education especially at the lower level (say, by raising the minimum school leaving age) will, *ceteris paribus*, improve income distribution in a given country as it will push a segment of the population that otherwise would have low incomes towards the mean.[22] Conversely, the provision of higher education must be inequitable as those with above mean incomes (say, the control group of secondary school graduates) will have even higher incomes because of the university degree.[23]

But there exists another way it has been claimed that higher education is inequitable by examining the 'who-pays-who-benefits' finance structure. According to the original argument by Hansen and Weisbrod, since it is rich families that mainly send their children to higher education, the latter being financed by the general taxpayer's money, rich families receive an effective subsidy from poor families that also pay taxes but do not send their children to higher education, at least at the same rate as rich families do.[24]

Although the empirical validity of this argument has been subject to debate,[25] Le Grand has found that it might apply to the UK as well, in the sense that the middle-class takes up far more educational resources than their proportion in the population justifies.[26]

On the other hand, recent research using the micro-data of the UK General Household Survey has shown that the provision of education has a greater impact on the subsequent earnings of children of low social origins. For example, the returns on investment in education by father's occupation are as follows:[27]

Father's Occupation	*Rate of Return to Education*
Agriculture worker	13.1 per cent
Professional worker	7.9 per cent

It is in this sense that one of the equitable roles of education in our society is the compensatory one for adverse socioeconomic background. Given the fact that one's family origins are fixed and thus not subject to policy manipulation, the provision of education might give a child the opportunity to move up the income ladder. At least this is what the data indicate.

It is for the reasons mentioned above that one cannot easily accept arguments against the equitable role of education. However, one must confess that education as a policy variable is slow acting, especially in the intergenerational sense. Therefore, this policy should be pursued in connection with other, faster acting measures in an attempt to alleviate low incomes.

THE ROLE OF THE PUBLIC SECTOR

The state's involvement in education is not limited to finance. The public sector is a major employer of educated labour and it also runs schools directly. The public sector involvement as an employer is often thought of as introducing a major element of non-competitiveness in the labour market, hence invalidating the use of earnings as a proxy for the individual worker's productivity. Also, the issue that private schools should be banned is daily debated in the newspapers.

However, an analysis of the 1975 General Household Survey data makes one sceptical about the above propositions. If anything is likely to be the case, the private sector attributes a higher value to the education of the persons it employs, and on efficiency grounds, private schools are associated with a considerable income advantage of the graduate.

Table 8A. 1 in the Appendix gives the mean characteristics of a sample of 5500 employees in the UK in 1975, as well as those of two sub-samples in the 'private' and 'public' sectors of the economy.[28] Public sector employees do not in fact earn more on average relative to private sector employees. However, when one corrects for differences in productive characteristics between employees (Table 8A. 2) those in the public sector do not earn significantly more relative to those in the private sector (regression R2), especially when one treats the education variable as a string of qualification dummies (regression R4).

The converse is true regarding private schools (regressions R3 and R5). Those who have attended a private school earn on average 13 to 16 per cent more relative to those who went to a state school. Therefore, on private efficiency grounds, families who send their children to independent schools are in fact getting back a substantial monetary reward for their initial outlay.[29]

Fitting the regressions within the two separate employment sectors (Table 8A.3) yields the extremely interesting result that assessing the rate of return to investment in education (coefficient of the years of schooling variable) on the basis of public sector employment would *under*-estimate the true competitive returns by over two percentage points, which is a considerable difference (6.3 versus 8.7, respectively).[30]

EDUCATION AND LIFE CHANCES

This is a much debated theme originally starting from the work of sociologists and now being on the top of the economics research agenda.[31] The main difference between sociologists and economists was that the former stopped with the determinants of occupational status, whereas economists extended the 'path model' by one further step considering also the determinants of income.

But it was a sociologist who in an influential 1972 book purported to have found that in the United States 'Neither family background, cognitive skill, educational attainment, nor occupational status, explains much of the variation in men's incomes.'[32]

This conclusion has appealed to those who heard what they wanted to hear, backed by the statistics and figures of an eminant Harvard scientist, and served as a blow to the social role of education the world over. At close scrutiny, however, the conclusion that education does not matter in the determination of the life chances of an individual is a myth. Jencks's work has come under attack from different quarters[33] and application of the same path model in the United States and other countries has in my opinion proven that education does indeed matter.[34]

By means of an example I present below the determinants of the lifetime chances in the UK using data from the 1975 General Household Survey.[35] Numbers on the arrows represent the relative strength of one factor in affecting the next.[36]

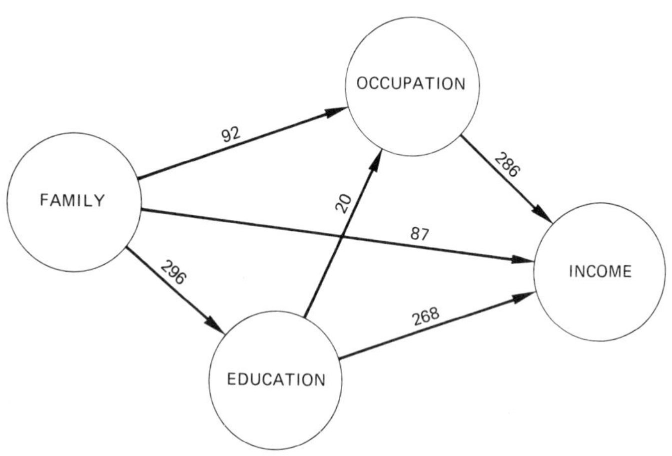

The message coming from this display is that the direct effect of family background in determining the respondent's current occupation and earnings is rather small (coefficients equal to 92 and 87, respectively) compared with the direct effect of education on earnings, which is rather big (coefficient 268). However, family background exerts an indirect influence on earnings by means of strongly affecting the level of educational attainment of the respondent (coefficient 296). The summary picture is that, even after standardisation for family background and occupation, education does indeed matter in the income generating process.

CONCLUDING REMARKS

In this paper I have reviewed a series of debated issues regarding the role of education in a modern mixed economy. The evidence presented seems to run against popular beliefs mostly based on anecdotal impressionism or political expediency. In particular, the following propositions seem to be supported by recent research findings:

1. Education is privately and socially a profitable investment.
2. The elusive social educational benefits can, to a great extent, be approximated by the market earnings of graduates.

3. Graduate unemployment is not a serious challenge to the social profitability of education.
4. The public sector involvement as an employer of educated labour does not invalidate the social profitability of education.
5. The provision of education contributes significantly, although slowly, to a more equitable income distribution.
6. The provision of education is likely to have a beneficial effect on those coming from low social origins.
7. Private school graduates carry a premium (other things being equal) relative to state school graduates in the labour market.
8. Education – whether state or privately provided – matters more than family background in the determination of the life chances of an individual.

By way of summary, these fact-based propositions are largely inconsistent with recent educational budgetary cuts in many countries which seem to tacitly rely on old myths regarding the role of education in a modern society.

APPENDIX

A rate of return to investment in education at a particular level is estimated *grosso modo*, by comparing the incremental costs of obtaining a given level of education (say, C_h per year for higher education) to the lifetime incremental monetary rewards associated with that level of education (say $Y_h - Y_s$ per year, where Y_h and Y_s are the earnings of higher education and secondary school graduates, respectively). An approximate formula for computing the rate of return to investment in education (r_h) in this case would be

$$r_h = \frac{Y_h - Y_s}{3(C_h - Y_s)}$$

on the assumption that the length of the higher education course is three years. Note that the foregone earnings of the higher education student enter on the cost side of the calculation. This basic formula can be varied to suit the particular application. (For further estimating details see G. Psacharopoulos, *Returns to Education: An International Comparison*, (Elsevier, 1973).

TABLE 8A. 1 Mean characteristics by economic sector

Variable	*Economic sector*		
	Private	*Public*	*All*
Annual earnings, (*Y*)	£2634	£3158	£2971
Years of schooling (*S*)	10.3	10.7	10.5
Years of experience (*EX*)	22.0	25.6	23.9
Qualification dummy			
None	0.57	0.37	0.49
1–4 O-levels	0.08	0.09	0.05
5+ O-levels	0.05	0.10	0.04
City and Guilds ordinary	0.04	0.03	0.05
City and Guilds advanced	0.02	0.03	0.03
ONC	0.01	0.01	0.02
HNC	0.02	0.08	0.05
A-level(s)	0.03	0.06	0.02
Degree	0.03	0.08	0.07
Other	0.16	0.16	0.16
Public sector dummy	0.00	1.00	0.07
Private school dummy	0.03	0.03	0.02
Number of observations	452	379	5509

SOURCE
General Household Survey 1975 tapes.
NOTES
Sample refers to male employees. 'Private' sector corresponds to SIC = 20. 'Public' sector corresponds to SIC = 24.

TABLE 8A. 2 Whole sample results (N = 5509)

Variable	*(R1)*	*(R2)*	*(R3)*	*(R4)*	*(R5)*
Constant term	6.400	6.400	6.405	7.156	7.158
S	0.080	0.080	0.079		
	(26.4)	(26.3)	(26.2)		
EX	0.058	0.058	0.058	0.056	0.056
	(32.3)	(32.3)	(32.3)	(31.5)	(31.4)
EX^2	−0.001	−0.001	−0.001	−0.001	−0.001
	(28.2)	(28.2)	(28.1)	(28.3)	(28.2)
Public sector		0.040		0.021	
		(1.67)		(0.88)	
Private School			0.159		0.126
			(3.68)		(2.9)
Qualification dummy					
1–4 O-levels				0.168	0.161
				(5.9)	(5.7)
5+ O-levels				0.240	0.232
				(7.8)	(7.5)
City and Guilds ordinary				0.140	0.140
				(4.8)	(4.8)
City and Guilds advanced				0.268	0.267
				(7.5)	(7.5)
ONC				0.308	0.308
				(6.5)	(6.5)
HNC				0.453	0.448
				(16.1)	(15.9)
A-level(s)				0.165	0.157
				(4.0)	(3.8)
Degree				0.700	0.698
				(28.4)	(28.4)
Other				0.088	0.088
				(5.5)	(5.5)
R^2	0.217	0.218	0.219	0.255	0.256

NOTE
Dependent variable is the natural logarithm of annual earnings. Numbers in parenthesis are t-ratios.

SOURCE
Based on General Household Survey 1975

TABLE 8A. 3 Earnings functions within economic sectors

Variable	*Private sector* (*R6*)	(*R7*)	*Public sector* (*R8*)	(*R9*)
Constant term	6.119	6.961	6.661	7.227
S	0.087		0.063	
	(6.2)		(5.8)	
EX	0.072	0.070	0.056	0.048
	(11.5)	(11.3)	(7.9)	(7.3)
EX^2	0.001	0.001	0.0009	0.0008
	(10.0	(10.0)	(7.2)	(6.4)
Qualification dummy				
1–4 O-levels		0.155		0.022
		(1.8)		(0.3)
5+ O-levels		0.074		0.370
		(0.7)		(4.7)
City and Guilds ordinary		0.151		0.202
		(1.2)		(1.4)
City and Guilds advanced		0.275		0.283
		(1.5)		(2.0)
ONC		0.658		0.392
		(2.4)		(1.8)
HNC		0.384		0.371
		(2.6)		(4.2)
A-levels		O.414		0.358
		(3.0)		(3.6)
Degree		0.789		0.704
		(6.0)		(8.0)
Other		0.102		0.091
		(1.6)		(1.4)
R^2	0.256	0.280	0.174	0.278
N	452	452	379	379

NOTE:
Dependent variable is the natural logarithm of annual earnings. Numbers in parenthesis are *t*-ratios.
SOURCE:
Based on General Household Survey 1975.

NOTES

1. See T. Husen, *The School in Question: A Comparative Study of the School and its Future in Modern Society* (Oxford University Press, 1979).
2. For a review of such studies see H.A. Averch *et al.*, *How Effective Is Schooling*? (Educational Technology Publications, 1974).
3. For a non-technical elaboration of some of these points, see G. Psacharopoulos, 'Educational Planning: Past and Present', *Prospects*, no. 2 (1978) and G. Psacharopoulos, 'Academic Work and Policy Formation', *Prospects*, no. 4 (1979).
4. Averages are from G. Psacharopoulos, *Returns to Education: An International Comparison* (Elsevier, 1973). The private rate of return cited might be a gross underestimate given the high returns to primary education in some countries.
5. *Ibid.*, p. 86.
6. From G. Psacharopoulos, 'Investment in Education and Equality of Opportunity', in K. Alexander and K. Forbis Jordan (eds.), *Educational Need in the Public Economy* (University of Florida Press, 1976).
7. Of course this is a sweeping average statement that has to be qualified in particular country or educational level settings.
8. For different versions of this hypothesis see K. Arrow, 'Higher Education as a Filter', *Journal of Public Economics*, July 1973; P. Taubman and T. Wales, 'Higher Education, Mental Ability and Screening', *Journal of Political Economy*, January/February 1973; and P.J. Wiles, 'The Correlation between Education and Earnings: The External-Test-Not-Content Hypothesis (ETNC)', *Higher Education*, no. 1, 1974. On the continuing debate on this issue see P. Taubman, 'Earnings, Education, Genetics and Environment', *Journal of Human Resources*, Fall 1976, and Z. Griliches, 'Sibling Models and Data in Economics: Beginnings of a Survey', *Journal of Political Economy*, October 1979, Supplement.
9. See G. Psacharopoulos, 'On the Weak Versus the Strong Version of the Screening Hypothesis', *Economic Letters*, no. 4, 1979; and R. Layard and G. Psacharopoulos, 'The Screening Hypothesis and the Returns to Education', *Journal of Political Economy*, no. 5, 1974.
10. See L. Thurow, *Generating Inequality* (Basic Books, 1975).
11. For example, see the earnings functions results presented later in this paper.
12. See D. Gordon, *Theories of Poverty and Unemployment* (Lexington, 1972).
13. See G. Cain, 'The Challenge of Segmented Labour Market Theories to Orthodox Theory: A Survey', *Journal of Economic Literature*, December 1976; G. Psacharopoulos, 'Labour Market Duality and Income Distribution: The Case of the UK', in W. Krelle and A. Shorrocks (eds.), *Personal Income Distribution* (North Holland 1978); and R. McNabb and G. Psacharopoulos, 'Further Evidence on Labour Market Duality in the UK', *Journal of Human Resources*, vol. 16, 1981.
14. See C.D. Wu, 'Education in Farm Production: The Case of Taiwan', *American Journal of Agricultural Economics*, no. 4, 1977; and for a review of many case studies in this respect, D. Jamison and L. Lau, 'Farmer Education and Farm Efficiency', World Bank, 1978 (mimeo).

15. For such evidence in a developing country see B.C. Sanyal *et al.*, *Higher Education and the Labour Market in Zambia* (Unesco, 1976) and for a documentation of the fact that returns to education remain high even after the unemployment correction, see M. Blaug, *et al.*, *The Causes of Graduate Unemployment in India* (Allen Lane, 1969).
16. See G. Psacharopoulos, 'Investing in Education in an Era of Economic Stress: An Optimistic's View', *Journal of Educational Finance*, no. 2, 1980.
17. For a debate on this issue see 'An Exchange', *Journal of Human Resources*, no. 1, 1980.
18. See F. Welch, 'Education in Production', *Journal of Political Economy*, No. 1, 1970; G. Psacharopoulos and K. Hinchliffe, 'Further Evidence on the Elasticity of Substitution between Different Types of Educated Labour', *Journal of Political Economy*, no. 4, 1972; and J. Tinbergen, *Income Differences*, (North Holland, 1975).
19. This is the thesis of the dual labour market school cited earlier.
20. See S. Bowles, 'Schooling and Inequality from Generation to Generation', *Journal of Political Economy*, May/June 1972, Supplement.
21. The data refer to male employees aged 35–45 years.
22. On the probable effects of raising the school leaving age (ROSLA) on income distribution in the UK, see M. Blaug, C. Dougherty and G. Psacharopoulos, 'The Distribution of Schooling and the Distribution of Earnings: Evidence from the British ROSLA of 1972', Institute of Education and London School of Economics, 1980 (mimeo).
23. See A Marin and G. Psacharopoulos, 'Schooling and Income Distribution', *Review of Economics and Statistics*, no. 4, 1976.
24. See W. Lee Hansen and B. Weisbrod, *Benefits, Costs and Finance of Public Higher Education* (Markham, 1969).
25. See R. Pechman, 'The Distributional Effects of Public Higher Education in California', *Journal of Human Resources*, Summer 1970.
26. See J. Le Grand, 'Who Benefits from Public Expenditure?' , *New Society,* 21 September 1978.
27. See J. Papanicolaou and G. Psacharopoulos, 'Socioeconomic Background, Schooling and Monetary Rewards in the United Kingdom', *Economica*, November 1969.
28. The public sector corresponds to those employed in public administration and the private sector to those in distributive trades. Given the information on the data tapes this is the most readily available possible split between the two sectors.
29. The issue whether the higher market value of private school graduates has a quality counterpart cannot be investigated with this data set.
30. This proposition is based on the assumption that earnings differences in the private sector reflect true productivity differences.
31. For a review see G. Psacharopoulos, and J. Tinbergen, 'On the Explanation of Schooling, Occupation and Earnings: Some Alternative Path Analyses', *De Economist*, no. 4, 1978.
32. C. Jencks *et al.*, *Inequality* (Basic Books, 1972) p. 226.
33. For symposia on the work of Jencks see *Harvard Educational Review*, February 1973 and *Comparative Education Review*, October 1974.

34. See Psacharopoulos and Tinbergen, 'Explanation of Schooling' and Kiong-Hock Lee and G. Psacharopoulos 'A Model of Occupational and Earnings Attainment in Malyasia', London School of Economics (mimeo).
35. Education is measured by the years of schooling of the individual. Father's and respondent's occupation are measured on Goldthorpe and Hope's desirability scale. Income refers to annual earnings from employment. For further details on the construction of these variables see G. Psacharopoulos, 'Socioeconomic Background, Education and Achievement', *British Journal of Sociology*, September 1977.
36. Numbers on the arrows are standardised beta coefficients multiplied by 1000. The structural equations in natural units (non-beta) form are:

Equation	R^2
$S = 7.9 + \underset{(22.8)}{0.062F}$	0.088
$OCC = 35.9 + \underset{(6.5)}{0.068F} + \underset{(1.4)}{0.072S}$	0.010
$Y = -1740.5 + \underset{(6.8)}{12.7F} + \underset{(20.9)}{186.4S} + \underset{(23.2)}{56.4\,OCC}$	0.187

N = 5421 individual observations referring to male employees.
Numbers in parenthesis are t-ratios.

9 Energy Policy And The Mixed Economy

DAVID HOWELL
Member of Parliament for Guildford and Secretary of State for Energy

THE ENERGY REFORMATION

I have to confess to you that I have been thinking very hard about the right word to describe the energy events of the last eighteen months and their impact upon us, and I have had a good deal of trouble finding the right one.

'Adjustment' or 'adaptation' seems altogether too modest and trivial to convey the size and extent of the upheavals either in 79/80 or back in 73/4 when the first shocks were administered to the world energy system. 'Revolution' is perhaps a shade over-dramatic, although it is indeed the case that certain assumptions about energy supply and use have had to be revolved through 180 degrees and stood on their heads.

The word 'Reformation' has, I know, a particular historical and religious significance in our language, so I use it tentatively. But perhaps the changes which we are going through, when they are done, will not appear in retrospect to be entirely without comparison with the turbulence of the fifteenth and sixteenth centuries, although I would not press the parallel too far.

But the energy 'reformation' is undoubtedly having an historic impact, causing a major disturbance in international politics and in deeply settled patterns of living all over the world. Most people think of the 'energy crisis' as the two spasms which occurred in 1973/74, and 1979/80 when oil prices leapt up by dizzying amounts. In fact, the energy reformation is a steadier and more gradual process unfolding over many years. The spasms are merely the eruptions stemming from a deeper volcanic activity which goes on continually. And I suspect that there will be more spasms in the years ahead.

There has been a huge transfer of power and influence into the hands of the oil producers. That may prove to be transitory, but will surely last for several years ahead. Like all power it can be used for good or evil, so there are very great dangers. And even though a new equilibrium may eventually emerge, things will certainly never be the same again. Our ways of life and work, any many of our attitudes, will have been permanently and profoundly altered.

At the same time there is no doubt about the depth of fervour and feeling concerning the changes being wrought in our society by the multiplication of oil prices and the major change caused in the economics of all energy production and consumption. Many people are worried about the impact on society of vast new structures and complexes being thrown up around the world to capture and process energy, and the gargantuan concentrations of capital which these involve. The search is on for opportunities to reduce our reliance on highly centralised systems of energy production, and thus reinforce the general desire of the age to move away from big government and mass organisation, and to elevate again the individual and the small community.

Meanwhile new perspectives open up in the developing world as well, as high cost oil promotes a great burst of inventiveness in using other both new and much older energy forms, neglected and forgotten when oil was cheap and easy, such as the energy locked in the wind or the sun or rivers and tides.

But this great bacterial stew of change and innovation is going to take a long time, as do almost all energy alternative developments: whereas oil prices can, and have, doubled in the space of a few months. So while it is right to look to the enormous longer term implications and potential of the energy reformation, the plain fact is that in an industrial country like ours the early impact of the events which have set it off is ugly, uncomfortable and dangerous.

I estimate that we have at least a decade of danger ahead during which our oil-based economies will remain hopelessly vulnerable to OPEC oil policies, or political accidents around the world. It would be fatal for us to assume in Britain that our own North Sea oil and gas excuse us from the need to reduce oil dependence. The existence of North Sea oil may give us a fraction more room for manoeuvre than is available to those industrialised countries which have no indigenous oil at all, but our dependence on international trade means that our economic welfare is affected by the extreme vulnerability of their oil supplies. So like them we must reduce our dependence on oil as an energy source. It would be catastrophic if Britain emerged ten or fifteen years from now still geared to massive oil reliance when North Sea supplies will probably be dwindling.

The danger in the intervening years will be mitigated if progress can be made, as I believe it must be, in establishing common ground with the OPEC producers about the need to avoid a repetition of the oil price earthquakes of the seventies. But the danger lies not only in possible attempts by OPEC to raise the price of oil through deliberate production cuts. It lies in political upheaval in the oil producing areas and no amount of talking with OPEC can bring certainty on that front. The reality is that however 'moderate' the oil policies of the OPEC countries, whether in relation to price or production, and no matter how finely-tuned their economies, the sooner that we get 'unhooked' from such massive reliance on oil, the easier we will be able to breathe. And that means following policies which give the fullest incentive to changes in our own energy supply and use patterns, and doing so without further delay.

THE IMMEDIATE IMPACT

Today I only have time to touch on a few of the ways in which the energy reformation is having its immediate impact on our own energy production and consumption, so that there will be much that goes unsaid. But the first point I wish to make, at the risk of stating the obvious, is to stress that the effect is both huge and very uncertain. It is not just a question of *oil prices* leaping upwards as the consequence of political upheavals and 'accidents'. The quantum jump in oil prices means that the prices which people are prepared to pay for *all other forms of energy* goes through the ceiling, too. And that alters totally all energy investment decisions. Thus every time the oil price changes significantly, all the figures for all forms of investment in energy production, not just for oil itself, and energy conservation have to be reworked.

So it can be seen that energy prices and hence pricing policy are really at the heart of the whole energy reformation process. If the price of oil is held below the world price in one market or country this has the double effect of maintaining consumption at inflated levels, *and* of delaying investment and the appropriate diversion of brain-power and effort into alternatives.

This is the lesson which the Americans learnt in the 1970s at enormous cost to themselves and the whole world. Indeed the full and appalling cost of keeping US oil prices below world levels may yet have to be paid in the form of much greater danger to world stability than anything experienced so far. For a nation to allow itself, over the space of about eight years after 1970, to drift away from oil self-sufficiency and into reliance for half its daily supplies on oil drawn largely from one of the most politically sensitive and unstable areas on the entire planet, surely ranks as carelessness on a historic scale. The current change of emphasis in US energy policy towards realism is all the more welcome.

The consequences would be no less dangerous if we were to attempt to hold down other energy prices, as people turn away from high cost and unreliable oil. Once again double chaos ensures from such a course of action. Demand is inflated by artificially restrained prices, and supply discouraged by artificially low incentives to invest in expanded production. Such a course, however tempting in the short-term leads with absolute inevitability to convulsions in energy flows which it is then far too late to do anything about.

It is instructive to trace how the different energy sectors in Britain have coped with these forces over the last eighteen months, during which time oil prices have risen by well over 100 per cent. I want in particular to draw the contrast in behaviour between the market sector – chiefly the production, distribution and consumption of oil and its products – and the state sector which embraces gas, electricity and coal. (Perhaps I should include conservation, in itself a major resource, in the private or market sector).

In the oil sector market forces have been allowed pretty well full scope to operate, both at the production and the consumption ends of the chain. In other words British oil companies buy in at full world market price, whether from the UK Continental Shelf or anywhere else, while refining and selling have been free of all price controls.

The result has been a very rapid accommodation at all levels to the new and vastly different price levels. At the production end large new incentives have helped lead to an upsurge in the search for new oil deposits, both offshore and on land. World pricing has also of course led to large and increasing profits accruing to oil producers, a substantial part of which has then been taken in tax.

At the other end, the sales end, once the disastrous price controls which I inherited were removed – which were forcing North Sea Oil overseas – the shortages and queues of early 1979 quickly vanished.

We are now seeing the initial very high profit margins characteristic of a very tight supply situation giving way to smaller margins as competition begins to operate again. The signs are that with the huge price increases being allowed to work through freely to the consumer, there has been a major incentive to reduce oil consumption, and this is reflected in the quarterly figures of consumption. True, in the motor spirit sector the impact has been smallest. But the real retail price of petrol which involves a large tax element only rose above its 1970 level one year ago. And whilst more economical driving of existing vehicles has its effect, the opportunity to trade down to a smaller-engined car only comes round, on average, once every two years. So it is hardly suprising that the process takes time. One can, however, see the process getting under way in the second-hand car market as the price of 'gas-guzzlers' is marked down and the search for fuel economy really gets going.

Inevitably the public tends to react very differently to price rises in the oil sector, and to price rises announced by the state energy industries. On the whole, people seem ready to grit their teeth and accept the market-driven decisions of the oil sector. But not so with the state sector. Because the state sector industries often supply virtually captive markets, and are widely believed to be under tight government control, many believe that their price rises must be the result of deliberate acts Government, taken almost on a whim. As the oil price increases work through to energy price rises in the state sector, these are regarded not as market pressures but as highly political decisions.

In reality, the rise in prices is more a reflection of reduced government involvement than of arbitrary interference. It has been this Government's policy to try to let the correct price signals work through all energy industries. Government is responsible for controlling the overall finances of nationalised industries on the taxpayer's behalf, but beyond that we have moved away from control where previously this existed.

Needless to say, the rapid rise in energy prices has been unpopular and unsettling; and led to very understandable cries for protection from the icy blast of high cost energy. It has also led to frequent allegations that the Government is 'forcing up' the price of energy.

All this illustrates, I suppose, the point that if the energy industries were all in the private sector, life might be easier for Ministers during a turbulent period of energy reformation such as the once we are passing through. The laws of economics might then be allowed to operate with less political 'aggro' and there would be a greater long-term chance of reaching a new equilibrium in energy supply and demand without storing up trouble for the future by delaying necessary but unpalatable adjustments.

Not that governments would have any less responsibility than they have now to see that the impact of the enormous price increases in eased by help for those individuals and groups who are especially badly hit and especially poorly-placed to adapt quickly. This Government has been alerted to such problems and remains alert to them. The programme of help announced this year for domestic consumers most in need in face of higher fuel prices is the largest and most comprehensive yet devised in Britain. The plight of specific firms with a high use of energy, faced with a grim rise in their bills, has been recognised by Government and transitional help offered.

CHANGING SUPPLY AND DEMAND TRENDS

Meanwhile, with energy prices generally in both the private and public sectors being allowed to move in the direction of world market levels, vast ranges of new projects have come into the potentially economic zone. The coal investment programme has started to look much more attractive on strictly economic grounds and we have fully maintained it, indeed increased it. Nuclear electricity economics have begun to look even more robust, despite the imperative need to improve construction times. Vast new investment in gas development has been embarked upon, with a £1 billion new project for gathering gas in the northern North Sea, from both oil and gas wells, on the slipway.

The economics of the so-called 'renewables' have also begun to look much more interesting, as have the economics of combined heat and power schemes. The Government's job here, as I see it, is not to try and do the impossible and pick 'winners' on the basis of wild guesses about the future course of fossil fuel prices or the commercial viability of alternatives, but to fund the research and development necessary to keep as many doors open as possible.

Some of the 'renewables' are never going to make the grade as far as large-scale energy supplies are concerned, although in particular locations and for particular uses they may make a lot of sense. Others may become justified when conventional fuel costs get above a certain point, although on the basis of present technology that point will have to be considerably above the present real oil price.

The moment when a project, be it a tidal barrage or an aerogenerator system, is worth picking up out of the R&D phase and carrying forward commercially is one of the most difficult of all to assess, and on the whole governments are not best placed to make the necessary judgment. What Government can and must do as far as possible, is see that the opportunities are kept open so that others can make the decisions to go commercial and to carry the risks.

On the demand side the response to changing energy prices is also clearly discernible. Of course, since investment in energy use is undertaken by millions of individual decision makers both industrial and domestic rather than being included in a visible public sector programme, it attracts less attention. But in practice the level of conservation investment in the domestic sector particularly has grown enormously. The latest figures suggest that over £400 m. were spent by home-owners last year on various forms of home insulation to increase the energy efficiency of their homes. This is an increase of more than 30 per cent over the previous year. On the industrial front energy efficiency investment is rather less buoyant at present than I would have hoped, but many sectors of industry have already become aware of the enormous potential for using energy more efficiently and can be expected to achieve that potential reasonably soon. On the whole the conservation response in Britain is coming rather faster than I personally expected and demonstrates the formidable impact of economic pricing on previously established patterns of behaviour, especially when it is understood that this is not just a passing phase but a permanent shift in the pattern of realistic prices.

The energy supply industries are also beginning to appreciate the probable benefits for them of steadier and more restrained energy demand. They are therefore no longer anxious simply to supply their product on request but to ensure that it is used to maximum efficiency so that more customers' needs can be met both in the short and longer term.

In all this the key is once again price. The Government has, in my view three roles in the conservation process – to encourage the correct price signals which promote greater energy saving, to support energy saving with a positive information and advice campaign so that conservation possibilities open to people are disseminated as widely as possible (which in our case includes demonstration projects to show industry how new technology can be applied), and thirdly, to establish a modest pattern of regulation when this seems justified. Perhaps a fourth role should be added, namely to ensure that the public sector itself sets a good example in energy economy.

I am not so impressed by the argument that the state should necessarily step in with elaborate subsidies for energy conservation since investments in such schemes usually pay for themselves in a remarkably short time (frequently only two or three years). I agree with the excellent recent Ford Foundation study on energy which gave government subsidy a low place in conservation programmes, provided, as is now largely the case in the UK, that energy prices reflect true economic cost. However I can see that people who measure the impact of policies by the size of Departmental spending upon them may not share this view.

LONG LEAD TIMES MEAN HIGH RISKS

Yet of course, while any data about either the past or the present is often incomplete and our view of the future is at best hazy, the decisions that have to be made need, in contrast, to be hard, firm and substantial. You cannot start a nuclear power station or a tidal barrage scheme and then unstart it. You cannot, as we have seen, start building power stations on the assumption of cheap oil and then stop three-quarters of the way without great cost. You cannot–except with enormous penalties–stop half way through tearing an oil-fired system out of your factory and replacing it with coal-fired because the economics have changed. So the immensely long lead times required to build new energy systems merely add to the uncertainties of energy prices.

It is this kind of unavoidably blurred vista which brings the central planners out of their corner arguing that the whole of energy policy should somehow be parcelled into a single, beautifully co-ordinated long-term plan. This is the way, so the argument goes, to free the energy issues from the vagaries of price and commercial calculation and allow the energy technicians to get on and produce pre-determined quantities and forms of energy at pre-determined dates in the future by carefully chosen technologies.

Given the uncertainties and the immensely long lead times for projects, one can understand this instinct, although it is in my view a thoroughly misguided one. In each separate energy sector there certainly have to be long-term plans. The oil companies plan decades ahead. The gas industry tries to plan its investment years ahead, although its estimates can be badly thrown out, as we have seen, by violent oil price movements. The NCB plans its long-term investment in coal production; the electricity supply industry have to think up to a decade ahead before they lay a single brick for a new power station.

So in all these areas if there is to be investment at all it has to be very long term and is therefore inherently risky. But can the central planners produce master plans which will reduce these risks? Admittedly, sector plans embarked upon on the basis of future fuel prices estimates and energy demand growth estimates can be seriously wrong, especially if the plans are unduly rigid and inflexible. But if there is doubt along this path there is grim certainty about the alternative. If sector plans are 'co-ordinated' not through intelligent use of price projections and information in each industry but on the basis of bureaucratic plans heavily influenced by political fashion, then you can be 100 per cent certain that they will be colossally and disastrously wrong. The decisions of the 1960s to build power stations galore under the ill-fated National Plan are Britain's monument to this particular brand of folly. Most centrally planned economies have made even worse mistakes.

The hankering after a totally co-ordinated energy plan springs from the knowledge that market-influenced decisions can lead to mistakes. The problem is that official centrally planned decisions invariably lead to bigger mistakes. So we have to live with error and suppress the impulses of articulate politicians and brilliant adminstrators in every generation to make even bigger errors.

SECURITY OF SUPPLY

There is one further area of dilemma facing the energy policy maker in which market-influenced factors pull one way and other equally vital considerations pull another. I am referring to the concept of national security of energy supply which no government can neglect and which in times of energy uncertainty and price upheaval becomes very prominent indeed in the thinking of governments in every nation.

In a sense the dilemma is resolved once one major energy-consuming nation steps in and intervenes to control energy and divert to itself supplies. Other governments can either stand by and see the international system distorted to their disadvantage or they can take compensating action. And of course there is no choice but to take such action. With the whole world full of governments all nervously seeking to secure future energy supplies we have no choice here in Britain but to ensure that our supplies are secured well into the future and that any such scheme for international sharing in times of real crisis is equitable and fair.

In particular, there is much to be done through close international collaboration, both at the EEC level and at wider levels, to ensure that the defensive action taken by each country is limited and not self-defeating, and thus to head off the sort of scramble for oil that we came very near to seeing in 1979 and which was only just prevented from turning into real disaster.

If one major consuming country neglects energy conservation by refusing to face price realism and holding down its fuel prices the efforts of all the others are undermined. If one country ignores the need to develop alternatives and sticks to oil, that is at the direct expense of everybody else. If one country arranges government to government deals at inflated prices, that plays into the hands of the producers quite unnecessarily.

That is why EEC energy co-operation, IEA co-operation, indeed Summit co-operation are all absolutely vital and fully merit the enormous time and effort which Energy Ministers spend on these things. Certainly our own security of supply must have priority. But it is dangerous and shallow illusion to believe that we can be comfortable and secure while others flounder and gasp for energy 'oxygen', however great our natural energy advantage. In the end we have to act in concert or we destroy each other.

Sovereign governments, then, are bound to make some decisions which are more strategic than economic. They are bound to embrace the view that it may be more important to have the most certain energy supplies than to have the cheapest energy supplies, although there is no reason why one should not have a damn good shot at getting both.

Certainly this is the guiding thought behind our decision to keep on the elaborate oil participation and trading operations undertaken by the BNOC. It is the thought behind our decision, which I announced recently, that the Government might delay certain oil field developments so as to prolong the lifetime of the North Sea oil province and to give us the potential for net self-sufficiency as long as possible into the future. And it informs the expectations the Government has of the sense of obligation to UK oil consumers which oil companies operating in the North Sea will display.

It is also one of the thoughts leading to the view that we ought to keep a thriving indigenous coal industry, especially since, taking a reasonable medium-term view, solid commercial considerations point the same way. To succumb to the temptation to build up reliance on foreign coal supplies in the belief that they were always going to be cheaper, and always freely available, would I think be a move which the country would come bitterly to regret. Having gone some way to escape the dangers of interrupted oil supplies through whatever political accident or whim that comes along, it really would be folly to let our increasingly coal-hungry economy of the future be exposed to just the same risks. There will always be a balance to be struck: we simply could not afford a grotesquely and suicidally uneconomic coal industry. That would give us no alternative but to go abroad. But I do not believe our coal industry, or the people in it, will allow that to happen, and that is why have taken the longer term view and given it the enormous support which we have.

ENERGY INDUSTRIES AND THE HUMAN SCALE

I have given you some of the reasons why market influence and economic pricing provide the best basis for sane and sound energy development but why governments nonetheless have been dragged into the centre of energy supply issues. The energy reformation is not changing this, I'm afraid, although it is somewhat altering the way the cards are dealt. The vast leap in energy prices has brought home to energy consumers the ability which they have to meet the challenge by using energy more efficiently. That in itself is a gigantic energy resource which is created through millions of individual decisions of the kind which I described earlier. The energy price increases have also produced, at least on the horizon, the possibility of small-scale energy supply through a variety of alternative 'green' methods which previously were just not remotely worthwhile except as hobbies and eccentricities.

But the oil upheaval has also driven both governments and energy industries all round the world into bigger and more complex projects and plans for a less oil dependent future than ever before. The scale is titanic. Structures which dwarf cathedrals rise up to handle and manufacture energy. Programmes are drawn up in which 'billions' become almost the smallest unit of currency. Power for decision becomes concentrated in unnervingly few hands, whether they be those of the managers of great energy industries or those of administrators and Ministers.

There are those who believe that our state institutions can cope with all this, but I must say I am not one of them. The burdens on the state are already far too great in the energy field. I concede that the pattern which has developed in the USA, when nominal private ownership of energy supply industries has now been continued with an almost suffocating blanket of regulations, controls, and consumerism gone mad, offers a no more attractive alternative. But there is no evidence at all that people are the least reassured by the knowledge that a particular industry is under state control and ownership and therefore, theoretically, accountable to the public. Nor is there any sign of enthusiasm for the corporatist alternative which began to be developed in the seventies in Britain and which tried to secure democratic legitimacy for state power by bringing in on the act a few other great corporate interests to achieve a claimed consensus.

My own view is that we would do far better in satisfying individual and family aspirations in today's dangerous world if we try to find a middle path between the Orwellian prospect of ever-growing state power and ownership and, at the other extreme, the paralysing mixture of over-regulation and shackled private enterprise in which the USA has found itself.

That middle path will best be found, I believe, by redefining the concept of public ownership as we have known it since the great Morrisonian period of nationalisation after the Second World War. Public ownership should mean just that – ownership spread as broadly as possible amongst the widest possible number of families. Indeed it is a curious paradox of our time, difficult I suppose for those of a centralising turn of mind of grasp, that the more fragmented, dispersed and widely shared the ownership pattern of our society, the greater the sense of common cause and the stronger the wish to work together. The more diffuse the power, the greater the unity.

Apply this principle in the energy sector and a number of limited but significant possibilities open up for at least easing, if not resolving the dilemma between the fact of large and centralised energy supply industries and the fear of over-concentrated and over-centralised state power. Increased competition, reduced monopoly, wider private capital participation, smaller units of ownership alongside the large –

all these are going to be not merely the desirable, but the essential features of the more supple pattern of energy supply which the energy reformation and the end of the cheap oil era is now bringing upon us.

It will be a slow process and, for those whose minds are fixed upon the easy assumptions of the sixties and seventies, and the familiar industrial structures embodying those assumptions, a jarring one, too. But the change that has come upon us is very great and our minds must stretch wide and long if we are to ride that change and yet retain our valued objectives of safe and secure supplies of energy delivered to a free and civilised industrial society through the dangerous years ahead. In the words of the Prince's son, Tancredi in that marvellous book *The Leopard*, 'if we want things to stay the way they are, things will have to change'. I hope that is not too indigestible a political thought to put before such a distinguished scientific gathering or with which to close my remarks on the energy reformation.

10 Finance in the Mixed Economy

ANDREW BAIN
University of Strathclyde

The Committee on the Functioning of Financial Institutions[1] (the Wilson Committee) whose report was published last June, conducted its enquiry against the background of a mixed economy. Yet this particular aspect of the UK economy played little part in either its deliberations or its Reports. The fact that government borrowing takes place for many different purposes, including the finance of investment by public sector enterprises, was fully recognised, but the whole question of the scale and composition of public enterprise financing was an issue which the Committee chose not to discuss. The provision of finance for industry and trade, not finance for the public sector, was at the heart of the enquiry.

Nor is the mixed economy a prominent feature of the financial sector itself. Amongst the financial institutions, direct public sector involvement is not at present very significant in quantitative terms, though the same does not necessarily hold good in a qualitative sense. The National Savings Bank fulfils important social functions, but acts as a source of funds only to the public sector. The National Giro plays a comparatively minor part in the payments system. And neither the National Enterprise Board nor the Regional Development Agencies dispose of large amounts of funds for investment in new projects at present. Other public sector financial institutions, such as the National Research Development Corporation or the Council for Small Industries in Rural Areas, are also highly specialised. The limited role of public sector institutions stands in contrast to the scale of public sector involvement in financial markets, which is very substantial, thanks to the size of the UK national debt, to the need to fund the public sector borrowing requirement (PSBR) and refinance maturing stocks, and to central bank activities.

Rather than deal directly with public sector financing or the respective roles of public and private sector institutions in the financial system I propose to discuss a somewhat broader issue concerning the functions of the financial system in a mixed economy, one which was the subject of some disagreement within the Wilson Committee. This is the question of how far the financial system contributes to macroeconomic balance in the economy, a question which is closely bound up with the determination and role of the rate of interest and takes us back to the debate between loanable funds and liquidity preference theorists in the 1930s.

Most of the other functions of the financial system are uncontroversial. The financial system mobilises savings, and makes them available to potential investors; it transforms maturities so that the conflicting preferences of savers and investors can be satisfied; and it helps to spread risk. These functions are all well understood, though the efficiency with which the systems in different countries perform them can be disputed, as can the means for remedying any weaknesses. But nobody would argue in principle that financial systems are incapable of carrying out these functions.

No similar consensus exists concerning the task of balancing the supply of saving with the demand for investment in the economy. It is a vitally important issue, because differences of view have implications for the kinds of government intervention in financial markets, and the scale of such intervention, which are deemed appropriate. Classical and neo-classical economists would argue that the *prices* which prevail in financial markets – the rates of interest on loans, the yields on equities and property, and the other terms attached to the supply of credit – adjust to maintain this balance. But this proposition was hotly contested by Keynes and his followers, on the grounds that disequilibrium affected both the supply of saving and the demand for investment and that interest rates would in any case be slow to adjust to changing circumstances.

The Wilson Committee has been criticised for the way it handled this question: S. Brittan[2] refers to 'the misleading examination essay-type Chapter 11 on problems of high theory'. Two alternative theories of interest rate determination, described as the flow of funds approach and the liquidity preference approach, were discussed in this chapter. The former is essentially a loanable funds theory which claims that the rate of interest balances the supply of saving (*ex ante*) plus any abnormal change in the quantity of money with the demands of borrowers (*ex ante*) plus any abnormal change in the demand for money. The propensities to save and invest are expected to be the dominant factors in the long run. In contrast the liquidity preference approach (in an extreme version) claims that interest rates are entirely dependent on monetary conditions and expectations in the capital market, and are unaffected by the propensity to save or the anticipated yield on investment, other than as a result of any effects that changes in these factors may have on the level of income.

The high theory had to be given an airing and the disagreement within the Committee brought out because it has important practical implications, which no doubt influenced the recommendations made by different members of the Committee. In particular, those who believe that the rate of interest balances saving and investment (or more broadly the supply of and demand for funds) may argue quite consistently that a high PSBR raises the cost of capital for industry, and may conclude from this that a cut in the PSBR would help industry to raise funds more cheaply. For the other camp, the effect of a cut in the PSBR would depend on its impact on the money supply and expectations, and would not necessarily be beneficial. In order to reduce the cost of industrial finance they would therefore be more likely to recommend the granting of subsidies or setting up of special institutions. The determination and role of interest rates was not, therefore, a side-issue to which the Committee could turn a blind eye. It was central to part of the Committee's terms of reference, viz. 'to review in particular the provision of funds for industry and trade'.

The view that propensities to save and invest are the principal determinants of interest rates in the medium term is often attacked on the grounds, *inter alia*, that:

- saving and investment do not vary independently;
- both saving and investment are highly inelastic with respect to the rate of interest;
- saving and investment flows are swamped by other factors;
- there is no plausible mechanism through which an *ex ante* surplus of saving can make itself felt in capital and credit market.

The alleged interdependence of saving and investment rests on the Keynesian model of income determination, in which incomes are the main determinant of consumer spending, so that a change in investment affects incomes and saving through the familiar multiplier process. However both theory and practical experience in recent years have led to the primacy of *income* as a determinant of saving being questioned. Personal saving in Britain, as in many other countries, has risen sharply in a period when real incomes have been depressed and the economic outlook has been clouded. Other factors, notably wealth, have come to play an important part in explanations of consumer behaviour. Moreoever, the multiplier process, with its dependence of saving on investment, is a feature of cyclical behaviour in which the level of activity is variable. This short-run interdependence of saving and investment does not rule out the possibility that investment prospects, and hence the demand for funds, may change at full employment, or indeed at any other level of economic activity, and that savings propensities may also undergo changes for reasons unconnected with the level of income. Proponents of the flow of funds approach to interest rate determination do not deny that changes in the level of economic activity may play some part in balancing the supply of funds with demand in the short-run. What they contest is the overriding importance of this mechanism, and argue instead that changes in interest rates are required to bring about a permanent adjustment to changes in savings or investment propensities.

This does presuppose that saving, investment, or both are sensitive to changes in the rate of interest. The Wilson Committee gave some consideration to the effect of the cost of funds on industrial investment. While firms themselves put little stress on the cost of funds in determining investment – emphasising instead the prospects for profitability – the cost of capital is an integral component of investment decision-taking methods many firms employ, and it also enters into lenders' assessments of the viability of projects which they are being asked to finance. In consequence, *a priori* argument and factual evidence are to some extent in conflict. Nevertheless the Committee concluded[3]

> Investment is an inherently risky activity. When funds are expensive the prospective reward to the businessman is whittled away by the cost of finance; some projects will fail to pass the test. Perhaps more important, financial uncertainty which militates against equity issues and increases the risk of debt financing adds an extra dimension to the uncertainty which businessmen face; caution will prevail more often. And when balance sheets have little equity to spare and funds are dear, the attitude and objective of businessmen will be to preserve what they have rather than to seek out new opportunities. For all these reasons we believe that over a long period a high cost of funds will decrease the level of investment.

Private investment in the enterprise sector amounts to only about 40 per cent of total investment, and is not likely to be the most sensitive to financial conditions, because the relevant time-horizon is often fairly short. Again, *a priori* argument suggests that the sensitivity of long-term investment should be higher, and much of long-term investment consists of housing or of investment connected with activities carried out by the public sector. Private house-building is affected by mortgage costs – the size of mortgage a person can afford to service depends on the rate of interest charged – but the financial controls applied to public sector investment imply that the response of investment in this sector to changes in interest rates is unlikely to be appreciable. The relatively high proportion of investment which falls within the public sector in the UK's mixed economy probably reduces the sensitivity of investment to the cost of capital in this country.

The effect of interest rates on saving is uncertain, but unlikely to be very large. It is by no means inconceivable that high real rates of interest may actually reduce private saving: high real rates reduce the pace at which mortgagees can pay off the capital they have borrowed, and target savers, such as pension funds, require lower contributions to achieve their objectives. Against this, lower security prices reduce the level of consumption which can be financed by realising assets.

The conclusion must be that the balance between saving and investment is likely to show some sensitivity to the rate of interest, but that the responsiveness may not be very high, particularly for the large component of investment undertaken within the public sector.

The third ground for attacking the flow of funds approach is that flows of saving and investment are likely to be swamped by other factors. In particular, changes in liquidity preference–the desire to hold short-term, liquid assets rather than long-term assets – and in the money supply will have a much greater bearing on interest rates than flows of saving and investment. To some extent the difference between the two theories might be regarded as one of degree: the flow of funds approach to interest rate determination does not deny that monetary factors will have some influence on interest rates, but it relegates them to secondary importance in the medium term.

The importance of shifts in liquidity preference and changes in the money supply for interest rates is really an empirical issue, but it is one on which fully satisfactory evidence is almost impossible to obtain. For if interest rates alter as a result of changes in liquidity preference, the *ex ante* magnitude of such shifts – the changes that would have occurred in the absence of interest rate changes – cannot be observed.

Fortunately, this difficulty does not prevent us from saying something on the subject.

First, the relative importance for interest rates of shifts in the desired composition of the existing stock of financial assets as against the flows of new financial assets created by saving and investment in the economy will depend on the time period considered. Shifts in liquidity preference are usually a consequence of changes in confidence or uncertainty. When the future appears particularly uncertain, wealth holders put a premium on liquidity because it enables them to alter their portfolios in future if changes should seem desirable: liquidity provides manoeuvrability. As events unfold uncertainty is gradually reduced and the apparent need for liquidity becomes less pressing. Indeed, since liquid assets generally yield less than long-term assets, there is an incentive for wealth-holders to have their funds fully invested. Thus, while in the short-term swings in confidence may have considerable effects on the demand for liquidity, in the longer run these swings are likely to even themselves out. By contrast, saving and investment flows are cumulative: the longer the period considered the more important these flows become.

Secondly, the factors which influence investment behaviour need to be considered. Long-term institutional investors, who now hold about half of the listed securities in Britain, have fiduciary obligations and other liabilities which inhibit large-scale switching between categories of securities. Many private holdings are administered by trustees who are subject to similar constraints. Large holders face the additional problem that dealing on a large scale may be impossible without incurring excessive costs (in terms of inducing unfavourable price movements). The result is that institutions are much more willing to build up liquidity by delaying investing accruing funds than by liquidating any substantial part of their existing portfolios, and this limits the scale of any movements. That is not, of course, to say that on occasion such movements may not be large. In the exceptionally disturbed conditions of 1974 the life assurance and pension funds used about half their accruing funds to build up liquid assets (compared with an average figure of about 5 per cent); these were run down again subsequently. More usually fluctuations in liquidity are much less significant, often being linked to short-run expectations of interest rate changes in the gilt-edged market. But institutional investors generally dislike holding substantial funds uninvested, over and above their normal requirement for liquidity, particularly if short-term running yields lie below those they expect to earn on long-term assets.

Thus if, having built up liquidity by holding off the market for a period, their expectations of a fall in security prices are not realised, they are likely to return quite quickly to the market as buyers, in order to employ both their continuing inflow of funds and, eventually, to run down their liquidity to its customary level. If this description of institutional investment behaviour is correct it suggests that swings in liquidity preference may indeed swamp savings and investment flows as determinants of interest rates in the short run, accounting as it were for the ripples on the surface of the water, but that their influence is unlikely to be durable.

Major swings in the growth of the money supply also have an important effect. If money is allowed to expand an excess of investment demand over saving (*ex ante*) may be reflected in money creation rather than in a rise in interest rates; or action by the monetary authorities to hold down interest rates may generate excess investment demand financed by money creation. This is exactly what happened in 1972, when interest rates fell to a very low level; the reverse is closer to the truth now. But again, this is not a situation that can persist indefinitely; for excessive monetary expansion will be reflected eventually in a higher rate of inflation, and lead to higher – not lower – nominal rates of interest. While nominal rates of interest would reflect the rate of monetary expansion, real rates of interest would continue to be governed by saving and investment flows.

The final ground for attacking the flow of funds approach is that there is no means by which a surplus of saving can exist in the economy, and so exert downward pressure on interest rates. Indeed, some liquidity preference theorists claim that

> there is a logical flaw in the flow of funds argument that the level of interest rates in real terms is determined mainly by the flows of saving and investment. Correctly defined, the flow of saving in any period will always be equal to the flow of gross investment in the same time period. Any sector's deficit (or surplus) must therefore always be matched by an equal and opposite surplus (or deficit) elsewhere. Consequently, a divergence between saving and investment cannot explain changes in interest rates, because no surplus or deficit of saving ever actually exists.[4]

This charge seems to reflect a simple confusion between *ex ante* and *ex post*, such as bedevilled discussion of the Keynesian model in its early years. The fact that *ex post* supply and demand in any free market are equal does not prevent excess demand from influencing the price or prevent changes in price from playing an integral part in the mechanism which brings supply and demand into balance.

It is not difficult to illustrate how the process might work in the financial markets. Let us assume initially that the money supply is held constant. First consider the case of a rise in investment demand reflected in a greater demand for bank loans and a higher level of rights issues of shares. Faced with this higher demand for loans banks will bid more actively for deposits and possibly sell securities, thereby raising interest rates; and investors who are channelling more of their funds into rights issues will have less available to buy (or hold) other securities, again raising security yields. The rise in interest rates is likely to be spread across the financial system as a whole, and must be sufficient to deter some potential borrowers (or increase saving) until saving and investment are again in balance. Notice that although the pattern of spending in the economy may change there need be no effect on aggregate demand.[5]

Next suppose that households choose to save more, and that the additional saving is held in the form of building society shares. The counterpart of the increased saving is, of course, a reduction in demand for consumer goods and services. Building societies may react to the increased inflow of funds in a number of ways: at first they may simply build up liquidity; then they may ease the terms of lending or impose a milder degree of credit rationing; if the higher inflow continues they may eventually cut the interest rates paid on shares and charged on loans. I shall return to what happens if they build up liquidity later. But if lending is increased the rise in demand for capital goods (house building) matches the reduced consumption demand in the economy. Although explicit interest rates do not necessarily change, the way in which building societies administer their interest rates and other terms of business helps to equate saving and investment in the economy.

Next assume that there is an increase in contractual saving through life assurance or, more probably, pension funds. Again, higher saving, considered in isolation, implies lower aggregate demand in the economy. But, as noted above, the long-term institutions are in the business of long-term investment, and the increased inflow of funds will be reflected in increased purchases of long-term assets, whose prices will therefore rise. The reduction in the cost of capital (combined with its greater availability) will eventually stimulate investment to match the higher saving flow.

These examples illustrate how interest rates might in practice be influenced by saving and investment flows. But two problems remain, the first concerning timing. The reduction in demand as people switch from spending to saving is immediate; the stimulus to investment from lower interest rates or easier credit terms may follow some time afterwards. There could be an awkward gap during which consumer demand was weak but investment had not yet increased to take up the slack, a gap which could in principle set off a Keynesian process of income contraction.

It is easy to make too much of this problem of lags. Most changes at the aggregate level in the economy are not the once and for all, short, sharp shifts of the theoretical models. On the contrary, they usually take place gradually, allowing time for the economy to adapt. The pattern of demand in the economy is changing continually and there is a fair degree of flexibility in the economy – sufficient to avoid a sharp reaction to a temporary disequilibrium. Nevertheless the possibility that time lags may be a problem in some conditions cannot be dismissed – sharp changes in commodity prices or tax rates are examples which come to mind. Moreover, long-term investors may sometimes be slow to recognise the need for a change in long-term yields, and choose for a time to build up or run down liquidity rather than buy or sell securities at seemingly high or low prices respectively.

The second problem concerns the money supply and monetary policy. If the money supply was fixed rigidly and if a rise in saving led to an increase in the demand for money, interest rates might rise, perversely, rather than fall as is required. For example, firms faced with a reduction in demand for their output might be compelled to increase their overdrafts, rather than reduce liquid balances, and if they could not expand their balance sheets banks would need to sell securities or deny loans to other potential borrowers in order to meet this demand for finance. In fact, it is not at all unlikely that part of an increase in saving will take the form of an increased demand for money, either by savers themselves or by institutions with which they place their funds. This is exactly what would happen if the building societies were to build up their liquidity in the previous example. To avoid a perverse increase in short-term interest rates the money supply must be allowed to expand in line with demand.

Provided that changes in the propensities to save or invest take place gradually, and provided that there is sufficient flexibility in monetary policy to permit an expansion of the money supply in response to the increase in demand, the problem of perverse interest rate changes will not arise. But it is important to recognise that elasticity in the money supply makes an important contribution to the flexibility and stability of the capital markets; that 'short-term variations in the demand for money . . ., far from damaging the economy, may play a vital part in helping it to function smoothly'.[6] This was one of the considerations which led the Wilson Committee to stress the need to set monetary targets in a way which did not impede short-run fluctuations.[7]

The possibility of perverse interest rate changes in the short run is worth pursuing a little further, because some members of the Committee felt, with varying degrees of conviction, that the pursuit of monetary targets had probably contributed to a vicious circle of rising interest rates and increased public sector borrowing. One version of the argument, consistent with the flow of funds theory of interest rate determination, runs as follows.

Thanks largely to inflation and a deteriorating business environment, the propensity to save has been high and the desire to invest has been low in recent years. In the absence of any change in public sector borrowing the combination of high private saving and low investment demand would lead to a reduction in the equilibrium real rate of interest. However, the required fall in real rates of interest has not occurred, for two principal reasons. First all all, governments for some time pursued counter-cyclical fiscal policies, and quite deliberately set out to mop up surplus saving in an effort to moderate the contractionary effect on economic activity. Higher public sector borrowing absorbed much of the surplus saving coming into capital markets and thereby removed most of the downward pressure on interest rates which would otherwise have been present. Secondly, long-term financial institutions were slow to adjust their interest rate expectations downwards. The nature of their liabilities makes them reluctant to buy long-term securities at low expected real rates of return, and the combination of high and volatile inflation with low real profitability made it difficult for them to judge what real returns they could reasonably expect. When interest rates or equity yields seemed too low they chose to hold off the market and build up liquidity. In normal circumstances a failure to place their funds on the desired terms, with a consequential gradual build-up of liquidity, would cause them sooner or later to revise downwards their view of what long-term yields were acceptable. But a build-up of liquidity fell foul of the authorities' objectives for monetary growth. The authorities responded by raising interest rates – both long and short term – to curb monetary expansion. They did not wait for the situation to correct itself of its own accord, and if they were to abide by their short-run monetary targets they could not have done so. The higher interest rates widened the potential gap between private saving and investment, contributing to further contraction in the economy, putting pressure on the government to raise its own borrowing still further, and validating the institutions' belief that a fall in interest rates was unlikely. Such, on this view, are the perverse effects of a combination of downward stickiness in interest rates and over-rigid short-run monetary targets!

CONCLUSIONS

What conclusions can be drawn from this discussion for the effects of the financial system on the stability of the mixed economy?

First, rates of interest act to balance saving and investment in the economy in the medium-term: other things equal, an increase in the propensity to save or reduction in the anticipated yield on investment entails lower equilibrium rates of interest.

Secondly, when *ex ante* saving and *ex ante* investment are unequal at prevailing rates of interest mechanisms exist within the financial system to bring about the adjustment in interest rates needed to restore balance. But the process of adjustment may be slow, particularly in the downward direction.

Thirdly, smooth adjustment of interest rates will be assisted by flexibility in the monetary system, such as to allow temporary changes in the demand for money to be accommodated. The pursuit of rigidly defined monetary targets in the short run is likely to impede desirable capital market adjustments.

These conclusions have some rather obvious implications for government policy today. First, unless there is a further rise in private saving – which is unlikely – or a further weakening of profit expectations from new investment – which is undesirable – a cut in the public sector deficit (the extent to which the public sector absorbs private sector saving) is the most obvious means of bringing about a fall in real rates of interest.

Secondly, the stress which is now being placed on the *medium-term* aspect of published monetary targets is welcome, but it needs to be combined with a greater willingness to tolerate short-run variations in monetary growth if the financial markets are to work properly.

Finally, there is a possibility that long-term interest rates may turn out to be sticky when a fall is needed, and there is a danger that when the public sector's demands on the financial system are reduced, interest rates may fall less quickly than is required to maintain the balance between saving and investment. The prospect of a rapid fall in interest rates has been made less likely by the high rates of inflation experienced in recent years and the fear that, even if inflation can be curbed for a while, there will be a resurgence in the future. If interest rates do not adjust quickly it may be necessary for the authorities to take a hand in ensuring that the terms on which borrowers can obtain funds reflect the volume of savings becoming available in the economy.

One approach, which circumvents the problem of inflationary expectations, would be to encourage borrowers to issue index-linked securities. The Wilson Committee agreed that experimentation by industrial borrowers was desirable, and that the present impediments should be removed,[8] but they were divided on the desirability of indexation in the house mortgage and government debt markets. Another, recommended unanimously by the Committee,[9] is a refinancing scheme for bank loans, to ensure that the supply of short and medium-term finance by the banks is not constrained by monetary policy at a time when long-term savings institutions have surplus funds. But what will matter will not so much be the means which the authorities choose to employ to deal with a situation of this kind, but their willingness to recognise that the situation exists and to take some measures to resolve it quickly. For by prolonging and deepening the current recession, delay could cause unnecessary suffering and avoidable damage to the economy.

NOTES

1. Cmnd. 7937.
2. *Financial Times*, 26 June 1980.
3. Cmnd. 7937, para. 504.
4. *Ibid.*, para. 581.
5. The rise in interest rates might, however, decrease the demand for money and, in the absence of supply constraints, be associated with an expansion of income.
6. *Ibid.*, para. 615.
7. *Ibid.*, paras 613–15.
8. *Ibid.*, para. 870.
9. *Ibid.*, para. 953.

11 The Mixed Economy in an International Context

BRIAN HINDLEY
University of London

This paper is about international trading problems and the mixed economy, so I should start by making plain my belief that there is no inherent *logical* connection between the two. In principle, incentives to managers and workers in nationalized industries and firms could be structured in such a way that their actions would be similar to those of the managers and workers in privately owned joint stock companies. Trade policies – tariffs, subsidies, and so on – then would have approximately the same effect on state-owned as privately owned companies, and the reactions to trading opportunities of the two would not systematically vary.

But while I believe this proposition to be logically correct, I also believe it to be practically vacuous. Industries and firms are not nationalized to reproduce the actions of their privately owned predecessors, but for some other reason. Trade policies are applied to obtain some effect. The interesting subject matter of the present topic lies in the relationship and interaction between that reason and that desired effect.

This means that there is an inevitable awkwardness for an economist writing to this title. The workmanlike approach would be to start with a well-ordered and tested explanation of the state's ownership and control of some activities within the economy and a similarly well-tested account of its objectives in regulating trade flows; and would then go on to discuss their interaction. But unfortunately this approach is precluded by the absence of both the first and the second of these hypotheses, at least in a well-tested and widely accepted form. The conventional text-book analysis of nationalization as a response to the problem of natural monopoly evidently cannot be applied to those nationalized industries – such as coal, steel, shipbuilding, airlines, aircraft, and motor cars – with an actual or potential heavy involvement in international trade. Similarly, the standard theorems of international economics offer no route to an explanation of existing trade policies beyond making clear that to explain them as the actions of an intelligent government primarily concerned to maximize the aggregate economic welfare of its residents is very difficult indeed.

Lack of relevant theory and testing is not the sole source of awkwardness in my topic however. The other major difficulty lies in the range and scope of the means for intervention in trade flows available to a modern government. The breadth of this range raises the question of whether the category 'mixed economy', used in the traditional sense to denote the co-existence of privately owned and publicly owned enterprises, has any fundamental relevance of analysis of international trade problems. Certainly it is not obvious that the policy-induced distortions of trade flows primarily affecting private sector firms are less serious than those affecting, or engineered through, public sector enterprises (consider for example textiles, agriculture, and electronics). Moreover, while nationalized industries have been used in all countries possessing them to intervene in trade, the trade effects of these interventions could have been achieved by other means, by and large, if the industries had not been nationalized.

The general flavour of what is now described as 'industrial policy' is conveyed by an OECD report on the subject.[1] The study lists the following instruments: . . . 'financial and fiscal incentives; technical assistance, training and a wide range of consultative and advisory activities; policies within the framework of government procurement and contracts for technological development (R and D contracts); and direct State participation in industry.' The study does not list what has since become a major support of European industrial policy and the industrial policy of individual European countries: the negotiation of 'voluntary' export restraints limiting the European sales of foreign suppliers and thus protecting European firms (whether nationalized or privately owned), as in steel, shipbuilding, textiles, electronics and motor cars.[2]

Seen against this background, nationalization appears from the viewpoint of international trade as merely one set of techniques for distorting trade flows among a much larger set. However, before assessing the significance of this fact, I shall briefly describe those techniques associated with nationalization.

NATIONALIZATION AND TRADE DISTORTION

Consider for example coal. The average pit-head cost of British coal is more than double the extraction cost of strip-mined coal in the United States and Australia. Many authorities believe that coal could be landed here more cheaply than it is produced in the average British pit, even taking account of the transport costs and the costs of constructing the port-handling facilities that would be needed for a substantial increase in coal imports, and clearly, the relative extraction costs provide a considerable margin for these factors.[3]

The International Energy Authority has made a powerful case for liberalizing international trade in coal. It estimates that European coal imports will rise to 200–300 m. tonnes in the year 2000 (as against 55 million tonnes in 1976); but also estimates that European imports could economically rise to nearly 470 m. tonnes in 2000 if barriers to trade in coal were removed and the necessary transport infrastructure constructed. But in the British case, liberalization does not entail the removal of tariffs – there is no British tariff on imports of coal. Some 75 per cent of National Coal Board output is taken by other nationalized industries – roughly two-thirds by the CEGB and the remainder by British Steel; and given the ownership structure of the coal-using industries and control of port-handling facilities, a British government could in principle pursue a policy of virtually complete protection of the home industry without any tariff at all. The speeches of delegates to the current (July 1980) conference of the National Union of Mineworkers ('not a single pit closed') suggest an awareness of this position.

Similar relationships exist between the British Aircraft Corporation and British Airways (where both the types of aircraft and the number of types that have been forced upon it by successive governments are sources of complaint); and between British Steel and British Shipbuilders and British Leyland.

The general problem raised by this kind of policy is that of subsidization of home production of goods that could be imported (and in some cases, exported). Of course, such subsidization occurs more directly. British Leyland, British Steel and British Shipbuilders provide obvious examples: had the Government not been willing to finance their losses by one means or another, they would have moved more quickly to a solution of their problems or they, or large fractions of them, would have ceased production some years ago. These examples also serve to introduce a possible explanation of why the subsidization demands of the public sector are so heavy. Typically, industries and firms selected for nationalization have not been among the most flourishing.

It is a standard theorem of international economics that if the object of policy is to maintain the scale of an import-competing industry, the economically efficient way of doing so is by a subsidy to the output of the home industry: for any level of gains (or loss-avoidance) to the factors of production employed in the industry, the aggregate cost to the other residents of the country will be less with a subsidy to output than with any other policy. That nationalization is a means of paying such subsidies provides the most generous interpretation of the nationalization of industries producing internationally tradeable goods.

Such an account leaves unanswered several major questions, however. Among these are the issues of why there could not be subsidization without nationalization; of whether the theorem applies in the case of subsidization through nationalization, which is essentially the issue of whether nationalized industries produce as efficiently as privately owned industries; and the question of why it should be desirable to maintain the scale of all of such inefficient import-competing industries? I shall return to the first and third of these at later points. For the moment, it is more important to note that subsidization via the activities of nationalized industries can also occur more indirectly than in the examples given above, and that the possibilities extend well beyond the nationalized industries themselves.

In Britain, the nationalized industries account for roughly one-sixth of total investment, and, of course, in specific areas very much more. Thus, to take obvious examples, the sometimes privately owned firms producing communications equipment, heavy electrical generating equipment, machine tools, ball-bearings, mining machinery, rolling stock and computers can be helped or hurt in competition with foreign suppliers by the actions of nationalized industries which are open to political influence and suggestion. As this paper is being drafted (July 1980), the newspapers are reporting the complaints of ICL that it may not be given a preference in bidding for a contract to instal a computer system at the Inland Revenue (it has been official policy for many years to give ICL a preference in bidding for government contracts); of union spokesman that the Civil Aviation Authority has purchased foreign radar equipment rather than domestic; and of Mr Jeff Rooker MP that a Rolls-Royce manager was bribed to buy machinery from an Italian rather than from a UK supplier (an allegation that Mr Rooker has now admitted to have no foundation). Evidently the prices, qualities, servicing and delivery dates quoted by foreign suppliers now count in the purchasing decisions of nationalized industries and firms: evidently the possibility of eliminating them as a relevant consideration in those decisions is well recognized. But the purchase of a good by the government or one of its agencies at a higher price that would otherwise be paid (there is *some* price that would lead to a *free* choice of a British supplier) is tantamount to paying a subsidy to the producer of that good.[4]

Another method of partial nationalization and subsidization of growing popularity is the state investment company, empowered to buy with public funds shares in private business, presumably at a higher price than the shares would have in the normal course of events. Italy, Spain and Portugal had such organizations in the 1930s, when these countries were experimenting with similar types of relationship between the economy and the state. Until the formation of the Industrial Reorganization Corporation in 1966 (abolished in 1971 but succeeded by the National Enterprise Board in 1974), no other European country created one. In the period 1970–4, however, the West European position in this respect was transformed; by 1974, every major country but West Germany possessed a state investment corporation.

Such organizations and practices often make the quantification of effective subsidies very difficult, particularly when, as often happens, they are combined with one another: indeed, difficulty with quantification might be regarded as a hall-mark of public sector subsidization. I do not want to suggest, of course, that there are no difficulties in the private sector case. That is far from being true, in any contemporary economy. As a matter of economic logic, since in order to subsidize the government must tax, not all activities can be subsidized (though no doubt politicians like their constituents to believe otherwise); nevertheless, the complexity of modern fiscal systems often makes it very difficult to know whether a particular private sector activity is net subsidized or net taxed. But whereas the details of taxes and subsidies obtainable through the fiscal system are generally openly available, and the difficulty in assessing their impact primarily computational, the nationalized industries receive, and permit the payment of, subsidies by administrative means, and their true values are difficult or impossible to know, not merely for computational reasons, but because basic information on amounts is lacking. It is unlikely that even those responsible for arranging the subsidizing transactions can be aware of the true amounts involved.

A second difference between subsidization of private sector and public sector activities is true by definition. Since there is no privately owned capital in public sector activities, the benefits of any subsidy to such an activity is received by the labour employed in it (which should, in this context, include management). The point, though definitional, is not without possible substantive implications. To pay a subsidy to the labour employed in a private sector activity without benefiting the owners of capital engaged in the activity is very difficult. A government wishing to pay such a subsidy to labour but not to privately owned capital might therefore contemplate nationalization as a means of achieving that goal. On the other hand, any other objective arguably could be accomplished as well or better by some other policy than nationalization. It follows that a governmental desire to subsidize labour in an activity provides a possible starting point for an economic theory of why nationalization occurs.[5]

However, I do not think that these distinctions are of primary importance in the present context. Much more important is the fact that while the existence of nationalized industries permits the payment of subsidies in a variety of forms and directions, these payments have their rough counterparts in the private sector. To maintain the domestic coal mining industry at higher levels of output and employment than would otherwise obtain by (say) instructions to other nationalized industries is not fundamentally different from maintaining the domestic textile industry by negotiating 'voluntary' export quotas with India and Hong Kong, or the domestic TV assembly industry by persuading the Japanese industry to increase the price they charge us for their sets. In each case, the effect of the policy is to collect a tax from one group of UK (or European) residents in order to make a payment to another group of UK (or European) residents. The method of collection and payment might vary between public and private sector, and this has possible implications for the ratio of the aggregate value received by recipients to the cost of the tax for those who pay it (a ratio that will be less than one in all cases). But that is secondary. It is the collection of such a tax and the payment of such a subsidy that is fundamental: and subsidies are paid in the private sector as well as in the public.

THE GENERAL ADJUSTMENT PROBLEM

Alternatively stated, one characteristic of an open economy is that the number of jobs it offers in a specific activity and at a particular wage is partially determined by what is happening elsewhere in the world. Thus, the unsubsidized wage for the current number of British coal miners is not indepedent of whether abundant coal is discovered in Australia or India, or of changes in the cost of extracting or transporting such coal, and that of the current number of British shipyard, steel, motor car or textile workers is not independent of the wages or efforts of Japanese, Korean or Indian workers in these occupations.

No developed country government has shown any great willingness to permit downward changes in the economically appropriate wage for a domestic activity to be reflected in actual wages (or, what amounts to the same thing, all have been reluctant to permit a 'too rapid' decline in affected activities). Manipulation of nationalized industries and nationalization have been two means of resisting adjustment to external events. But the basic problem is the failure to adjust: not that nationalized industries and nationalization have been two among several means of delaying adjustment.

The attempt to manage an economy on this basis inevitably leads to trade distortions. 'Policy' comes to be the problem of how to hold constant the quantity of labour in a threatened occupation (or how to allow it to decrease at a 'socially acceptable' rate) at a wage too high for that labour to be willingly demanded. In broad terms, the problem has only two solutions – either subsidize the threatened employment directly (perhaps by nationalization) or subsidize it indirectly by taxing substitute outputs (usually by tariffs or voluntary export restraints).

In Britain, this process of thought is observable at both the macro and micro levels. At the marco level, it appears in the 'Cambridge' position that Britain (and the USA) should adopt policies of overall tariff protection. The basic postulate of the argument is that real wages are given and not amenable to policy measures; while the level of employment taken to be 'full' is treated as if it is independent of real wages. Thus, economic policy must adjust to these givens, and on the Cambridge view, this implies a general tariff. At the micro level, the same proposition on the invariance of real wages, this time applied to real wage rates in particular activities, is typically left implicit. It is nevertheless at the root of the various demands for selective protection of threatened industries, in suggestions for 'buy British' policies, and, most significantly for the present topic, in proposals for further nationalization 'to halt and reverse the decline of British industry'. Such proposals are often explicitly connected with the possibility of granting subsidies to state-controlled industries and firms, and of causing such firms to divert their purchases or investible funds into the British economy.

The micro level proposals raise quite different issues from the Cambridge macro position in its current formulation. Apart from their common foundation stone of real wage rigidity, the only thing they share is the property that policy based upon their premise will bias observation in the direction of making it appear true. In the present context, however, it is the micro level proposals that are the more relevant and I shall focus on them.

As already noted, whether employment in an industry is subsidized by protection of one form or another or is subsidized by nationalization or some other means, the effect is to benefit those employed in the industry at the expense of a tax raised on those who are not employed in it. I now turn to the issue of the circumstances under which this might be considered a sensible policy. There seem to be five propositions which, in one combination or another, exhaust the content of arguments for subsidization. I shall consider them in turn.

DISPLACED WORKERS HAVE NO OTHER JOB OPPORTUNITIES

This argument gains much force from current levels of employment. However, it was widely used when general unemployment was much lower, and therefore can be expected to survive when unemployment figures fall.

The contention that workers have no alternative employment raises a puzzle when combined with the assertion that real wages in the occupation will not fall. Can it really be true that a worker with no other opportunities will prefer to be unemployed rather than continue in his existing job at a lower real wage?

There is evidence of continuing confusion on the relationship between wages and unemployment (for example in Mr Eric Heffer's article in *The Times* of 28 July 1980). Keynes argued that in a *closed* economy, declines in the general level of money wage rates could not directly affect the general level of employment. That is a correct proposition within the Keynesian framework. But it is not correct if applied to a single *open* economy or to a single industry in such an economy. There is some wage at which all current British coal miners, steel workers, textile workers, even motor car workers, would be employed without subsidy. In some industries, the wage at which this would occur might indeed be so low that workers would prefer to be unemployed rather than accept it, but in others it will not be. In any event, Keynes's proposition provides not the slightest reason to doubt that unemployment in particular industries (and the open economy as a whole) will be increased by reductions in wages.

Whatever the answer to the question of why occupational real wages will not fall when workers have no other opportunities (and indeed to that of whether the statement is true if there really are not other opportunities), the argument proceeds to the conclusion that it is better to use VERs or subsidies to have such a worker produce textiles or motor cars than to have him unemployed and producing nothing. From an economic point of view, however, that may or may not be the case. If the true cost to the rest of the country of subsidizing his employment is £Y per annum, if transfer payments to him when unemployed are £X per annum, and if $Y > X$, the rest of the country will be better off to have him unemployed.

An alternative form of the argument, which meets this objection, is that the rest of the country should be prepared to pay up to £X per annum in subsidy if the alternative to doing so is that he will be unemployed. However, such calculations translated into policy raise problems. Suppose the government makes it plain that this policy applies to the Z industry, which is not currently under threat. Will not the Z union (or unions) have an incentive to push up Z wages by £X per annum? And since, when employment in the industry is threatened (as probably it then will be) the government will provide a subsidy of £X per annum per worker, employers in the Z industry (or the management of British Z) have little or no incentive to resist this development. Alternatively, if the industry is threatened without any such wage development, there is little incentive on either side of the wage bargaining table to ask for, or offer, real wage reductions.

A government that creates an expectation that it will subsidize on this basis courts the risk that it will be obliged to subsidize very much more frequently than would otherwise be the case (which will in turn confirm the expectation). If such a policy is pursued at all, there is a strong case for employing it only when real wages in the occupation have fallen to such a level than there is no reasonable doubt that workers in it would rationally prefer to be unemployed rather than employed at that wage. The only real significance of the contention that workers have no other employment opportunities is that real wages in the occupation might then fall to such a level.

The argument that workers have no other possible employment than the one they already have is an extreme form of the more general proposition that the costs of adjusting to a new trading opportunity are so high (in terms of workers finding and securing new jobs) that it is not worthwhile to take the opportunity. In some large part, this notion is likely to be based on the idea that movements of factors of production between industries are necessary to obtain gains from trade. But that idea is false. To obtain the *maximum* benefit from a trading opportunity, movement of factors between industries is likely to be necessary; but the economy will still gain, in aggregate, even if there is no movement of factors at all, so long as factor *prices* in an industry facing lower output prices adjust to maintain its level of output at that lower price.[6] Movement of labour from low to high wage industries then increases the aggregate gain, but will presumably only take place if workers judge the increase in earnings sufficient to cover the costs of movement.

IT IS UNFAIR THAT WHEN THE COUNTRY AT LARGE GAINS FROM A TRADING OPPORTUNITY, FACTORS OF PRODUCTION EMPLOYED IN THE DOMESTIC INDUSTRY SHOULD BEAR ALL OF THE LOSSES.

This ethical argument is cogent. It was not, after all (to take an historical example) the Cornish tin miner's fault that abundant cheap tin was discovered in Bolivia, and he could not reasonable be expected to have foreseen this event. Why should he suffer, whether through lower wages, or through the costs of transfer to another occupation, or through unemployment, when the rest of the country is benefitting from the cheaper imported tin? Should he not have been compensated from these gains of others?

However, to accept this ethical case is not to agree that a subsidy to protect *employment* in Cornish tin mining would have been appropriate. Such a policy has the effect of making compensation conditional upon workers remaining in the threatened occupation: those who leave do not receive it. To remove any such element of conditionally could be better both for tax-payers and workers: essentially because it compensates workers *and* permits those with the opportunity to do so to transfer to other occupations in which the value of their product is higher.

The extent of justified compensation is often posed as a problem for this position. For example, should be owners of capital in affected industries be compensated too? Whatever the answer to that question, it is clear that the ethical case for compensation extends to workers displaced for any reason that is not of their own making: in particular because of technological progress, which is almost certainly a very much more important cause of worker displacement than changes in international trade. However, it is also true that governments have been very much more prone to respond with subsidy programmes to keep workers in place when the threat to employment has come through international trade than when it has come through technological progress. One might speculate on whether this is due to foreigners' lack of domestic votes. What it means, however, is that the urgent need is to find policies to replace those which are now blocking international trade.

SUBSIDIZATION OF EMPLOYMENT IN A PARTICULAR OCCUPATION PRESERVES EMPLOYMENT IN GENERAL

This proposition is often taken to be self-evidently true but is not. This is most easily seen in the case of a flexible exchange rate. Abstracting from international capital flows, the exchange rate will then adjust so that the value of imports is equal to the value of exports.

The effect of subsidizing employment in an import-competing industry, however, is to reduce the value of imports below the level it would otherwise have had; and it follows that the exchange rate must appreciate (compared with the value it would otherwise have had) to reduce the value of exports to a similar extent. Hence there is an offsetting loss in employment elsewhere in the economy.[7]

Nor is this position altered under fixed exchange rates. A reduction in imports then might provide the opportunity to expand domestic demand and employment with an unchanged trade balance. The same is true of an effective devaluation or a general tariff however. The alternative to protecting employment in the specific industry is to increase employment in general. There is no net gain of employment: simply a redistribution of it as against what would otherwise have been possible.

DOMESTIC SOURCES OF SUPPLY OF THE THREATENED GOOD ARE NEEDED AND THE INDUSTRY SHOULD BE MAINTAINED EVEN THOUGH FOREIGN SOURCES OF SUPPLY ARE LESS EXPENSIVE

The classic case of this argument is that from the needs of national defence. In the era of the four-minute warning, its force is less than it was. In any event, national defence needs could not possibly supply a rationale for the range of goods we protect or for the scale at which we protect them.

However, the national need that has now supplanted defence is technology. Not, it should be noted, a need for the *use* of technology, which can evidently be fulfilled without domestic manufacture, but a putative need to domestically *manufacture* high technology goods: a procedure that in fact might well reduce technology *use* by making it more expensive or less effective.

Two propositions are often confounded in this kind of discussion. The first is that as traditional industries decline, either new ones or expansion of other established industries is needed to replace them. That is true. The second often is presented as a corollary of the first: that therefore new industries should be subsidized. That is false, or at least is very far from being self-evident. If the industry *needs* subsidization from public funds to survive, the factors of production employed in it are paid more than the value of their product. Why should public funds be used to sustain that position rather than those factors reducing their take? Either they have better opportunities elsewhere, so that the employment argument fails, or they do not, in which case there is no obvious economic reason to maintain their current income.

In general, there is a case for subsidizing an activity if its presence on national soil generates some benefit for those domestic residents *not* employed in it; and in most cases, it is difficult to see how this could justify the extent of subsidy given. The infant industry argument, incidentally, provides no intellectual basis for subsidizing new industries. Properly analysed, it proves to require some inappropriability to investment in the industry, and from an economic point of view, it will always be better to remove that innappropriability than to subsidize the industry.[8]

OTHER COUNTRIES SUBSIDIZE THEIR Z INDUSTRY, THEREFORE WE SHOULD SUBSIDIZE OURS

Though widely used, this is on its face a *non sequitur* unless some need for the domestic industry has been established and the foreign subsidies threaten its existence. That foreign governments subsidize the same industries as ourselves is quite likely: Britain is not alone in this activity. But what does that signify? If foreign governments use their tax-payers' wealth to offer us goods at less than the resource cost of producing them, should our government rush to put our tax-payers on the block too?

There is, of course, very often some notion of fairness behind the attitude that would affirm that our government should indeed do that: if our people can produce Z for less than foreigners when both are unsubsidized, it is *unfair* that subsidies by foreign governments should reduce the scale of our Z industry. The argument seems to imply that there is some form of harder foreign competition that *is* fair. It would be more impressive if one were confident that in the event of a shift of comparative advantage (presumably shifts in comparative advantage are fair if anything is) members of a domestic industry would without complaint turn their hands to other things. However, that is not the real issue.

The real issue is whether international trade is viewed as a means to make better use of domestic resources or as a matter of national rivalry (for example, as a competition to see who can bear the heaviest unnecessary burdens: unfortunately those countries who might be regarded as our natural rivals now have the wealth to outclass us by a substantial margin in such competition should they choose to). On the former view, does it matter whether foreign steel or motor cars or television sets become cheaper due to changes in comparative advantage or as a result of subsidies granted by governments? It is hard to see why it should. In either case, the good is available to domestic residents on better terms than before and they would benefit if the allocation of resources were adjusted accordingly.

A more relevant distinction is between permanent and temporary shifts in foreign prices. It is often said, for example, that the prices we are charged will be raised if the domestic industry vanishes and foreign producers find themselves able to exploit a monopoly position: therefore the domestic industry should be subsidized. Obviously, the force of this contention depends upon the likely conditions of competition in the rest of the world in the absence of a British industry. If the rest of the world supports sufficient producers that there will be competition, then the case for subsidizing the British industry to protect us from a foreign monopoly fails. On the other hand if there are so few foreign producers that oligopolistic behaviour is likely, there is every chance that a rescued British industry will act in tune with producers in the rest of the world, so that its rescue provides us with no protection against higher prices.

I do not wish to argue that it is inconceivable that foreign subsidies could create circumstances in which counter-subsidies or protection by our own government became rational economic policy: merely that this is unlikely to be an over-crowded category and is certainly smaller than the number of claims for subsidies which rest upon it. The observation that economic policy should respond to permanent or long-term subsidy programmes of foreign governments as though they were shifts of comparative advantage is likely to have much wider practical application.

The point of this litany of arguments and counter-arguments is to suggest the weakness of the economic case for subsidy programmes to keep workers in place when their employment is threatened by foreign competition. That it is so weak raises the question of why governments undertake so many such programmes.

The question may be more of a puzzle for some economists than for laymen, who, by and large, long ago accepted (if they ever doubted) that governments intervene in trade flows with the primary purpose of redistributing income between their residents, and that in this process, considerations of economic efficiency play at most a secondary role. Judging from newspaper editorials, for example, the intelligent layman sees some protection as bad (for example that preserving the incomes of European farmers?) and only explicable in terms of the electoral interests of governments, and some as good (for example that preserving the jobs of British textile workers?) and therefore justifiable in terms other than the electoral interest of the government. Rather unstarry eyed economists, however, are likely to take this kind of argument a step further by arguing that, such policies not being explicable in terms of rational welfare maximizing economic policy, and members of governments not being evidently or grossly irrational, *all* such policies are likely to be best explained in terms of the perceived electoral advantage of members of governments.

It would be beside the present point to dwell upon all of the implications of this hypothesis, which, whatever its other merits, engages Anglo-Saxon moral feelings at a very basic level. Perhaps this is because it threatens the foundations of a needed belief that members of governments (and the managements of nationalized industries?) strive to do good things for the community at large; or at least that such behaviour is sufficiently common and plausible as to provide a sensible standard for judgement of actual members of governments. This apolitical proposition is in sharp and fundamental contrast with the alternative extreme contention that the political system produces tolerable results only because it places constraints upon the actions of self-interested politicians. On this latter view, subsidy programmes occur because of an imperfection (one of many) in the system of political constraints.

THE INTERNATIONAL ISSUES

Whatever the genesis of such programmes, however, a fact of overriding importance in the context of this paper is that in the course of using them to redistribute domestic income, governments inevitably cause changes in income and wealth and its distribution abroad. One consequence of restricting textile imports into the UK is that income is redistributed from British textile consumers to British textile workers (and, of course, to owners of capital employed in textile production in the UK). But another is that textile workers in India and Hongkong are worse-off. It is this fact, generalized, that calls for some set of rules on appropriate governmental actions and reactions in trade matters. So far as the world is concerned, this set of rules is currently embodied in the General Agreement on Tariffs and Trade (GATT). Member states of the EEC are also affected by the rules of that organization.

Over the past ten or twelve years, the GATT system has taken something of a battering. While industrial tariffs as such have been progressively reduced throughout the post-war period, and will be further reduced as a result of the latest multilateral tariff negotiation (the Tokyo round MTN), voluntary export restraints and non-tariff barriers to international trade have become very much more prominent: partly as a direct consequence of the declining importance of tariffs and partly, perhaps, because governments, with tariffs bound under the GATT and thus deprived of tariff increases as an instrument of policy, have turned to alternative means of achieving the same objectives. In turn, this has provoked a reaction within the GATT, albeit as yet mild, against the use of such instruments. It has become clear that further liberalization of world trade, or even realization of gains expected through past and present negotiated tariff reductions, require action against such non-tariff barriers.

In much of this paper, I have treated trade barriers associated with nationalization as equivalent to other barriers. That is appropriate on one level of analysis because the domestic and trade effects of the different policies are broadly (though not in detail) equivalent. However, I shall now concentrate on those GATT and EEC rules most likely to affect nationalized industries and which, hence, have most bearing on nationalization as a tool of policy when trade flows are involved.

Two codes among the several dealing with non-tariff barriers that were negotiated during the Tokyo round are therefore in principle relevant — the Agreement on Government Procurement, based on the principles of non-discrimination and national treatment, and the Code on Subsidies and Countervailing Duties. In practice, however, only the latter has current significance for nationalized industries. The purchasing 'entities' covered by the Agreement on Government Procurement include central government and its agencies but not nationalized industries: hence the Agreement bears upon the Inland Revenue's purchase of a computer system but not upon the CEGB's acquisitions of heavy electrical generating equipment.[9] The same is true of the Council of the European Communities Directive of 21 December 1976 (77/62/EC). So far as GATT is concerned, this occurs because of the *de jure* independence of nationalized industries from central government: in the EEC by a list of exempt industries which are in fact the nationalized industries. Whether this position can survive establishment of the principle of non-discriminatory procurement remains to be seen. However, it is of more immediate importance to turn to the Subsidies Code, which contains a radical and relevant departure from former practice.

This consists of bringing within the GATT rules *domestic* subsidies. Hitherto, GATT rules have been based upon a distinction between 'domestic' and 'international' policies. Thus, tariffs, quotas, export subsidies and foreign exchange restrictions were international policies and subject to discussion and negotiation with other countries. All other economic policies were 'domestic' and regarded as the exclusive concern of the country employing them. Whatever the legal merits of this distinction, it makes very little economic sense: an industry is just as damaged if its sales are cut by subsidized exports into its home market as if its exports are cut by subsidized import-competing production.

This shift in emphasis was the *quid pro quo* for US agreement to introduce into its law a requirement that countervailing duties be conditional upon demonstration of injury to a US industry. For many MTN participants, this amendment to US law was a major objective. (Countervailing duties were mandatory in the case of subsidies to exports in the pre-MTN US law, without reference to injury. GATT rules require a demonstration of injury, but the USA was not obliged to conform to this because its legislation on the subject pre-dated GATT and therefore, also by GATT rules, took priority over GATT obligations.)

The potential implications of this change are very great. For the first time, there is a legal basis for the government of country A 'to request consultations' with that of country B if it believes that B subsidy policies are damaging an A industry either through displacement of the A industry's exports to third countries or through import substitution in B. Moreover, if a 'mutually acceptable solution has not been reached within thirty days' then 'any signatory party to such consultations may refer the matter to the (GATT) Committee (on Subsidies and Countervailing Duties) for conciliation'. Examples of subsidies explicitly mentioned in the Code are: government financing of commercial enterprises, including grants, loans or guarantees; government provision or government financed provision of utility, supply distribution and other operational or support services or facilities; government financing of research and development programmes; fiscal incentives; and government subscription to, or provision of, equity capital.

As an eminent commentator on these matters has written:[10]

> (The Agreement does) put in place a machinery which, if it were to be used vigorously by complainants, and if there were to be willing and adequate co-operation from those complained against, could, over a period of time (which might be considerable), build up a body of case law and precedent. This would be very much, indeed, the way that the GATT worked during the 1950s and early 1960s – the period in which it made its greatest contribution to the civilisation of international trade relations. Whether this can be achieved again depends on the conditions for the conduct of world trade, and the attitude of governments, over the decade ahead.

What these moves portend is an increase in the levers available through international and EEC law (the Commission has recently approved a directive designed to make the accounts of nationalized industries more 'transparent' so that the true extent of subsidization is easier to ascertain) to limit or prevent the use of nationalized industries to distort trade. Thus, at a time when British newspapers seem every day to bring fresh proposals for the future nationalization of this, that, or the other thing, we may, depending on viewpoint and belief, either hope or fear that in the future the ability of government to use such industries to intervene in international trade flows will be curtailed – perhaps severely.

CONCLUSIONS

1. The nationalized industries have impeded, or have been used to impede, domestic adjustment to changing cost conditions in the rest of the world. However, lack of adjustment is not a characteristic that is specific to the public sector: adjustment has also been deferred in the private sector, though the policy means have differed.

2. Despite the rhetoric surrounding them, policies to resist adjustment have minimal social or economic justification. They are often based upon the proposition that sectoral real wages cannot be reduced, but the policies themselves will produce that state of affairs. In so far as they are supported by some idea of fairness, both workers and tax-payers could be made better-off by the adoption of policies that did not require workers to remain in a threatened industry as a condition of receiving compensation. Moreover, the more extensive become programmes to keep workers in place, the more dubious becomes their ability to maintain the real wage of any worker above the level he would receive in the absence of any such policy: subsidies to workers have to be financed by one form or another of tax, which inevitably falls primarily upon other workers.

3. From an international standpoint, these policies (which are not in any sense unique to Britain) are likely to have deleterious effects upon income and the distribution of income abroad. There is a clear foreign interest in such domestic policies, and this is reflected in the activities of the European Commission and in newly negotiated GATT rules.

4. The world is therefore impinging in two ways upon the development of the mixed economy. First, changes in comparative cost in the rest of the world are threatening the existence or scale of some established activities in the UK and other industrial companies. One response to this has been nationalization and protection and calls for yet more widespread nationalization and protection, apparently designed to maintain or increase real wage rates while foreclosing the opportunities for economic efficiency offered by international trade and specialization. Second, the activities of governments in blocking

changes in trade flows by this means has provoked the beginnings of a response in the GATT and the EEC, the thrust of which is to limit the possibilities of impeding trade *via* the practices associated with nationalization. Since disposable real wages are likely to be higher and to rise faster when we do make full use of the opportunities offered by international trade, the British government would do well to support and encourage such more as a matter of long-term policy. It would also do well to re-think its attitude to adjustment to changes in comparative cost affecting the private sector.

NOTES

1. The Aims and Instruments of Industrial Policy (Paris: OECD, 1975).
2. Brian Hindley, 'Voluntary Export Restraints and Article XIX of the GATT', in J. Black and B. Hindley (eds.), *Issues in Commercial Policy and Diplomacy* (London: Macmillan for the Trade Policy Research Centre, 1980) provides some analysis of this instrument.
3. The facts for these paragraphs are taken from the evidence of Professor Colin Robinson to the public enquiry on the North East Leicestershire Coalfield.
4. For a more complete analysis of public procurement policy see B. Hindley, 'The Economics of an Accord on Public Procurement Policies', *The World Economy*, June 1978.
5. A stimulating historical analysis appears in Robert Currie, *Industrial Politics* (Oxford: Clarendon Press, 1979) Chapter 4 has particular relevance.
8. For a simple demonstration of the point, see B. Hindley, *Theory of International Trade* (London: Weidenfeld and Nicolson, 1974) p. 15.
7. For a more complete analysis, see E. Tower, 'Commercial Policy under Fixed and Flexible Exchange Rates', *Quarterly Journal of Economics* (Aug. 1973).
8. Harry G. Johnson, 'Optimal Trade Intervention in the Presence of Domestic Distortions', in Robert Baldwin *et al.*, *Trade, Growth and the Balance of Payments* (New York: Rand McNally, 1965).
9. For an empirical assessment, see Barbara Epstein, 'Power Plant and Free Trade', in Duncan Burn and Barbara Epstein, *Realities of Free Trade: Two Industry Studies* (London: Allen Unwin, 1972).
10. Sidney Golt, 'Beyond the Tokyo Round', *The Banker*, Aug. 1979, p. 49.

12 The Mixed Economy And British Trade

SIR DEREK EZRA
Chairman of National Coal Board

INTRODUCTION

The activities of the publicly owned sector of the economy of the United Kingdom span a broad spectrum of United Kingdom enterprise, from heavy industry through most elements of the energy and transport sectors to the high technology of British Aerospace and the advanced telecommunications systems employed by the Post Office. Together, the publicly owned sector represents some 12 per cent of gross domestic product and employs about 8 per cent of the national labour force.

The enterprises which now form the publicly owned sector were brought into public ownership with the objective of managing the resources in their respective fields to the best advantage of the public interest. In many cases, a specific duty was laid upon the Board or Corporation to secure the efficient development of the industry concerned, but in all cases considerable emphasis has been placed upon planning and implementation of a concerted programme of technological advancement. The enterprises have worked closely with their private sector suppliers in this field. Thus, in furtherance of their primary duty of managing resources within their fields of activity to the public's best advantage, the enterprises have established, through their research and development programmes, a position in which many aspects of their technology and methods of operation have attained pre-eminence in comparison with those of enterprises in their respective sectors overseas. Similarly, where the enterprises are major users of products from the private sector, these products are in many instances recognised internationally to be among the best available in their fields.

For some of the public sector enterprises direct sales of their products and services overseas have always been a prime aspect of their activity. For those, where direct exports may represent (as in the case of the National Coal Board) a small proportion of total turnover or where (as, for example, in the energy utilities) there is little or no scope for direct export activity, their technological position now gives considerable scope for overseas earnings through consultancy, project participation and the support of sales of equipment by their suppliers. This potential has been recognised by amendments to the statutory framework of more than one enterprise; in the case of the National Coal Board, for example, the Coal Industry Act 1977 made it clear that the Board had power to do anything outside Great Britain which appeared to them 'requisite, advantageous or convenient, and which the Board are required or authorised to do in Great Britain', subject to the consent of the Secretary of State.

There are many respects in which the individual public sector enterprises can benefit from each other's experience in activities by collaboration between the public sector enterprises, their customers and suppliers. A number of the major public sector enterprises recognised the need for more effective co-ordination through the establishment, in 1976, of the Nationalised Industries' Overseas Group (NIOG) with these terms of reference:

> With the object of raising UK exports, to promote collaboration between:
>
> (i) the nationalised industries and
> (ii) those industries and their customers and suppliers to them of plant and equipment and consultancy services;
>
> with particular reference to:
>
> (i) direct exports
> (ii) overseas consultancy and project management
> (iii) turnkey projects and
> (iv) the scope for standardisation of plant orders placed with UK manufacturers, to help their exports.

Membership of NIOG now comprises twenty-three enterprises; the National Economic Development Office and the Projects and Export Policy Division of the Department of Trade are also members of NIOG which additionally maintains close contact with the Foreign and Commonwealth Office (FCO), other Government Departments, the British Overseas Trade Board (BOTB) and the British Consultants

Bureau (BCB). The current members of NIOG are listed at the end of this paper.

The total direct overseas earnings of the members of NIOG amounted to £2881 m. in 1979/80, representing about 4½ per cent of the total (visible and invisible) overseas earnings of the United Kingdom; it is not possible to quantify the total overseas earnings of NIOG members' suppliers arising from export promotional and support work in which the public sector enterprises have played a major part, but the total is undoubtedly very substantial.

The public sector enterprises can also play an important role in improving the United Kingdom's balance of trade through a 'positive purchasing' policy. The majority of the public sector enterprises are substantial purchasers of goods and services; subject, of course, to the conditions set by European Community and other international obligations on fair competition, the enterprises can play an important part in reducing the total volume of United Kingdom imports through a policy of purchasing competitively from United Kingdom sources wherever possible. In cases where no suitable product or service is immediately available in the home market, the public sector enterprises can do much, by consultation with, and assistance to, potential suppliers, to ensure that United Kingdom sources can adjust their approach to enable these gaps to be filled. The public sector corporations, with the encouragement of the Secretary of State for Industry, are currently undertaking an exercise to establish the scope for activity further to improve their performance in this field. Apart, therefore, from the role of some public sector enterprises as major direct exporters, in which they act in the open market in the same way as do private sector concerns, the public sector enterprises play a major part in improving the United Kingdom's balance of trade through

(1) consultancy and project management, independently and in collaboration with the private sector or other public sector enterprises;
(2) technical and promotional support for their suppliers' export activities including co-ordination work where a number of major concerns may be involved in preparation of a major project;
(3) 'positive purchasing' to reduce to a minimum consistent with legislative requirements the degree of import penetration within their own purchasing programmes.

This paper discusses the general steps which have been taken in each of these areas of activity, and deals in more detail, as an example, with the measures which have been adopted to maximise the overall overseas performance of all sectors of the United Kingdom coal industry.

THE ROLE AND ORGANISATION OF NIOG

Within the broad terms of reference as stated above, NIOG seeks to act as a forum for action on general matters of common interest to members' overseas activities, as for example on relations with the international lending agencies which now fund much major investment in the developing countries; as a central register for the collation of information on overseas business in hand or under negotiation, by product sector and geographical area, details of which are circulated quarterly to members, and therefore as a framework within which members may readily find opportunities to link interests if business considerations suggest such a course; as a vehicle through which to bring the wide range of products and services available from members, and from their suppliers, to the attention of overseas governments and other agencies (including nationalised industries) either directly or through briefing of the diplomatic and commercial staff of United Kingdom Posts overseas; as a means of co-ordinating the development of members' policies on relations with the private sector, and in particular the private sector consultants; as a method by which to compile advice or representations to Government Departments or other agencies on overseas matters concerning the public sector enterprises, as for example during the last year on Japanese trading practices and on the review of the Export Credits Guarantee Department's services; and as a forum in which to exchange information and develop policy on members' own organisation for overseas business.

ORGANISATION

The full Group, on which all members are represented at Main Board or senior official level, meets quarterly to review developments and policy. The Group is supported by an Advisory Committee (which includes as a member a representative of a leading merchant bank with extensive experience in export related activities), a number of territorial working parties (currently covering Latin America, the Middle East and North Africa, South East Asia, Africa, People's Republic of China and Portugal) and a small permanent secretariat. The membership of the territorial working parties includes representation from UK Government agencies and Departments, as for example the Overseas Development Administration and the Crown Agents for Overseas Governments and Administrations, and from the private sector, where this is judged particularly appropriate for the area concerned.

GENERAL MATTERS

On the general matters of common interest, NIOG has been active in a number of fields, the most important of which has probably been the clarification for members of the procedures necessary to secure eligibility for consultancy work funded by the many international lending agencies. Direct contacts have been established with the World Bank, which has assumed particular importance in view of the decision last year to allocate greatly increased resources (up to $1500 m. per year by the fiscal year 1983) to the energy sector in which several NIOG members have substantial potential interests, with the Inter-American Development Bank and the regional development banks in Europe, Africa and Asia. An investigation of the United Kingdom's relative lack of success in securing European Development Fund contracts was carried out during 1980, as a result of which members gained a better appreciation of the administrative contacts which were required to secure reasonable prospects for success in obtaining consultancy contracts; a further review of progress is to be made towards the end of 1980.

COLLATION OF INFORMATION AND JOINT PROMOTION OF MEMBERS' INTERESTS

In the field of collation of information on members' overseas business in hand and in negotiation, the quarterly summary which is circulated to members has proved its value as a means by which members' representatives making overseas visits can readily obtain information on other members' activities and identify the scope for collaboration, which is often attractive to administrations in countries where there is a high degree of central planning, or for promotion of each other's interests. The register of information is also of considerable value in providing a ready source of information for briefing diplomatic staff.

BRIEFING ON MEMBERS' ACTIVITIES

The promotion of awareness of the range of products and services available from the United Kingdom public sector enterprises has been carried out by the mounting of direct NIOG missions to a number of overseas states, by a NIOG presence at a number of major international exhibitions and by briefing of United Kingdom diplomatic and trade staff and of resident and visiting representatives of overseas states and agencies. Direct contacts over the last two years have included missions to Mexico and the German Democratic Republic, participation in seminars on public enterprise in Portugal and the signature of a framework agreement on co-operation with the Spanish Instituto Nacional de Industria, participation in a mission to Colombia mounted by the Committee on Invisible Exports and NIOG representation on United Kingdom Government Joint Commissions with Bulgaria, Czechoslovakia, India, Mexico, Romania and Saudi Arabia. All HM Ambassadors and High Commissioners proceeding to their Posts on first appointment are briefed by NIOG, both centrally and by individual members with particular interests in the countries concerned. Briefing meetings for senior officials of the Foreign and Commonwealth Office and of the Departments of Trade and of Industry in London have also been held to ensure that these officials, who might not otherwise have come into direct contact with NIOG, may become fully aware of the facilities offered by NIOG's members. NIOG has taken part in state or official visits from a number of countries including Nigeria, Portugal, Hungary and Bangladesh, and has also established links with a number of Embassies and High Commissions in London.

RELATIONS WITH THE PRIVATE SECTOR

Many United Kingdom public sector enterprises have traditionally maintained very close relations with their suppliers, in particular on research and development and on specification for equipment requirements with export potential in view. On this latter point, some enterprises (for example the NCB and the Post Office) require their suppliers to report to them any element of a specification for domestic supplies which could possibly be detrimental to export orders for that particular supplier. The enterprise is then able to take a decision at that stage as to whether the specification can reasonably be modified to improve export potential. The NCB's procedures for liaison with their suppliers will be discussed in more detail later. A number of enterprises have also established overseas co-ordinating bodies, or jointly owned companies, on which their private sector suppliers are represented.

As far as more general liaison with the private sector is concerned, NIOG has placed great emphasis on the fostering of closer relationships. NIOG joined the British Consultants Bureau as a collective member in 1978, and is represented on the BCB Executive Committee and on all BCB territorial and professional sub-committees. Direct liaison has also been established with a number of individual consultancies; throughout, considerable emphasis has been placed on the specialised assistance which can be made available by the public sector consultancies to their private sector counterparts.

In addition to these means of collaboration, there are a number of other practical ways in which NIOG members support enterprises in the private sector. Members provide facilities for the demonstration of suppliers' equipment to potential overseas customers under operational conditions; members also provide training on United Kingdom equipment for overseas operators, and staff for commissioning such equipment overseas.

Some public sector enterprises have also made major efforts to promote a single United Kingdom approach to important areas of potential new business. The co-ordinated deployment of all available resources to the greater benefit of the United Kingdom as a whole, rather than to the interests of individual United Kingdom concerns, is of considerable importance if the maximum success is to be achieved in these highly competitive fields. There has often, unfortunately, been considerable reluctance on the part of the private sector suppliers to involve themselves in the preparation of unified United Kingdom 'package bids' of this type.

CONTACTS WITH GOVERNMENT DEPARTMENTS AND OFFICIAL AGENCIES

The head of the Projects and Export Policy Division (PEPD) of the Department of Trade is a member of NIOG, and PEPD is the official channel of communication with the Government. PEPD consult NIOG frequently on all aspects of overseas project business, and have appointed a public sector industry member of the Department of Trade's Overseas Project Board to provide links with NIOG for this purpose. Contact has also been established with several of the Area

Advisory Groups of the British Overseas Trade Board: the European Trade Committee, the East European Trade Council, the British Overseas Trade Group for Israel and the North America Advisory Group.

Close Liaison is also maintained with the Foreign and Commonwealth Office (including the Overseas Development Administration)–mention has already been made of the provision of briefing for United Kingdom Heads of Mission overseas on initial appointment–and with the Departments of Energy and Industry.

Contact has been established with the Simplification of International Trade Procedures Board, representatives of which now attend NIOG Advisory Committee and Working Party meetings on an *ad hoc* basis wherever advantage is seen in this arrangement.

MEMBERS' ORGANISATION FOR OVERSEAS BUSINESS

The differences of structure among NIOG members have inevitably led to a variety of internal arrangements for the management of overseas activities. Some members have made a single Board member responsible for the overall co-ordination of overseas activities; in other industries (such as the electricity supply industry) the internal structure makes this course impracticable, but in almost every case responsibility for the co-ordination of overseas activities rests at Board or most senior executive level.

A number of members have established subsidiary companies to co-ordinate and undertake overseas activities (for example British Steel Corporation (Overseas Services) Limited, British Airports International and British Electricity International). The NCB and British Rail have established co-ordinating bodies (British Coal International and the British Railway Industry Export Group respectively) on which, as indicated above, the industry, their subsidiaries and associates with overseas activities and their suppliers are represented. The Post Office, GEC Ltd, Plessey Ltd and STC Ltd have established a joint company, British Telecommunications Systems Ltd, to promote the System X switching system in overseas markets.

NIOG has provided a valuable forum for exchange of information on individual members' organisation for overseas work; although overall operational and organisational constraints make it impracticable for all members to adopt a common approach, a number of valuable general lessons, and also lessons relevant to particular markets, have been learned through such discussion.

NIOG: CONCLUSION

Of the three main areas (other than direct exports of products) identified above in which the public sector enterprises can assist in improving the United Kingdom's trade position, NIOG plays an important role in assisting members to perform to the best advantage in two; consultancy and project management, and technical and other support for suppliers' export activities. The remaining area, 'positive purchasing' to reduce to a minimum import penetration of public sector enterprises' own requirements, falls outside NIOG's scope and, relating as it does directly to the enterprises' main activities, is a matter very much for direction at main Board level. As already indicated, the scope for improvement in this field is currently under review by the Nationalised Industries' Chairmen's Group.

A quantitative assessment of NIOG's success in increasing the overseas business of the publicly owned enterprises and their suppliers cannot readily be made because of changes in membership since NIOG's inception and because of refinement of the methods of assembling financial information. The indications are, however, that members' direct overseas sterling earnings have remained fairly stable, at a level of a little under £3000 m. per annum, over the last two years, during which the developing world recession and the appreciation of sterling have caused increasingly difficult trading conditions.

What can, however, be said is that in July 1980 NIOG's members had 721 overseas contracts in hand and 477 contracts in negotiation, in about 100 countries. It is also undoubtedly the case that NIOG's role in promoting United Kingdom trade is now widely recognised and supported, and that the publicly owned enterprises' place in support of overseas work is increasingly appreciated in the private sector. In speaking of NIOG's activities, the chairman of a leading firm of engineering contractors recently made the unprompted comment that NIOG was a 'mechanism to foster'. This confirmed NIOG's own assessment of its chief utility and of its specific contribution to the overseas business of the United Kingdom.

I shall now consider in more detail ways in which one particular industry organises and manages its own overseas activities.

THE OVERSEAS ACTIVITIES OF THE UNITED KINGDOM COAL INDUSTRY

The United Kingdom coal industry has established a very high international reputation in the technology and safe operation of the longwall system of underground coal mining. The NCB has also developed internationally recognised expertise in coal exploration and project planning and appraisal techniques and in training for all aspects of mining operations, and has a world lead in the design and implementation of underground remote control and monitoring systems. In the coal utilisation field, the NCB have long experience with the blending of coals to meet stringent conditions for combustion and, in particular, for carbonisation to form high-grade blast furnace and metallurgical cokes and with the operation of coke ovens. The NCB and manufacturers in the private sector have developed a range of improved combustion techniques centred around 'fluidised bed combustion'. These have almost unlimited scope for application overseas given the greatly increased reliance on coal which has been predicted by OECD leaders at the Venice summit, and by a number of major studies, including most recently the WOCOL World Coal Study, published in May 1980. The NCB have also developed considerable expertise in novel methods of conversion of coal to gas and liquid fuels. Among other interests, the NCB are also associated with a specialist international coal trading company.

The United Kingdom coal industry, including the NCB's subsidiaries, associates and private sector suppliers and collaborators, can therefore offer services to overseas states and agencies in almost any field connected with coal. International competition particularly from Germany, France, the USSR, the USA and Poland, in various sectors, is, however, intense; the NCB decided, therefore, that there was a need to develop a comprehensive structure to enable the industry to develop overseas opportunities to the full, and to perform as efficiently as possible in the international market.

This organisation would have as its aim the generation of the greatest possible overseas earnings for the United Kingdom coal industry and its suppliers through

(1) the identification of potential new markets for all sectors of the industry;
(2) the deployment of the industry's resources to maximum effect in promotion of the industry's services in potential new markets;

(3) the development, wherever possible, of a unified United Kingdom coal industry approach to negotiations for major mining and equipment packages overseas;
(4) the development of existing overseas activities to the greatest benefit of the whole industry;
(5) the collection and exchange of statistical information on the industry's overseas activities.

In 1977 the NCB took the lead in establishing British Coal International as a co-ordinating body with this aim in view.

BRITISH COAL INTERNATIONAL

The current membership of British Coal International (BCI) comprises

(1) *The National Coal Board*;
(2) *NCB (Coal Products) Ltd*, the NCB's wholly owned subsidiary which manages the NCB's coking and coking by-products/chemicals activities;
(3) *NCB (Ancillaries) Ltd*, the NCB's wholly owned subsidiary which manages, *inter alia*, the NCB's computing services and the Board's interests in certain jointly owned companies;
(4) *British Mining Consultants Ltd*, a mining consultancy (covering all aspects of coal and non-coal mining work) with an established international reputation, jointly owned by NCB (Ancillaries) Ltd and the Powell Duffryn Group;
(5) *Coal Processing Consultants Ltd*, a consultancy owned jointly by NCB (Coal Products) Ltd, British Petroleum and the Babcock Group, which provides a wide range of services on coal combustion and blending technology and on all other aspects of the use of coal, including liquefaction and gasification;
(6) *Horizon Exploration Ltd*, a joint venture with English China Clays Ltd and NCB (Ancillaries) Ltd as major shareholders, acting in land and marine geophysical data collection, processing and interpretation;
(7) *Intercontinental Fuels Ltd*, a company in which the major shareholder is the British Fuel Company, a partnership jointly owned by the NCB and AAH Ltd. Intercontinental Fuels Ltd is active in

the marketing of thermal, metallurgical and anthracite coal from worldwide sources to widely spread customers. Intercontinental Fuels Ltd is also able to provide advice on shipping, insurance, port and handling facilities and other related aspects of the international sea-borne coal trade;

(8) *Overseas Coal Developments Ltd*, owned by the NCB, Intercontinental Fuels Ltd, the Shell Group and Austen and Butta Ltd, an Australian coal mining company, which has been established to identify major opportunities to participate in substantial new overseas coal development projects, and to provide associated consultancy services for foreign agencies;

(9) *The Association of British Mining Equipment Companies*, the trade association representing over ninety United Kingdom companies which can provide a wide ranging mining capability covering designing, manufacturing and supplying equipment to meet almost every mining need;

(10) *The Coal Preparation Plant Association*, the trade association comprising ten British firms engaged in the design, procurement, manufacture, construction and commissioning of coal preparation plants, and in associated test work and consultancy and in the preparation of feasibility studies.

All members of BCI are represented on the BCI Council, which meets quarterly. Representatives of the Departments of Industry, Energy and Trade also attend Council meetings by invitation.

Administrative support is provided by a Director, who is also the NCB's Director of Overseas Mining, a Secretary and a small staff, all of whom are employed by the NCB.

I shall now consider in more detail the methods by which BCI seeks to act to the best effect in the five areas identified above.

IDENTIFICATION OF POTENTIAL NEW MARKETS

BCI has established contact with a wide range of organisations which can provide information on potential opportunities for members. These include NIOG, the British Overseas Trade Board's Export Information Service, the international lending agencies, the appropriate sections of the Departments of Industry, Energy and Trade, the Overseas Development Administration of the Foreign and Commonwealth Office and United Kingdom Posts overseas. BCI is now well known to these organisations, who provide a flow of information on possible opportunities and in many cases on the activities of our overseas competitors.

BCI also obtains valuable 'leads' from its own members' wide network of overseas contacts; with members currently operating in over 100 countries, developments of potential interest to other members in the same country, or in nearby countries, often come to the attention of members' representatives travelling overseas.

Useful information can also be gained from direct contact with representatives of foreign countries and agencies visiting the United Kingdom; the appropriate government departments make a point of ensuring that such representatives visiting the United Kingdom are met by a BCI representative wherever there seems to be any likelihood of interest to a BCI member.

Information gathered from all these sources is assessed by the Director of BCI and is sent to the members who appear most directly to be concerned; these members then take appropriate action. All significant information is also collated in the Director's quarterly Report to the Council.

PROMOTION OF THE INDUSTRY'S SERVICES

Many of the same routes are used for the promotion of members' services as are used for the collection of information. Promotional literature describing the range of members' services is available in a number of major languages and is distributed through Posts overseas and by members' representatives when they visit potential new markets. BCI participation, either centrally or through particular members, has been arranged at a number of major coal and energy related international exhibitions including the 1980 American Mining Congress International Coal Show in Chicago, and, during 1979, the exhibition associated with the World Mining Congress in Istanbul. Other exhibitions in which BCI have participated have included those at Beijing, Sao Paulo, Houston and Mexico City. BCI has also placed advertisements and arranged publication of major features in a number of international coal and business periodicals.

BCI, apart from participating in NIOG missions, has also mounted missions to a number of countries where major new business is in prospect. In many cases, leads are most appropriately followed up by the member with the greatest direct interest–although that member will, of course also take every opportunity to promote the interests of other members. In some cases, however, particularly where government bodies are closely involved in detailed energy planning, a mission representing BCI centrally is more appropriate. This has been the case over the last two years in Brazil and China; in each case, when requirements have been identified in sufficient detail the members most directly concerned have taken over negotiations.

Opportunity is also taken to brief other NIOG members visiting countries of interest, and general United Kingdom trade missions, on BCI interests.

The Posts overseas play a particularly valuable part in following up contacts on BCI members' behalf, a service which is of great importance when dealing with government agencies, who are the potential customers in most of the developing countries.

UNIFIED UNITED KINGDOM APPROACH TO MAJOR COAL PROJECTS

A number of the United Kingdom coal industry's competitors in major projects business overseas have developed arrangements whereby their appropriate organisations arrange for the submission of a single 'package' bid for large coal development projects. This approach promotes a satisfactory image of united purpose on the part of their industry. Such a unified approach, particularly when coupled with a financing proposal on advantageous terms, has given a substantial competitive advantage to foreign coal industries in a number of instances. BCI has made considerable efforts to promote such an approach by the United Kingdom industry, but has met difficulty through the reluctance of individual manufacturers to agree to co-operate. This attitude, although understandable on the part of the individual manufacturer, is unfortunate in the overall context of the overseas performance of the coal industry as a whole. BCI have made considerable progress through the adoption of a broadly centralised approach to negotiations in India, accepting, however, that individual manufacturers should tender in competition once detailed specifications for equipment had been agreed with the Indian side. A lengthy negotiation with China, which was initially conducted on a central basis, resulted eventually in a separate bid by one manufacturer, supported by a number of other interests; it remains to be seen whether this approach will be successful.

There is little doubt that the success of United Kingdom approaches to the major project market in general could substantially be increased were the private sector contractors and manufacturers to be more ready to agree to joint tender approaches. The public sector enterprises are generally ready to provide the facilities for central co-ordination and suppoprt; it remains up to their private sector associates to take the steps necessary to move further towards this aim.

DEVELOPMENT OF EXISTING OVERSEAS ACTIVITIES

There are many occasions on which existing overseas activities of individual BCI members can provide subsequent opportunities for business for other members. The most obvious field in which this applies is that of mining consultancy; work by British Mining Consultants Ltd can provide valuable 'leads' for substantial sales of United Kingdom mining machinery. Although British Mining Consultants Ltd must and do take care to maintain their independent stance in order to preserve their high international reputation and to meet the requirements of the major international lending agencies who fund much of their work, the BCI structure provides an excellent vehicle to allow British Mining Consultants Ltd to keep the manufacturers fully informed of developing opportunities.

A similar purpose is fulfilled by direct contact between other individual members; in addition, the quarterly summary of business prospects and work in hand, and the discussion of it at the Council meetings, gives an opportunity for all members to give regular consideration to approaches in conjunction with work already in hand.

A further important area of work in connection with the development of existing opportunities is the support given to the manufacturers in the development and demonstration of their products. As already indicated, the NCB include in their specifications for new equipment a requirement that the manufacturer inform the NCB if they consider that any element of the specification inhibits the export potential of the equipment concerned. Apart from this direct orientation of new equipment development towards the export market, the NCB also provide facilities for rigorous testing of manufacturers' equipment to ensure that it meets the NCB's standards; although differing safety standards in different countries do sometimes cause some difficulty, most manufacturers regard the granting of the NCB's approval as one of the most important 'selling points' for their equipment.

In addition, the NCB provide facilities for manufacturers to demonstrate their equipment to potential customers while in use underground. During the first six months of 1980, 246 such visits for manufacturers' potential foreign clients were arranged by the NCB; a further 338 visits by overseas personnel were also arranged in connection with general collaboration and other aspects of the industry's overseas activities. The NCB permit their training and operational facilities to be used by manufacturers for the training of overseas operators of exported equipment.

COLLATION AND CIRCULATION OF INFORMATION

The need for a comprehensive collation of information on members' current and prospective activities overseas is clear from the foregoing paragraphs. Quarterly returns of business in hand and in prospect and of opportunities for new business are collected from all members and are then analysed, commented upon and circulated, as part of a quarterly report to the Council which reviews all major developments.

BCI: ACHIEVEMENTS AND CURRENT STATE OF BUSINESS

There is no doubt that the formation of BCI has increased considerably the effectiveness of the UK coal industry's activities overseas and has also greatly increased overseas awareness of the facilities and services which are available. As in the case of NIOG, changes in membership and refinements to the method of reporting business make direct comparability of annual results difficult. Results for 1978 and 1979 are, however, available on a comparable basis; the key elements are as follows:

United Kingdom coal industry's overseas earnings, 1978 and 1979

	£ Million	
	1978	*1979*
NCB Group: sales of products	76.0	100.0
ABMEC/CPPA: sales of products	91.0	182.0
Sales of services	2.4	2.7
Total earnings (rounded)	170.0	285.0

NOTE
sales of services exclude Horizon Exploration Ltd, who were not members of BCI in 1978.

At the end of 1979, contracts or product sales were in hand or in negotiation in over 100 countries; within this total, business other than equipment sales by ABMEC or CPPA members was in hand in 41 countries, and potential business was under negotiation in 31 countries. At the end of 1978, contracts or product sales were in hand or in negotiation in about the same number of countries; within this total, business other than equipment sales by ABMEC and CPPA was in hand in 42 countries and in negotiation in 26.

Thus, in the face of a progressive deterioration in external trading conditions, BCI's total earnings increased substantially from 1978 to 1979, largely due, albeit, to one major ABMEC contract in China. After elimination of this erratic factor, the underlying trend remained encouraging, with a significant increase in value of business continuing on into 1980 and a slight increase in the number of countries in which members were pursuing new opportunities.

There is every indication that the BCI organisation, which is now firmly established, will assist in the further development of this trend.

CONCLUSIONS: THE MIXED ECONOMY AND UK TRADE

The established technical reputation of the United Kingdom's public sector enterprises, and the resources which they can bring to bear in support of the overseas efforts of their suppliers and other associates, place them in a position greatly to assist the overall United Kingdom export effort. The enterprises have established NIOG to co-ordinate their efforts, jointly and in collaboration with the private sector, and to provide a forum for the discussion and development of general policy on their overseas activities. Individual enterprises' overseas organisations vary, as is inevitable given the variation in the enterprises' structure, but almost all are now placing considerable weight on the promotion of the overseas interests of all concerned within their sector. Other than in the case of those enterprises whose major business is to sell in international markets, the majority of the enterprises draw little direct benefit from their overseas work; the major benefits fall to their suppliers. The public and private sector elements of the varied and important areas of the economy covered by the public sector enterprises therefore play a valuable combined role in the promotion of United Kingdom exports.

MEMBERSHIP OF NATIONALISED INDUSTRIES OVERSEAS GROUP

FULL MEMBERS

British Aerospace
British Airports Authority
British Airways
British Gas Corporation
British Railways Board
British Shipbuilders
British Steel Corporation
Cable and Wireless Ltd
Civil Aviation Authority
Electricity Council
National Coal Board
National Economic Development Office
Natural Environment Research Council
National Freight Corporation
National Water Council
Post Office Corporation
Projects and Export Policy Division, Department of Trade
United Kingdom Atomic Energy Authority

ASSOCIATE MEMBERS

British Transport Docks Board
British Waterways Board
London Transport International Ltd
National Bus Company
Placon Ltd
Remploy Ltd
White Fish Authority

Index

Agency theory, 39–42
impact of regulation on managerial performance, 47
in medical services, 131, 141
related to non-trading public sector, 45
Agreement on Government Procurement, 202
Airlines
overmanning in Australia, 70–1
relationship between BAC and British Airways, 189
Alchian, A., 40, 61
Amalgamated Union of Engineering Workers, 18
Australia, airline overmanning in, 70–1
Austria, incomes policy, 12
Averch, H., 78
Aylen, J., 101, 106

Bank of England, style of management, 6–7
Banks, state ownership, 5–6
Bennett, J.T., 73–4
Beswick, Lord (Frank Beswick), 102
British Coal International
achievements, 221–2
identifying potential new markets, 217–18
information service, 221
liaison with existing overseas activities, 220–1
membership and organisation, 216–17
promotional activities, 218–19
British Consultants Bureau, 212
British Leyland (BL), 117, 124
subsidies, 189
British Mining Consultants Ltd, 220
British Overseas Trade Board, 213
British Overseas Trade Group for Israel, 213
British Petroleum, management, 6
British Rail, hotel ownership, 5
British shipbuilders, subsidies, 189
British Steel Corporation, 94
criticism of management, 106–7
development plans over-optimistic, 104
failure to meet peak demands, 105
formation, 95; included many weak companies, 99
industrial relations, 103
initial development strategy, 99–100
investment programme, 98, 100
management time taken by government intervention, 102, 107
poor productivity, 105–6
price control, 101
reduction in capacity, 96, 98, 101
review of closure programme, 102
special steels production, 108
strike (1980), 102
subsidies, 189
Brittan, S., 176
Buchanan, J., 37
Budget policies
affecting industrial policies, 52–3
balanced budget theory, 43
Bureaucracy
effects of budgetary politics, 44
imposition of cash limits on, 45
reduction by dismantling regulations, 54
Burke, Sir Edmund, 3
Burns, Arthur, 12

Canada
  performance of railways, 82
  refuse collection costs, 74
Capital
  cost differentials, 64–5
  no direct control on movement, 19
  ratio to labour, 79
Capital market, indicating firm's performance, 41
Capitalism in the mixed economy, 19–20, 21
  self-seeking behaviour, 36
Cartels, protection against, 39, 50
Caves, D.W., 82
Central planning, 23
Christensen, L.R., 82
Coal industry
  international comparison of costs, 189
  international competition, 215
  liberalising international trade, 189
  ouptut to other nationalised industries, 189
  overseas activities, 215–22; areas of interest, 215–16; problems of presenting unified package, 219–20
  WOCOL World Coal Study, 215
  see also British Coal International; Energy: search for alternatives to oil; National Coal Board
Cochrane, A.L., 138
Code on Subsidies and Countervailing Duties, 202
Collective ownership, 3
Community consent, necessary for operation of mixed economy, 25
Competition
  as discipline on firm's behaviour, 40
  in free market capitalism, 23
  in medical care, 133
  in US electricity industry, 65, 81
  limited by regulatory instruments, 38
  protection by private sector, 120
  socialist support, 119
Confederation of British Industry (CBI), 125–6
Conservation of fuel stocks
  car engine size, 166
  government roles, 168–9
  home insulation, 168
Consultancy work, undertaken by public sector industry, 210
Consumers, power in the economy, 122–3
Co-operatives, 114
  Co-operative Development Agency, 124
  Meriden Motor Cycle, 117–18
Costs
  factors affecting, 63–4
  input prices, 79; variation, 64
  minimisation, 60–1
  of US water utilities, 69–70
  relative public/private sector efficiency, 63–5
  studies of US electricity industry, 66–7
Council for the Securities Industry, 14
Cowling, K., 50
Crain, W.M., 61, 69–70, 79

Dasgupta, Partha, 3
Davies, D.D., 61, 70
De Alessi, L., 61, 69, 76, 77, 78
Decision-making, by disinterested managers, 39–40
Defence, as state activity, 3
Demand management, 116
  encouraging investment growth, 124
Demsetz, Harold, 36, 40, 61
Dennison, Stanley Raymond, 16
Department of Trade, Projects and Export Policy
  Division (PEPD), 207, 212

East European Trade Council, 213
Economic expansion, predicting rates of, 32–3
Economic planning, allowed by public ownership, 115–16
Economic policy
  instruments distinguished from objectives, 4

inter-country comparisons, 13–14
macro- and micro-economic, 9; *see also* Macro-economics
philosophical aspects, 15–16
politicians' lack of caution, 16
see also Fiscal policy; Monetary policy
Economic systems, similarity of problems encountered, 20
Ederer, F., 138
Education
class-related aspects, 151–2
economic profitability, 146–7, 155–8
expenditure cuts, 146
private, advantages of, 153
problems of cost-benefit analysis, 145
productivity-enhancing role, 147–9
rates of return to, 146–7
related to life chances, 153–4
relationship with unemployment, 149–50
role in society, 145–58
social costs of qualifications, 147–8
state involvement, 152–3
value during recession, 149
Edwardes, Sir Ronald, 7
Edwards, F.R., 72
Electricity industry
in USA, 80; costs, 63, 65–9; tariff structures, 75–8
see also Nationalised industries
Employment
effects of technical change, 32
employers' selection by candidates' qualifications, 147
ethical arguments for protection, 196
in uncontrolled free market capitalism, 22
international influences, 193
of displaced workers, 194–6
threats from foreign competition, 200
Energy
need for international co-operation, 171
ownership of supply industries, 172–4
prices influenced by oil prices, 164
'reformation' of uses, 162–4
risks associated with long lead times, 169–70
schemes to ease price impact, 167
search for new sources, 163, 167–9
security of national supplies, 170–2
World Bank allocation, 210
European Development Fund, 210
European Economic Community (EEC)
directive on accounts of nationalised industries, 203
rules affecting trade of nationalised industries, 202
European Trade Committee, 213
Exchange rate flexibility, 197
Exports
of public sector industries, 207
UK trade promotion, 212
voluntary restraints, 188, 201

Finance of nationalised industries, 7
Financial sector
contribution to GDP, 19
functions, 176
little direct public involvement, 175
Fiscal policy
budget deficits, 43
effects, 10
objectives, 8
on industrial taxation and subsidies, 191
relationship to monetary policy, 14
Foreign and Commonwealth Office, 213
France, state-owned banks, 5–6
Free market
correlation of productivity with living standards, 15
uncontrolled, objections to, 22–3
Frey, B.S., 74
Furubotn, E., 61

Gaitskell, Hugh, 119

General Agreement on Tariffs and Trade (GATT), 201
  rules affecting nationalised industries, 202
Germany, incomes policy, 12
Gold Standard, 53
Government employment, 19
Government intervention
  in macro-economic sphere, 42–6
  in nationalised industries, 101
  in the mixed economy, 24–5
  in trade flows, 188
  justified by market failure, 36
  necessity, 118
  positive measures, 123
  preventive measures, 119
  trend to increase, 33
Government Procurement, Agreement on, 202

Hansen, W. Lee, 150
Hayek, Friedrich August von, 3, 4
Health services
  advantages of NHS over private medicine, 142–3
  agency role of doctor, 141
  as one aspect of total health policy, 139
  basic ignorance of patients, 132–3
  effect of life style and preventive measures, 130
  effectiveness unrelated to patients' rationality, 132
  equality of access, 130, 131
  income distribution, 136
  limits to availability of private medicine, 130
  non-profit motivation, 140–1
  political economy, 131–41
  positive health policies needed, 142
  private v. NHS, 128–9
  retention of ineffective treatments, 137–8
  supply aspects, 137–41
  uncertainties in diagnosis and treatment, 138–9
  unequal distribution of facilities, 30–1
  see also Medical insurance
Hicks, John, 122

Income distribution
  affected by subsidy programmes, 201
  inequalities in free market capitalism, 23
  inequalities in socialist countries, 24
  public policies to influence, 21–2
  related to individual effort, 129
Incomes
  adaptability, 12–14
  decline following oil price rises, 11
  determination under various economic systems, 26
  effect of education, 148–9, 150–1
  related to savings, 177–8
Incomes policy, 11, 27, 122
  effectiveness, 12
  justifying mixed economy, 28
  problems for implementation, 27
Index-linked securities, 185
Industrial policy
  future choices, 52–6
  OECD study, 188
Industry
  adjustment problems, 193–201
  compensation for effects of cheap imports, 196–7
  co-operation with government, 125
  effect of cost of finance, 178
  energy efficiency schemes, 168
  maintaining domestic supplies, 197–8
  regional policy, 123
  replacing declining sectors, 198
  structure, to preserve competition, 120–1
Inflation
  effects of deficit finance, 43, 44–5
  income determination in relation to, 26–7
Innovation, private process lost under socialism, 23
Interest rates
  adjustment mechanisms, 184–5
  affected by money supply, 182–3
  balancing savings and investment,

176, 177, 184
reasons for persistently high levels, 183–4
theories of determination, 176–7
Investment
balancing demand with savings, 176
effect of increased demand, 181
factors dissuading firms, 123–4
factors influencing, 180
in energy supply industries, 169–70
influence of cost of capital, 178
private, crowded out by government borrowing, 45
state investment companies, 191
Italy, state-owned banks, 5

Japan, flexibility of real incomes, 12
Jencks, C., 153
Johnson, L.K., 78
Johnson, M.H., 73–4
Junk, P.E., 65

Keynes, John Maynard, 6–7, 13
budgetary theory, 43
Kitchen, H.M., 74

Labour market, duality of, 148–9
Labour Party, attitudes to mixed economy, 113
Legislation
instruments of economic policy, 4
liability at law replacing regulation, 54
little restraint on private sector, 19
see also Government intervention; Regulation
Le Grand, J., 151
Lenin, I.Y., 119
Liquidity
by delaying investment, 180
fluctuations, 180
Liquidity preferences
influenced by perception of economic future, 180
influencing savings and investment, 179

MacGregor, Ian, 101
Macro-economics
contribution of financial system, 176
effects of industrial policy, 52–3
government intervention in, 42–6
Management and managers
dealings with regulatory bodies, 47
in labour market, 41
in public sector, 6; dead wood difficult to remove, 46; political appointments, 48
monitoring performance, 41–2
public/private sector efficiency compared, 59–61
Manufacturing industry, output of largest enterprises, 18
Market forces, in oil industry, 165–6
Medical insurance, 132
compulsory, 134–5
'loaded' premiums, 134
'moral hazard', 135
predictability problems, 133
Melchett, Lord (Peter Robert Henry Mond), 104
Mergers
need for study, 14
UK policy weaknesses, 119–20
Meriden Motor Cycle Co-operative, 117–18
Meyer, R.A., 66–7, 76, 80
Millward, R., 78
Mining consultancy, 220
Mixed economy
capitalist sector predominates, 20
criticisms, 21
future developments, 31–2
future socialist policies, 126–7
horizontal and vertical divisions, 118–19
international trading, 187–205
limits, 3
monetary nature, 19
not significant in financial sector, 175
performance assessments necessary, 24
political attacks on, 1–2
political attitudes to, 113
problem of defining limits, 3

Monetary policy
  effects, 10
  medium-term targets, 185
  objectives, 8
  relationship to fiscal policy, 14
Money supply
  affecting interest rates, 182–3
  creation mechanisms, 4
  expansion to finance deficits, 43
  flexibility, 183, 185
  influencing savings and investment, 180
Monopoly
  anti-trust machinery, 55–6
  control of, 8
  in medical practice, 140
  in mixed economies, 49–50
  internal management monitoring, 51
  need for fresh study, 14
  prevention, 120
  reasons for persistence, 52
Monopoly profits, 38–9
  in public sector, 44; deleterious effects of seeking, 45
  regulation affected by vested interests, 78
  rent-seeking by public enterprise, 48
Motor cycle industry, 117–18
Mueller, D., 50

National Coal Board
  areas of international expertise, 215
  overseas activities, 207
  working demonstrations of equipment, 220–1
  see also British Coal International; Coal industry
National Economic Development Council (NEDC), 125, 126
National Enterprise Board, 124, 191
National Health Service (NHS), 30–1
  doubts on future role, 128
  see also Health services
Nationalisation
  planning objective unrealised, 115
  to halt industrial decline, 194
Nationalised industries
  effect of GATT and EEC rules, 202–4
  energy, consumer education, 168; public reaction to prices, 166
  finance, 7
  import-competing, 190
  international trade of, 188
  link with subsidisation, 190
  monopolies, 8
  trade disortion, 189–92
  see also British Steel Corporation; National Coal Board; Public sector
Nationalised Industries' Overseas Group (NIOG), 207–8
  briefing civil servants and diplomats, 211, 213
  collation of information, 210
  contact with government departments and agencies, 212–13
  direct overseas earnings, 208
  members, 223; variety of organisation for overseas business, 213
  role and organisation, 209–14
  summary of activities, 214
Neuberg, L.G., 67
North America Advisory Group, 213

Office of Fair Trading, 14
Oil
  economic vulnerability to, 163
  effect of market forces in UK, 165–6
  power of producers, 163
  price increases, 162; effect on UK steel industry, 105; effect on western economies, 10–11; increasing prices of other energy forms, 164
Okun, Arthur, 15
Organisation for Economic Cooperation and Development
  (OECD) report on aims of industrial policy, 188
Organisation of Petroleum Exporting Countries (OPEC)
  likely future adjustments, 32
  political control of oil supplies, 164

see also Oil
Output, division between public and private sectors, 28
Overmanning
capital/labour ratio, 79
in British Steel Corporation, 106
in water utilities and airlines, 69–71
Ownership, characteristics of, 59

Pashigan, B.P., 81
Pejovich, S., 61
Peltzman, S., 61, 75–6, 77
Pensions, public commitment to increase, 27–8
Performance measures, 58
Pescatrice, D.R., 79
Pier, W.J., 73
Political considerations
economic preferences, 17
on subsidies, 200–1
Pommerehne, W.W., 74
Portfolios, diversifying holdings, 41
see also Investment
Posner, R.A., 38–9, 46, 50
Price
control, aiding innovation and investment, 122
charged by nationalised industries, 7; government control, 101
groups exerting market power, 18
growth rates in public and private sectors, 87
increases due to regulation, 39
related to level of competition, 121
tariff structure in UK nationalised industries, 77–8
US electricity tariff structure, 75–8
Primeaux, W.J., 81
Private sector, 3
effect of regulation on performance, 78–80
in monopoly position, 8
NIOG's relations with, 211–12
performance compared with public sector, 58–84
profit maximisation, 59–60
public intervention in mixed economy, 24
rent seeking, 38
suppliers to public sector, 206
Problem-solving, political stumbling-blocks to, 31
Productivity
related to income demands, 29
related to level of education, 148
related to state interference, 15
Profitability
economic, of education, 146–7, 155–8
incentives of disinterested managements, 39–40
of nationalised industries, 8
of UK public and private sectors, 61–3
subordinated to social necessity, 63
Protectionism, 200
Public choice, 35–8, 44
favouring regulation, 48–9
problems of alternative industrial policies, 54
Public sector
as percentage of GNP, 46
attitudes of disinterested management, 61
broad range, 206
confusion of aims, 48
confusion with state sector, 114
constituent parts, 18
criteria of efficient management, 60
effect of expenditure on government support, 44
employment, 19
finance, 175; relationship to prices charged, 7–8
importing foreign equipment, 190–1
manufacturing industry behaving like private sector, 115
motives other than profitability, 62
no guarantee of equality, 113–14
overseas trade, 207
performance compared with private sector, 58–84
purchases from domestic sources, 208
question of management, 6
reactions to spending cuts, 44

relations with private suppliers, 211
role in education, 152–3
services in free market capitalism, 23
suitable enterprises for ownership, 5
technological achievements and exports, 206–7
treatment of monopoly of utilities, 121
workers' commitment, 117
see also Nationalised industries
Public sector borrowing requirement (PSBR)
cut back to reduce interest rates, 185
need for study to relate to economic policy, 14
related to industrial finance, 177

Railways, performance in Canada, 82
Rawls, John, 3
Refuse collection costs, 71–5, 80–1
Regional industrial policy, 123
Regulation
effect of dismantling, 53–4
effect of private firms' performance, 78–80
political justification, 48–9
problem of definition, 46
Rent control, 29–30
Rents, *see* Monopoly profits
Restrictive practices legislation, 14
Risk bearers, hedges for, against firms' failures, 40–1
Rowley, C., 61
Royal Commission on Distribution of Income and Wealth, 28

Savas, E.S., 72, 73, 80
Savings
balancing with investment demand, 176
contractual, affecting investment, 182
division between public and private sectors, 28
effects of increased building society deposits, 181–2
personal, in UK, 178
Schultze, Charles, 16
Share prices, reflecting management actions, 60
Simplification of International Trade Procedures Board, 213
Smith, Adam, 3, 120
Social cost
of monopoly rents, 38
of rent seeking in public enterprise, 48
Socialism in the mixed economy, 19–20
defects, 23–4
State investment companies, 191
State ownership, *see* Public sector
Steel
demand related to GNP, 98
development of electric arc 'mini-mills', 95–6, 107
exports, 97–8, 110–11
failure to meet peak demands, 105
imports, 97, 110–11; to meet peak demands, 105
mixed industry, 94
private sector, development, 107–8; share, 95; technical backwardness, 107
rationalisation of special steel producers, 107
revival of demand in 1980s, 105
UK consumption, 97, 110–11
UK production, 97, 110–11
see also British Steel Corporation
Stephens, B.J., 72
Subsidies to public sector industries, 189
Code on Subsidies and Countervailing Duties, 202
conferring comparative advantages, 199
economic justification, 190
effect on industry in general, 197
ethical arguments in favour, 196
international consultation, 203
link with nationalisation, 190
public and private sector differences, 191–2

question of complementary international action, 198–201
questions on limits, 22
to maintain domestic supplies, 197–8
to maintain employment, 195
Switzerland, refuse collection costs, 74–5

Take-Over Panel, 14
Tariffs
to protect employment, 193
see also General Agreement on Tariffs and Trade (GATT)
Tawney, R.H., 118
Taxation
effect of shift from direct to indirect, 10
effect on government support, 44
Technology, effects on employment pattern, 32
Trade international, 187–205
non-tariff barriers, 201
see also Exports
Trades unions
membership as percentage of workforce, 18
role in come determination, 26
Transfer payments, 26, 32
Transport and General Workers Union, 18
Transport services performance studies, 81–2
Australian airlines 70–1
Trapani, J.M., 79

Unemployment
duration, among graduates, 149
job opportunities for displaced workers, 194–6
transfer payments related to subsidy costs, 195
Unit costs
in public and private sector, 62; growth rates, 87
United Kingdom
budget principles, 43
choice of medical services, 130
monopolies, 50; welfare losses due to, 51
profitability of public and private sectors, 61–3
thinking behind oil policy, 171–2
United States
budget principles, 43
effect of oil prices below world levels, 165
electricity industry, 80; cost, 63, 65–9; tariff structure, 75–8
energy supply industries, 173
law on countervailing duties, 202–3
monopolies, 50; welfare losses due to, 50–1
philosophy subordinated to practical issues, 16
refuse collection costs, 71–4
water utility overmanning, 69–70

Vernon, R.B., 73
Villiers, Sir Charles, 101

Wages
differentials related to education, 148–9, 150–1
inflation higher in public than private industry, 64
international influences, 193
just deserts of workers, 129
public/private sector growth rates compared, 86
related to unemployment risk, 194
Wallace, R.L., 65
Water utilities, overmanning in USA, 69–71
Wealth
opposing attitudes to, 25
socialist and capitalist attitudes to, 20
state control limiting political freedom, 23
Weisbrod, B., 150
Welfare economics, 35–6
challenged by public choice, 37
loss from monopoly, 50
loss from regulation, 46; and from

public enterprise, 47
Wicks, J.H., 73
Wiles, Peter, 13
Wilson Committee (on the Functioning of the Financial Institutions), 175, 176–7
on industrial investment, 178
recommendation on new financial systems, 185
Workforce, division between public and private sectors, 18–19
World Bank funds for energy sector, 210

Yunker, J.A., 66, 67

Zardkoohi, A., 61, 69–70, 79